"A real page-turner for those currently or aspiring to lead high performance teams. This compelling book provides a compendium of tried and tested tools, techniques and processes designed to build high performance teams"

—**Ken McGowan, Former Regional Director Asia, Lloyds TSB Bank**
Regional Consultant, Asia, Chartered Institute for Securities & Investment

"I like the Team Charter concept in this book, one gets excited already for the next leadership team event just by reading this chapter. I am convinced with such kind of signing-off, on the different Team Charter elements by each team member, the commitment is there right from the beginning"

—**Norbert Hentschel, Regional Managing Director,**
Asia Pacific & China at Nord-Lock

"What you can't measure you can't manage. Leadership and team performance can of course be measured by the associated business result. However using KPI's as feedback and a guidepost to improve team performance and leadership is only useful at the end result, and is not diagnostic in nature. Team Quotient gives both, leader and teams, the opportunity to measure and improve way before the business result becomes evident. And it's a good fundament for sustainable growth and stability."

—**Roman Kupper, President APAC, Member of Doehler Group Board**

Team Quotient is the insider's guide to building teams that win. In his cutting edge book, Douglas Gerber shares decades of personal experience with leading multinationals in some of the most challenging markets, leading and training platinum winning management teams. In Team Quotient, Gerber offers rare insights into the practical steps that will create competitive advantage.

—**Laurence Brahm, Author of 30 books including "Fusion Economics" &**
"Art of the China Deal", Founding Director, Himalayan Consensus Institute

"Team Quotient is an impressive and most useful overview of leadership team transformation, and an encyclopaedia of methods and tools in an easy to digest format. The case studies are informative, enlightening and well-integrated."

—**Glenn Frommer, Managing Partner, ESG Matters IVS,**
Former Head of Sustainability, Mass Transit Railway Corporation

TEAM QUOTIENT™

How to Build

High Performance
Leadership Teams
that
Win Every Time

DOUGLAS R. GERBER
FOREWORD BY MARSHALL GOLDSMITH

TURNER
PUBLISHING COMPANY

Turner Publishing Company
Nashville, Tennessee
New York, New York
www.turnerpublishing.com

Team Quotient: How to Build High Performance Leadership Teams that Win Every Time

Cover Design by: George Stevens
Editing by: Bryna Kranzler
Book design: Mallory Collins

Library of Congress Cataloging-in-Publication Data available upon request

9781684422487 paperback
9781684422470 hardcover
9781684422494 eBook

Printed in the United States of America
18 19 20 10 9 8 7 6 5 4 3 2 1

To all the aspiring teams moving toward high performance: may you enjoy the fulfillment, exhilaration, and benefits that are bestowed upon you for your persistence and dedication.

ACKNOWLEDGEMENTS

Five years ago, when I started writing *Team Quotient: How to Build High Performance Leadership Teams that Win Every Time*, I had been planning to offer best practices from my years of creating successful teams as both a corporate executive and consultant. It soon became apparent that this book would be so much richer with the stories and case studies of a diverse range of teams that followed the steps to achieve High Performance.

Therefore, I would first like to acknowledge my wonderful clients and friends who are, in so many cases, brilliant team leaders. These include: Achal Agarwal from Kimberly Clark; Dave Schoch from Ford Motor Company; Merle Hinrich from Global Sources; Penny Wan from Amgen; Dudley Slater, author of *Fusion Leadership*; Ed Sanchez from ProQC: Glenn Frommer from MTR Corporation; Dan Booher from Kohl's; Chris Geary from BSD Code and Design Academy; Hervé Gissersot, Yi Wang, and other leadership team members from GSK; the committed leaders at Roche; the many capable leaders from Swire, Ethos & Cathay Pacific Airways; Ron McEachern, and the talented people who worked with me at PepsiCo where I started the journey to create High-TQ teams. I am also eternally grateful to the many clients who have demonstrated the power of TQ and High Performance Teams.

Others have contributed to book by allowing me to reference their ideas and works, including Richard Warburton, for his edits and contribution to the Leicester story; Bryce Hoffman, author of *American Icon*; Steve Ellis; Pat McBay, & Jim Coley, talented coaches who have inspired ideas; Richard Howell from Cathay Pacific Airways; Tania Cook from Zurich Insurance; John Cook from Rock Lake, Andy Robbins from PCR Ltd. and Dan Harrison from Harrison Assessments.

A major source of inspiration comes from my mentor, the internationally acclaimed leadership and coaching guru, Marshall Goldsmith.

I would like to thank my friend and visionary, Gary Wang from Mindspan; as well as those who provided advice and inspiration, including Laurence Brahm, prolific author of 30 books; Frank Gallo, author of *The Enlightened Leader*; Dr. Gary Ranker, author of *Global Mindset Coaching*; Salvador de la Barrera, my expert on web and social media matters; my tireless editor, Bryna Kranzler; and my book designer, George Stevens, and my final sounding board, Anthony Somerset.

Finally, I am grateful to my mother, Beth, who served as a sounding board while I talked about ways of approaching this book; my daughters, Paloma, who effectively managed this entire book project over the long haul, and Maxine, who offered down-to-earth reality checks; and finally to my wife, Janice, whose patience and encouragement knows no bounds.

CONTENTS

PART II
THE TQ JOURNEY:
YOUR ROAD MAP TO CREATING
HIGH PERFORMANCE TEAMS

PART III
BUILDING
RIGHT INTENTIONS; RIGHT PLAYERS

PART IV

THE LEADER'S
OPERATING MANUAL

INTEGRATING THE EIGHT ESSENTIAL ELEMENTS
OF A HIGH-TQ TEAM

FOREWORD

MARSHALL GOLDSMITH, AUTHOR OF THE #1 NEW YORK TIMES BEST SELLER *TRIGGERS*

In my article "You Are Only as Good as Your Team," I write about coaching a client named Charlie and his team. Charlie was president of a division with more than 50,000 employees. His CEO recognized his talents and asked me to help Charlie expand his role, provide more leadership, and build synergy across the organization.

At the end of our project, I told Charlie about my observation: "I think that I spent less time with you and your team than any team I have ever coached, yet you and your team produced the most dramatic, positive results. What should I learn from my experience?"

Charlie thought about my question. "As a coach," he said, "you should realize that success with your clients isn't all about you. It's about the people who choose to work with you." He chuckled, and then he continued: "In a way, I am the same. The success of my organization isn't about me. It's all about the great people who are working with me."

There is a big difference between achievers and leaders. For the great achiever, perhaps someone on Charlie's team, the focus is all about "me" and reaching individual goals. For Charlie, one of the greatest leaders I've ever met, leadership is all about "them" and their success. He truly exemplifies the oft-quoted proverb, "The best leader, the people do not notice. When the best leader's work is done, the people say, 'We did it ourselves.'"

Douglas Gerber's book, *Team Quotient*, recognizes the power of "them." It's the power of a High Performance Team to create exceptional results for an organization. A team's success goes beyond the skill and genius of the leader. Success is the result when the *entire team* is galvanized around clearly aligned goals, and has a clear understanding of what's important. As a result of working with hundreds of teams, Douglas shares numerous examples from his corporate and consulting experience about what works, as well as the caveats of which to be aware.

Team Quotient identifies critical elements that "winning" teams possess. What they all have in common is that focusing on the team's success leads to success for each individual. It is also the most effective way to get noticed in the organization.

The book not only outlines the key elements of a High Performance Team, it also provides detailed instructions on how to achieve each one. For example, one key element is "trust." Douglas specifies what goes into creating trust and offers proven exercises that can be used to build it.

Each team is distinct. Its uniqueness is defined by the style of its leader, mix of its members, stage of development, and, finally, the type of business and industry. This book recognizes that uniqueness and addresses the differences between teams. It takes into account the need to develop awareness, acceptance, and appreciation of each of the team's members. No two team prescriptions are the same, just as no two teams are alike. Each team must embrace truly where it is and where it wants to go.

One of the leaders with whom I have had the pleasure of working is Alan Mulally, former CEO of Boeing and Ford. The genesis of many of his leadership and management principles came out of his work at Boeing. At Ford, he not only applied the best of those principles but also, and against all odds, transformed the culture and the company. He accomplished this by shifting the culture from an "individual" or "division" performance mindset to a "One Team" performance mindset. In the book's chapter on Ford, Douglas draws on many of his own experiences in working with the automotive giant, citing the common thread of

"Working Together" that was pervasive from Dearborn to Shanghai to Chennai.

With one of my clients, I developed a process called "Team Building Without Time Wasting" that benchmarks the current state of the team and measures progress. *Team Quotient* does exactly that: it measures a team's performance over time and identifies the behaviors that will lead to team success. TQ quantifies the degree to which team members work together effectively as a High Performance Team. It's a new way of looking at the IQ of a team as a whole. TQ is an easy and expedient way to measure the current state of the team and to chart a path to its desired future state. It forms a diagnosis of team areas to improve upon and objectifies the process, leaving out the guesswork and subjectivity.

My mission is simple: I want to help successful people achieve positive, lasting changes in behavior for themselves, their employees, and their teams. Douglas' book focuses on the team aspect, positing that in order to create success in an organization, it is vital to manifest change in team behavior, an element that is often overlooked. Most leaders recognize the time and resources required to improve their own leadership effectiveness and behavior, however they may not recognize the need to spend commensurate time and resources on developing their teams and aligning team behavior. As Douglas states: "Leaders are only as good as the teams they build." This book details the case for team development. It includes interviews with successful leaders at Ford, Kimberly Clark, GSK, AMGEN, PepsiCo and others, who can attest to the importance of developing a High Performance Team.

You'll find this book to be a comprehensive guide to moving your team from where it is now to high performance. Whether your team is currently dysfunctional or is already effective, *Team Quotient* will provide you with a clear and actionable road map to make it the best that it can be.

Marshall Goldsmith – The Thinkers 50
#1 Leadership Thinker in the World.

INTRODUCTION

IT'S LONELY AT THE TOP . . .
(BUT IT DOESN'T HAVE TO BE)

As a leader in your organization, do you feel somewhat alone with the weight of the world on your shoulders? If so, it's probably because you feel the pressure of having to make the final decision. And you are accountable for results. Your team members may or may not agree with or support your decisions, yet they must be made. Your success depends on the outcome of those decisions, and you and your team's ability to execute and deliver on them.

There is a better way. Many leaders experience that when reaching a certain executive level, success becomes less about their own capability. and more how to galvanize and motivate others. No matter how smart, talented, or experienced *you* are, true achievement only comes with getting *others* to execute, deliver, and win. Moreover, through an effective team, you can engage in a sense of shared ownership and commitment over decisions and goals. That's right; it doesn't have to be so lonely!

A case in point: Ronald is senior vice president of a consumer goods company. He leads a large and high-profile business unit nationally and is responsible for several billion dollars in annual revenues For two years, I served as Ronald's executive coach and got to know him and the issues he contends with quite well.

Ronald is tall, and his chiseled and attractive appearance enhances his gravitas. He touts an impressive pedigree, having come from a well-known business family. His Harvard MBA,

4

commercial acumen, and successful track record with several companies contributed to his being a much sought-after talent.

Yet for all his recognized strengths, Ronald felt a degree of insecurity. An introvert, he shied away from social gatherings and felt awkward with casual interactions. He intimated that "In business discussions or meetings, I'm well prepared, and my opinions are respected, but I tend to be quiet, only speaking up when necessary." Ronald's personality assessment revealed him to be a perfectionist who didn't take failure easily. He admitted, "I feel enormous stress when things are not going according to plan. I tend to hold it all in, and occasionally the pent-up emotion boils over, leading to unintended outbursts with my team members."

I asked Ronald what effect this has on those around him. He replied, "My team meetings tend to focus on business and have a serious overtone. I seem to miss what is really going on, and sometimes I'm the last one to hear the news." He sighed.

I probed further to learn more about his outbursts. "Even though they're few and far between, people are gun shy around me and kind of tiptoe around topics." When asked about team ambiance, Ronald confessed, "I just don't think my team members are enjoying our monthly meetings. They can hardly wait for them to end to have a drink with each other and unwind. I kind of feel those are a waste of time, so I don't usually attend. To be honest, I feel quite alone."

What we had in Ronald was a talented, and in some ways brilliant, leader who didn't display the classic charismatic, ballsy leadership common to many "folk hero" leaders. It was a conundrum. He knew that he should engage the team more, yet he felt awkward doing so. He realized that he needed to build stronger, more-engaged relationships but didn't enjoy it. And he felt lonely and somewhat isolated. What was he to do?

At this point, I had to shift Ronald's paradigm. As he believed that most decisions were funneled up to him, he felt enormous responsibility. I suggested to Ronald, "What if you shifted your mindset and pushed more decision making to your leadership team? What if you got your team to take ownership over the common business-unit goals and deliverables? What if you tasked your team members to lead key initiatives and redefined your role as supporting those initiatives?" Ronald sat up in his chair with a puzzled look. "What does that mean, and how can it be done"? I then outlined a leadership-team framework and journey to high performance. I described how to create a sense of ownership among all members on key initiatives. Ronald grasped how, through strong team bonding, effective meetings, and collaboration, much more could be accomplished, leading to with superior results.

Ronald gave the thumbs up. Utilizing the TQ HealthCheck (explained in chapter 7), we measured the current state of team. It was mediocre at best. So we embarked on a two-year leadership team journey with several offsite sessions and lots of integration back in the office. The team began the transformation process to high performance. It worked on bonding with deeper relationships and trust. It started collaborating and aligning with its vision. Team members took pride in "walking their talk," and the sense of team identity became palpable. The leadership team worked diligently to engage in effective meetings with full participation.

Then an amazing thing happened: Ronald started to relax and smile more with his leadership team. No longer feeling the pressure to lead and decide everything on his own, he could focus on what he did best—strategy and thought leadership. He could then support and encourage his team members to deliver on both individual and team goals. I was astounded to witness Ronald becoming likable and fun. He admitted, "I am still one of the quieter ones, but my team members know I am there to support them, and they go the extra mile."

You might be thinking, "That's fine. It's great that Ronald became comfortable in his own boots with a transformed team. But what about results?" Yes, let's talk about results, because they are one of the primary reasons you would want to develop a High Performance Team.

Ronald's business unit went on to become the top performer in the country in terms of revenue growth and profitability. Moreover, his team's "engagement scores" skyrocketed to one of the best in the company. And remember the TQ HealthCheck? Taking it again after two years, the team attained the top tier: high performance!

Ronald's future is bright. Through his team's transformation, Ronald himself has shifted from feeling distant, awkward, and alone to experiencing belonging, comfort, and confidence. And team members are enjoying the success of being a High Performance Team.

———

Of course, there are many types of leaders, and most are not as shy and introverted as Ronald. Consider Alex. She heads up the medical function nationally for a large pharmaceutical company. She is well respected as one of the best in the business. As a medical doctor and with a PhD in medical science, she is frequently invited to be the keynote speaker at medical seminars and workshops. Alex enjoys good relationships with her leadership team members. She works hard to listen and shows care and concern for each of them. She is decisive and shows up with authority in meetings.

Alex possesses some classic leadership qualities, yet not all is rosy. Alex acknowledged, "I tend to dominate in meetings, so sometimes people just don't talk. It's hard getting people's real thoughts out in the open. I know that some people suck up to me, while others withdraw."

I asked Alex about the leadership-team dynamics. "There are three cliques in the team, and they really don't get along. I push them to cooperate, but alas, to no avail." When queried about how she felt, Alex confessed, "I just feel so much pressure to look after all of the difficult characters on this team. When there are conflicts, it always falls back on me to resolve them. Sometimes I feel like a mother hen trying to corral all her chicks!"

It became clear that Alex was operating in overdrive, trying to control everything. I asked her, "What if you could just let go and empower the team to work out its own differences? Do this by creating a framework and expectation that they collaborate and get along; it's a part of their job as team members."

She protested, "But left alone, they just disagree, and only I can intervene to straighten them out."

I retorted, "That's part of the problem. You believe you have to solve all the problems. What the team really needs is a new way to communicate with one another. First, they need to engage in safe, structured feedback with a focus on the team's welfare above their own welfare."

Alex relented. "I know that we need a true sense of 'team.' I know we need to collaborate more and be more transparent. Okay; I'm game."

After taking the TQ HealthCheck, it became clear that Alex's medical team was just in functioning mode. The diagnostics revealed a need to work on trust, feedback, collaboration, bonding, and fun. We engaged in a two-day comprehensive offsite at a lovely mountain resort to allow team members to unwind, relax, and come together in a nurturing environment. Structured feedback and trust building were core aspects of the offsite. We explored and aligned on values and behaviors that everyone was expected to demonstrate back at work. With lots of practice, showing up as a "real team" back at the office, coupled with another offsite program, Alex's medical team was clearly transforming. One year after starting the journey, they took the TQ HealthCheck again, edging very close to high performance.

Alex's demeanor as a leader changed markedly. Still as passionate as ever about her work, she now sees herself as more of an enabler as opposed to a controller. When dustups arise, she lets them play out with the expectation that the team will resolve their problems using the framework they have been given. Having developed her reputation as a skilled leader of teams, Alex just got promoted to a larger role. Yes, building High Performance Teams can do wonders for your career!

Ronald and Alex represent just two of the myriad of leadership styles and their corresponding challenges. No matter what your challenge, your team is your ally. It can make the difference between your being considered "good" vs. "great." Leading a team is exciting because it affords you the luxury to build and manage it in any way that suits your own needs and the needs of the organization.

Teams are extraordinarily adaptable. They can move in any direction according to where you and its members want it to go.

Yes, there is a better way. You don't need to feel lonely at the top. In this book, we will show you how to leverage your team to create stellar results. We will outline a proven and effective team framework within the context of a team journey. We will provide the simple yet effective TQ measurement framework to establish a baseline for the team and track its progress. All the tools and methodologies you need on the journey are contained herein.

—————

HOW TO USE THIS BOOK

This book is laid out in several parts:

Part I, The Imperative, highlights the "why" and "what" of TQ, including lessons and case studies from business and sports teams.

Part II, The TQ Journey, illustrates the processes and methodologies of Team Quotient, and the framework for building High Performance Teams

Part III, Building, addresses types of teams and building them out, highlighting specific watch outs depending on the type of team you manage.

Part IV, The Leader's Operating Manual, is a "how to" guide for creating your own High-TQ Team. It provides all the detailed tools and approaches which you can use with your team.

CORE CONCEPTS OF TEAM QUOTIENT

Familiarizing yourself with a few core concepts will help put TQ into perspective, before you get started. Moving a team to high performance is a journey over time, which in our experience can take between 1 to 2 years, depending on the current state of the team and intentions of its members:

THE 2-STEP HIGH PERFORMANCE TEAM (HPT) JOURNEY
STEP 1—TRANSFORM: Assess, and Develop Team Culture
STEP 2—INTEGRATE: Embed, Renew, and Certify

The journey to become a High Performance Team entails two major steps or stages on the journey: "Transform" deals with understanding where the team is today, where it wants to go, then creating a new *team culture*.

"Integrate" deals with how to sustain and integrate the new team culture into the larger team or organization back at the office or plant, in order to ultimately arrive at the state of High Performance.

In order to Transform and Integrate, the team must develop and embody the Eight Essential Elements of a High Performance (or High TQ) Team. These eight elements are based on interviews with over 100 leadership teams over 15 years, on what constitutes a High Performance Team. We have condensed the results into the eight elements, summarized by the acronym VIVRE FAT:

$$
\begin{array}{l}
V \text{ision} \\
I \text{dentity} \\
V \text{alues} \\
R \text{esults} \\
E \text{ffective} \\[6pt]
F \text{un} \\
A \text{ligned} \\
T \text{rust}
\end{array}
$$

The detail of the TQ Journey and Eight Essential Elements can be found in Chapter 6. Then Part IV expands VIVRE FAT, demonstrating all the tools and processes necessary to incorporate the eight elements into your own team; essentially it's the operating manual for your team.

Most teams say they want to move to high performance, but how does it know where it is now? That's where "Team Quotient" comes in. Doing the TQ HealthCheck, gives your team a Team Quotient score, allowing it to measure and track its progress.

TQ SCORE GUIDE	
41–50	You are a High Performance Team!
34–40	You are a performing team.
27–33	You are a functioning team.
20–26	You are a barely functioning team.
10–19	You are a dysfunctional team.

TQ is an easy and expedient tool to measure the current state of the team and track potential future states. It forms a quantitative diagnostic for areas to work on and objectifies the process, leaving out guesswork and subjectivity. More details on measuring Team Quotient are highlighted in Chapter 7.

You can treat this book as a comprehensive guide for building High Performance Teams. If you are interested in first grasping the core concepts in detail, jump to chapters 6 and 7. Or, if you would like to cherry pick some specific element, say 'vision' or 'trust', check out those chapters. Alternatively, perhaps you are more intrigued by the real life team lessons and case studies such as Ford, GSK, Kimberly Clark or others. Whatever your interest, you are bound to take away some potent lessons on building and nurturing your own team.

Enjoy the High Performance Team journey!

PART I

THE IMPERATIVE

WHY HIGH-TQ TEAMS ACHIEVE SUPERIOR PERFORMANCE

1

TEAM QUOTIENT

CAN YOU BUILD A WINNING TEAM?

"An individual can make a difference,
but a team makes a miracle."[1]

Doug Pederson,
Head Coach of the Philadelphia Eagles,
after winning 2018 Super Bowl LII

You may have picked up this book because you are interested in building a High Performance Team. Or you may have tasted the allure of being on a great team, either—in business, sports, or elsewhere—and long for that feeling of being part of a well-oiled machine. Alternatively, you may never have experienced being part of a great team but can envisage its potential. Perhaps you are simply curious about the notion of TQ. Rest assured; you are in the right place!

The ensuing chapters will provide a road map for building a High Performance Team. The road map has built-in flexibility; you can start slowly and work steadily, or you can take the turbocharged approach and roar ahead (Chapters 6 and 7 detail the roadmap and methodology of Team Quotient).

The elegance of the model is that it allows you to move at your own pace. In other words, you can take a more basic approach, or proceed in a comprehensive manner. Whichever route you choose, understand that success will require the full buy in of your team. With knowledge, intention, persistence, and time, you will succeed. And a successful team carries tangible and palpable benefits.

THE GENESIS OF TEAM QUOTIENT

Fate is funny. When I began my corporate career more than 30 years ago as an aspiring and ambitious professional, the prospect of consulting on High Performance Teams was the farthest thing from my mind. However in 1998, when I was appointed vice president of sales for PepsiCo Greater China Region, I was given the mandate to take the sales and distribution function to the next level and had to build a team from scratch. Within five years, I had successfully built a High Performance Team that experienced minimal staff turnover. We had moved to the #1 market share position in all of our targeted cities and crossed the line to profitability. Moreover, we had transformed our go-to-market model.

It was during those years that I discovered I had a talent for team transformation and developed a passion for creating and nurturing teams. It was also during those years that I caught a glimpse of what was possible for other companies and teams to accomplish. Among other things, I discovered how a winning team can accomplish so much more than a leader can, alone, and how a High Performance Team is a rare, yet potent, phenomenon that can impact not only business but the lives and experiences of the team's members.

In 2003, after a successful tenure in the Greater China Region, in which PepsiCo transformed its business, I left to start my own consulting firm, Focus One. I wanted to share the benefit of what had worked so effectively for me by teaching other organizations how to build High Performance Teams. My transition into this field actually began ten years earlier when I had attended a corporate leadership program conducted by Dr. Marshall Goldsmith, one of the fathers of executive coaching. After reviewing my personality assessment and several discussions, Marshall challenged me with, "Douglas, what are you doing in corporate? Everything I see from your assessment shows that you'd be a great executive coach!" At the time, I laughed off Marshall's prodding, but his encouragement must have remained in the back of my mind, because ten years later I found my niche as a leadership team coach, encouraging leadership teams to commit to achieving high performance.

After working with hundreds of teams over the last 15 years through my company, Focus One, I realized that High Performance Teams possess certain traits or attributes that make them excel. These traits can be measured and tracked over time through what I call the "Team Quotient," or "TQ." Plain and simple: The formula works. It is repeatable and provable. Develop High TQ, and your team will move toward high performance.

So how did TQ come about? In my work with teams, I reflected on the fact that we, as human beings, like to measure everything. We have IQ (intelligence quotient), EQ (emotional intelligence quotient), and now even SQ (social intelligence quotient). One morning, the thought occurred to me: "Why not 'TQ?'"

Then something amazing happened. That afternoon, I was coaching an executive from Cathay Pacific Airways and chatting about team effectiveness and how to measure it. Out of the blue, my client said, "Yes. What we really need is TQ." My morning thought had turned into an afternoon reality!

SO WHAT IS A "WINNING TEAM" ANYWAY?

Perhaps you aren't convinced of the benefits of creating a winning team in your organization. What is a "winning team," anyway? Let's use this remarkable sports story as our example.

The Leicester City football team in England's Premier League was a poor team of nobodies that had never won anything in the Premier League in their 138-year history. Yet with new owners and a new coach, wild fans, and unbeatable team spirit, these unheralded players came out of nowhere to win the championship in 2016. It was an achievement considered by many to be the greatest ever seen in the history of team sports. It demonstrated how a small club with limited resources managed to defeat the might of the ultra-rich soccer giants: Arsenal, Manchester United, and others.

My friend, Richard Warburton, who hails from Leicester City and is passionate about his team, recounts the fascinating tale.

LESSONS FROM LEICESTER CITY

Stranded at the bottom of the Premier League for most of the 2014–15 season and expected to be relegated to the lower league, Leicester City found its form and won eight out of their last ten games to avoid the drop. That in itself was considered a miracle, but it was nothing compared to what was to unfold in the 2015–16 season. When Leicester City began the new season, oddsmakers gave it incredible 5000:1 odds to win the league. What were the key elements to their amazing success, and who was the team behind it?

Unable to attract the "superstars" of the league, Leicester's team consisted of a group of players from seven different nationalities, including a Danish goalkeeper, a French/Malian midfielder, and Japanese and Argentinian strikers. Each of these players had talent, but more importantly, their coaches saw them as a group that worked hard and played for each other rather than as individuals. Their "escape" from being dropped from the Premier League the previous season had instilled confidence in the team and a strong bond that continued to deepen as the season progressed. As results began to go their way, the team members started to believe that anything was possible.

> How did a small English football club with limited resources that had never won a championship in their 138-year history win the Premier League?

According to Fox Sports, Australia: "So, how has a humdrum team from central England that was nearly relegated last season managed, and was in administration seven years ago, overcome the mega-rich giants of the Premier League? TEAM SPIRIT. The seeds of Leicester's charge to the title were sown at the end of last season when the team pulled off the greatest escape from relegation ever seen in the Premier League. Seven wins in their last nine games lifted the Foxes from last place to safety, demonstrating the togetherness and ability in the squad. The team spirit was in place . . ."[2]

But the team didn't do it alone. Their success also required an innovative manager, open-minded owners, and passionate fans. These may seem like elements of "luck," but the Leicester City team did a lot of things right. Give much of the credit to the team's manager.

In his 30-year managerial career, affable 64-year-old Italian Claudio Ranieri had never won a European title—but he had come close. Known as the "Tinkerman" for constantly changing tactics and players, Claudio saw immediately that that would not be the right approach for this closely-knit team. Consequently, he kept the same lineup week after week, which increased the team's confidence and bonding. He was also quick to praise the players, taking them out for pizzas from time to time. He trusted his players, and they trusted him. On one famous occasion, Leicester had unluckily lost a game in the last minute of play to a major rival, Arsenal, and heads were down. He sent the team off to Dubai for a few days to relax, regroup, and do some light training—without pressure. This was a masterstroke. They came back with a vengeance, not losing in the next 12 games and setting themselves up for the title. Claudio also said that success was for the fans, referring to them as the "twelfth man." Ranieri gave credit to the "team spirit" after winning the Premier League. "The players have been fantastic. Their focus, their determination, their spirit has made this possible. Every game they fight for each other, and I love to see this in my players. They deserve to be champions."[3]

LEARN FROM THE BEST

Great teams are created by great leaders. What makes a great leader? In *Fortune* magazine's "The World's 50 Greatest Leaders,"[4] Geoff

Colvin identifies three key lessons taught by leaders who excel in today's environment: 1) acknowledge reality and hope, 2) bring followers physically together, and 3) build bridges. On point number two, Colvin writes, "Research shows that *when groups meet in person, face-to-face, they trust each other more, become better problem solvers, and are markedly more creative.* Those are outcomes every organization needs more of." Great leaders bring people and teams together in person—not just over the phone, video conference, or group chat. It is a key skill that many of today's leaders sorely lack. Later in this book, we will illustrate that no matter how much we communicate virtually or remotely, some degree of face-to-face meeting is essential to building a High Performance Team.

THE SIX PREREQUISITES TO EMBARKING ON THE TQ JOURNEY

Before you begin the journey of team development, you, the leader, need to ask yourself a few questions to ensure that you are ready. (These questions also apply to team members about to embark on the same journey.)

1. Are you willing to shift your own attitude to put the team first? As a team leader, you may need to make a fundamental change in your approach or attitude. This is because team members can feel it when you are committed to them; conversely, they know when you are not committed. Here is the good news: being open and willing to adopt a new attitude is the most important step. When you begin the team transformation process, you'll be taking the ride of your life, and the experiences you'll have will encourage and sustain you.

2. Are you committed to the journey, not just to off-sites and interventions? One of my missions at Focus One is to create awareness that we are not about *team building*; we are about *team transformation*. When I speak about building High Performance Teams, many people think that refers to classic "team building" involving entertaining activities and experiences that build team spirit. In fact, there is a whole industry of team-building companies that provide this function, such as Outward Bound, as well as other companies that offer team challenges, team day outings, rope courses, and specific activities designed for specific outcomes. One such organization with whom I work occasionally is Team Building Asia, that offers uniue and well executed programs along certain themes, such as "competitiveness," "creativity," "innovation," "icebreakers," "energizers," and so on. Each of these programs is effective in galvanizing a team around developing new team skills. There are a lot of takeaways and "aha" moments. The key is ensuring there is continuity back at the office or plant.

If you have ever participated in team-building activities and programs, ask yourself, "When we returned to the office, did we return to the same old habits?" Therein lies the challenge: *how to create team transformation, not just team experience.* The commitment and hard work begin the day you return to the office. Sure, there are enormous benefits to be gained from the first intervention, but the journey to high performance is ongoing and, in fact, never ends.

3. Are you clear that team success implies personal success, as well? I often ask clients and audiences a fundamental question; "Would you rather be a great player on a mediocre team or a good player on a great team?" Usually, 20 to 30 percent of people I ask would rather be a great player on a mediocre team. The reasons

> The journey is not about team building; it's about team transformation.

why include, "I can bring the team along," "I can raise the bar for the team," and "I can stand out more easily." The following story illustrates the fallacy of these arguments.

Lessons from a Top-Five Global Advertising Agency
A few years ago, I conducted a High Performance Team development program for the Singapore office of one of the top-five global advertising firms. Their challenges were formidable: the team ranked in the lower quartile in both customer and employee satisfaction. The team was fragmented and demonstrated palpable conflict.

Interestingly, there were several star players on the team who were very effective at what they did. Unfortunately for them, the perception of the team as one of the worst on the globe tugged at their collective self-esteem. Those star players carried the stigma of being on a "low-TQ team."

> Being a member or leader of a great team can do wonders for your own success and career!

Within 18 months of committing to move from a dysfunctional to a High Performance Team, things began to turn around. The unit transformed from being in the bottom quartile to the top quartile in company, customer, and employee satisfaction. The dysfunctional team became a star team. And what happened to those star performers? They were finally recognized and promoted to other units in the agency!

The lessons are clear: if you have a chance to be on or lead a great team, jump on it. *Being a member or leader of a great team can do wonders for your own success and career.* You will reap the benefit of belonging to a group of committed people who are rooting for you and are invested in your success.

4. Are you willing to let others shine, lead, and be in the limelight, or do you need to control everything? As a leader, you are expected to lead the team to success. This doesn't mean that you are expected to have all the answers, make all the decisions, or lead all the meetings. When working with clients, I stress that, during the team transformation process, the leader needs to occasionally take a backseat and let others lead. Often leaders have "positional power" with the ability to make decisions, lead, and manage team members as he wishes, however that doesn't necessarily translate into success. To accomplish change, the team leader needs to encourage a healthy mix of leading from the front and encouraging others to lead certain aspects.

Lessons from a Major French Bank

Recently, I conducted a program with a major French bank, and the team leader noticed that one individual had the kind of charisma that could bring people together. He then empowered the individual to lead some of the key projects that involved organizing people and galvanizing them around certain projects, with great success. The leader recognized this individual had the talent to lead and gave him the opportunity to demonstrate it.

When I do team interventions, I often ask the leader to sit back and act as one of the participants. It's amazing how this can unleash creativity, fun, and participation from other team members. To accomplish this, the leader needs to be willing to let go of control and trust in the process and other team players.

5. How is your "openness/transparency and ability-to-receive-feedback" meter? This is where being a great team in an organization tends to be different from being a great sports team. Leaders (coaches) in sports teams often possess strong command and control and are seen as strong authority figures. That is because sports performance is often 'in the moment' with a limited time window, and decisions need to be made on the spot. Not even the star quarterback with the multimillion dollar salary will question the plays that the coach sends in to the huddle. In a corporate organization, however, time frames are often much longer; projects and programs can involve many stakeholders over a series of interactions.

It isn't just team members who need openness and feedback. Leaders need to be open to feedback and be willing to self-correct. You want your people to feel free to give feedback on ANY aspect of leadership/management.

Lessons from the IT Team at Cathay Pacific Airways

A while back, I was hired to coach an IT team for Cathay Pacific Airways. The team leader was a strong visionary and had an oversized personality, but his confrontational nature caused people to shy away from him, dampening collaboration and openness. I encouraged this team leader to seek feedback from the team. Initially, he resisted, however he finally relented, and during the feedback session, he remained open and calm. He made a commitment to the team to take the feedback to heart. This was an enormously valuable exercise, and he changed some key behaviors as a result. Lessons that may have taken years to learn were gleaned in a matter of days, just through this feedback process!

6. Do you have the facilitation skills to lead the team through the process, or do you need help? Be honest. As the leader of the team, are you also a good facilitator? Are you willing and able to lead the team through the various steps required to develop a High Performance Team? Or do you feel more comfortable stepping back and allowing someone else to handle parts of the job? The process of leading the off-sites and modules, which you will learn in this book, requires skill and practice. The facilitator needs to be impartial and objective. Can you do that effectively? If you feel confident, that's great. If not, you might consider asking other people to facilitate parts of the program. This may be someone internal to your organization, such as someone from human resources, or a team member. Alternatively, it may be an external facilitator who is adept at leading teams through difficult issues and knows when to apply the right levers and ramp the energy up or down, as required.

I offer this perspective: every company is built upon scores of people and teams at all levels and functions, and of all types. It is not the *leaders* who get things done; rather it is the *teams* that execute, produce, and deliver the outcome that the leader desires. Therefore, as a leader, an essential trait is the extent to which you develop teams with High-Team Quotient. High-TQ Teams are intelligent teams that operate at the highest level of performance, however that performance gets defined by the team.

2

WHAT'S MISSING IS TQ

Lessons from a Pharmaceutical Leader

Jack had just been appointed as the new business unit head of a major pharmaceutical company. I was assigned to be Jack's coach in 2014. Jack was elated about his new job, but he had some concerns. His predecessor had left quite suddenly, and given his predecessor's relatively long tenure and strong relationships with his leadership team, Jack was concerned that some of the team members might leave, as well.

Jack's first priority was to stabilize his team. "How can I build a strong stable team when there are obvious loyalties to my predecessor?" he asked me.

I coached Jack on first building solid one-on-one relationships within his leadership team and then working on developing the team. I mentored him on shifting the paradigm by creating a new team culture—one that could supersede the influence of any previous relationship. The new team culture would create a powerful team identity. What the team needed and was missing was High TQ.

Jack agreed but lamented, "I don't know where to start, and I need to move fast!" I suggested that the entire team take the TQ HealthCheck to diagnose their current state. The results came back crystal clear: this leadership team needed to focus on trust building, feedback, camaraderie, and meeting effectiveness and to reinforce its identity. The TQ score came out as 38/50 (50 is the top score), meaning it was already a "Performing Team," but Jack wasn't satisfied, exclaiming, "I want to go for a High Performance Team!"

In December 2015, we engaged in a two-day off-site program to build the culture and identity of the team. Feedback, trust, meeting effectiveness, and camaraderie were stressed. At the end of the program, the shift was palpable; the team was clearly aligned on what kind of team it wanted to be and how to get there. Back at the office, the team practiced the new habits and rituals to which it had committed, and together members championed many team initiatives.

> Our team welfare is more important than team members' individual welfares.

After about eight months, Jack and I talked about how the team was progressing, He said, "I'm happy about the ongoing transformation, yet I sense some of the old habits and turf building creeping back in."

"It's normal that between six-to-nine months after a TQ-team off-site stagnation will set in," I noted. "That means it's time for 'round two.'"

In December of 2016, we proceeded to the second off-site program to take stock of progress, learn how to deepen the relationships and trust, and move forward. It was at this off-site that the team had its breakthrough realization that "our team welfare is more important than team members' individual welfares." The team identity was beginning to crystallize.

In mid 2017, Jack's team took the TQ HealthCheck the second time and earned a TQ score of 44/50. It was a major breakthrough, and we certified Jack's team as a High Performance Team! The leadership team had transformed those areas of weakness (trust, feedback, camaraderie) into strengths.

Yet the power of Jack's leadership team extended beyond itself to include the entire business unit team consisting of thousands of people. The company's highly visible annual engagement survey showed an improvement of Jack's entire business unit from 53 percent engagement in 2014 to 79 percent in 2017! Thus we witnessed a strong correlation between a High-TQ leadership team and high overall engagement. How did this happen? The leaders on Jack's team brought the energy, values, and focus they had gained as part of the leadership team into their own teams, as well, providing a potent effect. A strong leadership team affects the entire organization in a powerful way.

> A strong leadership team affects the entire organization in a powerful way.

But it didn't stop there. Jack's team went on to become the most successful team within all business units in key performance indicators. They surpassed their targets on most measures, becoming a star team.

For Jack's team, what had been missing was High TQ. The two years of focus, dedication, and willingness to spend the time and energy to move to High TQ paid off for Jack's team. It can pay off for your team, too. Now, let's define TQ and how to measure it.

WHAT IS TQ?

Over the past 15 years of working with teams, I have noticed that something was missing from the skill set and arsenal of most executives: TQ, or "Team Quotient", a concept which I coined and trademarked which means—*the degree to which team members work together effectively as a High Performance Team.* It's a new way of looking at intelligence from the perspective of the team.

There are two types of Team Quotient: Collective TQ and Personal TQ (outlined in more detail in Chapter 7):

1. Collective TQ. Collective TQ measures the *team's ability to operate as a High Performance Team.* A team with a high Collective TQ

- consistently and effectively delivers results
- aligns its goals and positions and collaborates well
- conducts effective, productive, and engaged meetings

- possesses high trust and openly gives feedback
- knows what is important and behaves in accordance with its values
- is highly motivated, enjoys working as a team, and enjoys strong relationships among team members.

Teams with a high Collective TQ possess a strong identity. Team members take pride in their work and enjoy collaborating with their teammates. A team with a high Collective TQ believes in itself and its capabilities and knows where it is going and how to get there. It's a team that celebrates its successes and constantly reflects and self-corrects.

I consult extensively with many executive teams. One of the big shifts that High TQ Teams experience is *adopting the attitude that "team success is just as important as individual success."*

Most people approach the team environment with individual agendas and the desire to shine and be recognized; it's human nature. In fact, some team leaders even encourage competition and conflict, believing that friendly competition will encourage team members to improve. What they should really be striving for is not competition but, rather, accountability to the team, the sentiment that "I, as a team member, want to do my best for the team and not let them down."

> High TQ Teams believe team success is just as important as individual success.

The notion of "accountability to the team" is considerably more powerful than "competition between team members." It engenders support, cooperation, recognition, and collaboration. The sense of accountability is strongest when there is clear willingness to put the team first.

Lessons from a Top-Ten Global Bank

One of my clients, a top-ten global bank, embarked on a High Performance Team journey. In the middle of an off-site workshop, one of the managers came forward after an impactful team activity and declared, "I just realized that

I've been putting myself first all these years, and what I really need to do is put the team first!" I was elated to hear his declaration. He got a core message naturally, without me having to spell it out.

Focus on the team's success leads to success for all. It is the best and surest way to get noticed in an organization. It is the fullest expression of TQ in action. But doing so requires a shift in our habitual thought patterns.

I often use questions to help team members reframe their team attitudes:

REFRAMING TEAM ATTITUDES

FROM	TO
How can I get noticed?	How can the team get noticed?
How can I shine?	How can I help others shine?
How can I get recognized?	How can I recognize team members?
How can I one-up you?	How can we both win?
How can I contribute a good answer?	How can we utilize our collective mind power to come up with the best answer?
How can I win this point?	How can we come up with the best solution for all?

Figure 2.1

2. Personal TQ. If Collective TQ is a measure of the entire team, then Personal TQ is the *degree to which each team member works effectively in the team*. High Personal TQ team members

- become effective communicators within the team context
- emphasize cooperation and collaboration
- have a well-developed awareness of fellow team members' styles, preferences, strengths, and development opportunities
- engage other team members and are very active in discussions
- are willing to challenge where necessary, but not to the point of creating personal conflict
- are good listeners and allow others to express their ideas

- recognize others frequently and provide and welcome open feedback to help each other grow and improve.

Personal TQ is distinct from being a "team player," which essentially means going along with and supporting the team. TQ implies a higher level of intelligence in working with the team. It may mean challenging other team members while maintaining good relationships. High and well-developed Personal TQ isn't limited to leaders. All team members need to develop Personal TQ to move to High Performance and increase the Collective TQ. Personal TQ is not natural; it is learned over time and requires consistent practice, feedback, and self-correction.

> Personal TQ is not natural; it is learned over time and requires consistent practice, feedback, and self-correction.

Personal TQ is not some ideal way of behaving or acting. It is, however, based on having the right *intentions* for others and the team, and incorporating *attitudes* conducive to moving the team to High Performance. It also requires *action* to make an impact on the team.

The Higher the IQ, the Lower the TQ!

Many highly intelligent executives have challenges leading or operating in High Performance Teams for several reasons. First, there is the IQ/EQ ratio. It takes decent EQ to nurture a great team. Many extremely bright executives err on the side of focusing on their own intelligence. Their intelligence may have gotten them where they are today, yet they now need to make a shift from "executive genius" to "team brilliance," taking their genius and applying it to the team. When high IQ is applied for the benefit of the team, both collective and individual TQ start to develop.

The other reason that highly intelligent executives are challenged to operate well in a team, is that they often have oversized egos. Their egos may have given them the drive, strength, and confidence to accomplish great things, but when building a High

Performance Team, it's time to park the ego. Focusing on *others* and helping them become great results in a High Performance Team. This implies a team that is proud of its work and accomplishments, wants to shine and win, and believes that it is, indeed, very important to the

> It is imperative to shift from expressing a big personal ego, to developing a big team ego.

company. *In order to win, it is imperative to shift from expressing a big personal ego, to developing a big team ego.*

HOW TO MEASURE TQ

Team Quotient is a measurable phenomenon. This is important because 1) what gets measured gets done, and 2) teams need to be able to assess how they're doing and what progress is being made.

There is a formula for scoring TQ (outlined in chapter 7) that allows teams to track progress, celebrate wins, and have a clear direction in which to work. TQ is measured on a scale of 10 (dysfunctional) to 50 (High Performance). The real utility of the tool is the benchmarking of progress along ten dimensions. Teams take pride in increasing their TQ, and arriving at High Performance is a major event. Importantly, TQ allows for a diagnosis of the strengths and the areas to work on.

The following chapters provide a step-by-step outline of how the team can develop and measure High TQ and move to High Performance, thereby winning with sustained competitive advantage.

The need to invest in your team may seem obvious. However leaders and organizations chronically underinvest in team development. Let's find out why.

THE FOUR REASONS TQ IS MISSING FROM MOST TEAMS

Your "personal development" and the "development of your people" or talent, are two key areas to which you probably have made commitments. The third, not widely recognized area is "team development," leading to High TQ.

Leaders usually start with personal development, then move on to people development, and finally, if at all, to team development. Yet it is an area in which tangible results can be realized.

Team development is unique in the sense that it is not a solitary or one-on-one relationship. Team development is a dynamic, multifaceted endeavor with potential for true synergy. There is no limit to the heights an effective team can reach.

> Team development is a dynamic, multifaceted endeavor with potential for true synergy.

Personal and people development are supported by the massive resources that organizations devote to these efforts. Human Resource departments dedicate "Talent/Learning and Development" functions to managing these initiatives. Such development efforts are high profile, whether they are achieved through executive education, leadership programs, executive coaching, or assessment centers. What is less obvious to many organizations—but is gaining steam—is the importance of team development. With its power to create extraordinary results, why is team development under recognized? Let's look at several reasons:

1. Building a High Performance Team is hard work. During team development sessions, I often ask my clients how many of them are married. Many participants raise their hands. I then ask if marriage is easy. Inevitably the answer is, "Marriage is hard work!" Imagine you are leading a team of eight people. Now multiply the hard work of marriage by eight. This illustrates the degree of complexity involved in developing a High Performance Team. The team must be developed within the context of eight different styles and personalities and within a complex array of relationships, all of which come with conflicts and a lack of natural team cohesion.

2. Team development requires expertise. One of the major reasons leaders don't spend more time developing their teams is that they don't know how to do it! Team development involves much more than running good meetings. It demands having a comprehensive view of the team in the context of mutual relationships and interactions, goals, culture, markets, clients, organizations, and stakeholders. It requires a view and a vision of what the team wants to accomplish over time and a road map guiding the members to the goal. The team leader needs to be a good facilitator (or have the wisdom to find an external one), and to possess a reasonable level of "emotional intelligence." Building High Performance Teams compels a leader to acquire this knowledge and experience.

3. Developing teams takes time. During my off-site team interventions, we take advantage of "low-hanging team fruit" and see noticeable results within one-to-two days. Yes, it's true; after two days, the team will start to visibly transform. But make no mistake: moving all the way to a High Performance Team takes time— usually from one to two years. That's why clients often engage consultative support over a series of interactions. What happens during team interventions is important, but what happens *between* interventions is equally vital. It's during the "back to the office" time that positive habits develop and sustaining interactions occur.

4. Developing teams doesn't happen naturally. What is "natural?" Beginning at birth, we are concerned with ourselves and our own special needs. As we mature, we find ways to meet those needs. In many Western societies, the prevailing axiom is, "Looking out for number one." In some Eastern societies, the "group" mentality is deeply engrained in the psyche, however even Eastern societies are increasingly trending toward individual focus. China's former one-child policy has caused the country to breed hundreds of millions of "princes and princesses." As a result, despite a strong nationalistic and collective awareness, mainland Chinese possess a high degree of individualism. Thus, in any culture, moving beyond "personal focus" to include "team focus" is not a natural mindset. It takes conscious effort to focus on the team ahead of the individual. That requires strong motivation and conscious intention. The paradox is that in order to engage successfully in a High Performance Team, members must operate from a strong "sense of team" and feel deeply that team welfare is paramount.

Given the above factors in regard to team development—that it is hard work, requires expertise, takes time, and doesn't happen naturally—less time and energy tend to be devoted toward that development. As a result, the "team" concept suffers.

Figure 2.2 represents the typical energy and time commitments allocated to the three developmental areas. However, after shifting the focus toward *team development*, the amount of time and energy spent by leaders will naturally shift. By spending between 30 and 40 percent of their time on team development as in figure 2.3, leaders can achieve more balance among all three developmental areas listed in figure 2.2

DEVELOPMENT AREAS	LEADERS' TIME AND ENERGY	REASONS
Personal Development	40–70%	Is controllable Is self-oriented Is flexible and manageable
People Development	20–40%	Is usually part of HR agenda Often has a provided structure Can be awkward Requires coaching/mentoring skills Is often paid lip service
Team Development (prior to embarking on the High Performance Team journey)	5–10%	Can be hard work Requires know how Takes time Is not natural Has fewer role models

Figure 2.2

DEVELOPMENT AREAS	LEADERS' TIME AND ENERGY	REASONS
Team Development (after embarking on the High Performance Team journey)	30–40%	Provides tangible benefits Gives high return on effort Has high impact on results and team Offers high visibility and recognition Results in positive energy and engagement and fulfillment

Figure 2.3

Focusing on team development requires a rethink of where the leader will spend their development time, energy, and focus. Through reflection, most leaders will realize that investment in their Team Quotient will yield a sizable return. Just like Jack's team, your team can reap the benefits of being a High Performance Team.

TEAM INTELLIGENCE IS THE NEXT STEP IN BUILDING GREAT BUSINESS

Organizations have focused enormous resources on developing strong, inspirational, and visionary leaders. Savvy leaders increasingly realize that going beyond personal development to include team development is essential to enjoying a competitive edge. Star players alone cannot create the desired success. The old saying that "A chain is only as strong as its weakest link" applies here. Apply this to business, and you discover that *"Leaders are only as good as the teams they build."*

How does an organization go beyond individual intelligence to team intelligence? The answer is simple: develop teams with High TQ. By definition, High TQ implies a High Performance Team, a team that knows itself, is aware of its strengths and development areas, accepts other team members' styles and preferences, and appreciates the team as it is, as well as for its potential.

A High Performance Team is clear about where it wants to go and its vision, and it is aligned on how all team members will exhibit its values and behaviors. It focuses on the big things that will create results. By its very definition, it performs at the highest level. High Performance Team members elicit a high degree of mutual trust and collaborate willingly with one another. Finally, they are energized and motivated to work together and enjoy a strong sense of team identity.

Team members with High TQ feel a profound sense of accountability to each other. They leverage the entire team intelligence to work synergistically, creating notable results. As an example, in this book you will read of the legacy of Alan Mulally, former CEO of Ford, who knew the power of teams and working together. He built a team with High TQ and, in the process, achieved sustained, superior results that outperformed competitors.

Throughout this book, we will explore how TQ creates superior results and how to create High TQ within your own team.

3

WINNING SPORTS TEAMS
POSSESS HIGH TQ

The Golden State Warriors' domination of the Cleveland Cavaliers in the 2018 NBA championship series was cringeworthy. The 4-0 sweep makes us pause. It became clear that while Cleveland relied on their top talent Lebron James, Golden State played as a team. When Steph Curry fell flat, Kevin Durant and others stepped up. This was the battle of *'team vs. man'*; there was no contest.

In the 2018 Super Bowl LII, Tom Brady and the stars at the New England Patriots withered against the Philadelphia Eagles superior team cohesiveness, spirit and determination, led by Nick Foles, the back-up quarterback. The proud Patriots could never catch the ambitious Eagles, who won 41-33. This was the battle of *'team vs. stars'*; the team wins.

The above iconic examples demonstrate that in team sports, the team is more important than any individual player. As described in Chapter 2, TQ is the measure of how effectively team members work together as a High Performance Team. Success or failure in team sports, depends on the extent to which the team can nurture High TQ. There is no better example of sucesss and failure than the German World Cup Football Team, the champions in 2014, dominating their opponents, and an embarrassment in 2018, crashing out early.

"DIE MANNSCHAFT"
Germany's World Cup Team in 2014

"In the 11th minute, the Germans scored from their first corner of the game. Thomas Müller escaped his marker, David Luiz, in the penalty box, and Toni Kroos's delivery found him wide open for a side-footed shot into the net . . . Germany scored again after Kroos and Müller combined to set up Miroslav Klose, who scored on the rebound after his initial shot was saved by goalkeeper Júlio César. It was Klose's 16th goal at a World Cup, passing Ronaldo as the all-time World Cup top scorer . . .

Klose's goal initiated a flurry of German scoring as Brazil lost control of the game. All five of Germany's first-half goals came within the first half-hour, with four of them coming in one six-minute period. Brazil had no shots on target in the first half. Many Brazil supporters in the crowd were visibly in shock or reduced to tears . . .

With the score at 7–0, the home fans (in Brazil) gave the Germans a standing ovation, applauding both Schürrle's goal and Germany's overall performance. Seconds later, Oscar received a long ball and scored in the 90th minute to make the score 7–1 . . . The Brazilian players left the pitch in tears to a chorus of boos."[5]

There are numerous examples of how High TQ is paramount to winning in team sports. None is more compelling than the 2014 World Cup in Brazil. All the stars of the participating teams played in this World Cup, including Neymar from Brazil, Ronaldo from Portugal,

And Messi from Argentina. Despite the fact that Germany's individual players were less acclaimed and not readily recognized on a global scale, "Die Mannschaft,"[6] the German National Football Team, dominated the Cup, thrashing Brazil in the semifinal and beating Argentina convincingly in the final.

> The real lesson of Germany's success is their High TQ, as evidenced from the backstory of how Germany prepared for the 2014 World Cup.

The real lesson of Germany's success is their High TQ, as evidenced from the backstory of how Germany prepared for the 2014 Cup. Well in advance of the Cup, the Germans invested heavily in their team with time and money, employing a novel strategy to become the best team ever. Coach Joachim Löw and General Manager Oliver Bierhoff made the calculated *investment in an intense training camp*—away from distractions—in a remote part of Brazil, as highlighted by Jeremy Wilson's article in *The Telegraph*:

> "It can be safely assumed that the 900 residents of the remote Brazilian fishing village of Santo Andre will never forget this World Cup . . .

> Why? Because while teams such as England simply checked themselves into a hotel in Rio—and then faced a daily battle through traffic for training—Santo Andre was handpicked by the German Football Federation (DFB) for what is a unique team base.

> '. . . This village has been a major factor in building up the special team spirit in the group today,' said left-back Benedikt Höwedes . . .

> '. . .The base was a very important point in the planning of the tournament for Germany,' says Lars Wallrodt, chief football writer of *Die Welt*. 'All the players have been talking

about it. The idea of living together in this way has been very good for team spirit. You have your own space, but the players are always bumping into each other around the resort."[7]

The Santo Andre training camp can be compared to "corporate off-sites" at which the team can "practice being a team" and, in essence, build up its TQ. After five weeks of practicing together, the German team would come to know and appreciate each other's strengths and weaknesses and develop a team spirit and identity, which would be hard to replicate. Knowing the success of the German experiment, I often encourage the idea of off-site environments, where the team can experience being together in a way not possible in the office. I would say to my clients, "If the German national team needed a five-week off-site to become 'world-class' competitors, couldn't your team invest one or two days?"

> After five weeks practicing together, the German team would come to know and appreciate each other's strengths and weaknesses and develop a team spirit and identity.

Yale School of Management's David Bach goes one step further, citing a sense of mission, inclusive culture, and shared values as key to Germany's success.

> ". . . Sound management cultivated a deep and broad pool of stars. And sound management forged them into a team with a mission and a plan. Peter Drucker reminds us that the task of management is to 'make people capable of *joint performance.*' A key to this, according to Drucker, is a 'commitment to common goals and shared values.' 'The mission of the organization,' he explains, 'has to be clear enough and big enough to provide common vision.'

> . . . What distinguished 'Die Mannschaft' was a combination of five factors: long-term capability development,

meticulous planning, an inclusive culture based on open communication and individual responsibility, competitive intelligence, and the confidence to deviate from the plan when circumstances required it."[8]

A few things in the Yale article stand out. First are the fundamental concepts of vision and mission. In Germany's case, these were identified years earlier. Germany's grandiose vision prompted a massive, multiyear investment in their team, borne out of a "burning platform" that, as we will discuss later in the book, is a key motivator for any team.

Next are "common goals and values," which were deeply embedded in all involved on the team. "An inclusive culture based on open communication and individual responsibility" is critical for team success. It is based on the distinction that it is inclusion, as opposed to competition, that creates a successful team in the long term. Open communication and feedback engender a sense of honesty and transparency, which are essential to team performance, allowing the team to shift and modify its approach as necessary. Ultimately "Die Mannschaft's" domination on the world stage in 2014 comes down to building the right team culture, which IS the hallmark of TQ.

WHAT HAPPENED TO "DIE MANNSCHAFT" IN 2018?

What goes up must come down. The German World Cup Football Teams contains two lessons of late; the 2014 team is a lesson in high performance. The 2018 team is a lesson in the *inability to sustain* performance. We can learn from both. Why did the 2018 team crash out so abruptly?

1. *Preparation*: in 2014, the Santo Andre training camp in Brazil was an uninterrupted investment in the team in a quiet, lush tropical oasis. Yet in 2018, Germany disrupted their preparation by splitting their training in two camps; one in Italy and the other in Vatutinki, 40 kilometers southwest of the Russian

capital. It was a dreary atmosphere with lots of rain, and not conducive to engendering a positive team mood and spirit.

2. *Distraction*: Players Mesut Özil's and Ilkay Gündogan's appeared to go rogue, meeting with the Turkish President Recep Erdogan at a sensitive time before the Cup, drawing disturbing noise and criticism from German fans and pundits.

3. *Lack of Team Unity*: in 2018 there appeared to be two camps on the team: the ambitious youngsters, and the experienced veterans who were part of the 2014 team. There is nothing which kills team spirit more than conflicting cliques or camps.

4. *Arrogance and complacency*: despite the poor showing prior to the Cup, and the dismal performance in the first matches, the Germans somehow believed everything would work out; instead they never found their rhythm, and bombed out.

5. *Loss of leaders*: the core leaders in 2014, including Philipp Lahm, Per Mertesacker and Miroslav Klose were missing from the 2018 squad. A dearth of on-the-field leadership ensued.

Ultimately "Die Mannschaft" was never able to live up to its expectations. It's a lesson for all teams, business or sports. You may achieve the state of high performance, yet, given a variety of factors; change of team members, external conditions, stress points, interference, and many others, the team can easily drop back down. As we will see in later chapters, the sustainability of high performance entails a relentless effort and intention to continuously improve; high performance is never enough!

LESSONS FROM TEAM SPORTS AND APPLYING THEM TO BUSINESS

In studying dozens of successful sports teams, I have derived eight characteristics that most of them share and that ultimately can be applied to business teams:

1. Mutual reliance (collaboration and cooperation)
2. Challenge to do your best (feedback)
3. Awareness

4. Identity and pride
5. Trust and confidence
6. Success and performance
7. Motivation and fun
8. Coaches encourage team commitment

If we apply these lessons to our respective businesses, what will the implication be for team members, the organization at large, the industry, competitors, and other stakeholders?

1. Mutual reliance (collaboration and cooperation).

Applied to Sports Teams:

Every team member plays his or her role. Without clear role identification, the team is handicapped. More importantly, team interactions are vital to success. In most ball games, kicking, passing, or throwing are the keys to scoring or being out of the game. These activities all require at least two participants. Therefore, team drills reinforcing how the team will work together represent the cornerstone of preparation and ultimate success.

Applied to Business Teams:

Imagine you could rely only on your team members for success, or nothing would get done. Imagine an environment in which the whole team needed to cooperate, have the right attitude, and collaborate with a sense of shared values. What could be accomplished when people truly reach out to each other with an awareness of what is required to win? The implication is that team members would be forced to develop strong and workable relationships. They could not afford to allow conflict to linger, and they would need to recognize that "my success is only as good as how successful I make you." There is nothing that can't get done when people are fully cooperating and collaborating unselfishly. Think it's impossible? If winning sports teams can do it, why not your team?

2. Challenge (feedback).

Applied to Sports Teams:

Whether challenged by the coach or by fellow team members, raising the bar of expectations is essential to continuous improvement.

Challenges come from all types of interactions: passing and tackling, but also cajoling, gesturing, etc. All these constitute different ways of providing feedback on the performance of an activity.

Applied to Business Teams:

In the corporate arena, accepting the challenge to do your best can best be translated into providing "feedback to improve." Frequent and constructive feedback is the key to increasing individual and team performance. Amazingly, most companies shy away from open feedback, preferring to give it in formal sessions. Human nature is such that, unless feedback is accepted and appreciated as an important process in the company, many people take offense to it. Companies that encourage a "feedback culture" move much more quickly and nimbly as team members become open and willing to learn from each other.

3. Awareness.

Applied to Sports Teams:

In all team sports, one key requirement is awareness of other team members—where they are and how they are playing. If you are a member of a crew team, you can literally feel your teammates' rowing; it's all about synchronicity. And to achieve it, you need a heightened awareness of your team members.

Applied to Business Teams:

Increasingly, successful companies are encouraging team members to become more aware of themselves and each other. The plethora of assessments used in the first decade of the 21st century is a testament to this trend. The key is not only self-awareness but also awareness of other team members' styles, ways of working, and preferences. Team members can then move on to the next level: acceptance. It is the acceptance of each other along with how we work. And finally appreciation, in which team members begin to appreciate the diversity and value that each individual team member brings to the table. Implicit in awareness—acceptance—appreciation (the A-A-A process covered later in the book) is the openness to give and receive feedback. A-A-A, a learned skill, engenders emotional intelligence and goes a long way towards creating High TQ.

4. Identity and pride.

Applied to Sports Teams:

In all winning teams, the sense of personal identity within the team is critical. This corresponds to the basic human need to belong. Being part of a winning sports team is like being a rock star, bringing with it adulation and various other rewards. Indeed, the team ends up engendering a whole *culture* unto itself, which affects the way players interact, the management style of the coach, and interaction with the fans–jerseys, memorabilia, colors, chants, cheers, and on-field displays.

Applied to Business Teams:

What if you went to work every day with a sense of pride that you were working for the "A Team," the best in the industry and the finest in the company? You would identify yourself with the team and all it stood for. When talking with co-workers you would proudly let others know you're an "A Team" member, and people would comment in admiration. You could cite accomplishments and projects and energize others in turn. This sense of identity and pride has legs; it's a notable point when speaking with friends, family, the industry, suppliers, etc. Furthermore, it strengthens the sense of meaning in your work, and you derive great satisfaction in being part of this team. Importantly there is a clear team culture that is shared among all team members.

5. Trust and confidence.

Applied to Sports Teams:

Team members are selected based upon their capabilities and their ability to deliver value in a particular position. There is a heightened sense of knowledge of who is good at what, and an implicit trust that fellow members can and will deliver. To support this, team members take care of each other to the best of their abilities.

Applied to Business Teams:

Now for perhaps the hardest element to imagine: all your team members possess a high degree of trust in each other. You openly give and receive feedback and act upon it. You work hard to gain and maintain trust. You can relax because you know that others have your back, and you have confidence that other team members are operating under the premise of what's best for the business and the team as a whole. When conflict arises, you recognize it, open it up, and seek to resolve it effectively. You believe that other team members are not operating any secret agendas; rather, the team agenda is the operational agenda.

6. Success and performance.

Applied to Sports Teams:

So powerful is team success that team members will do virtually anything to win. Players feel an imperative to "show up" for the benefit of the team. Conversely, team failure brings with it the litany of shame, blame, and discord, with some members invariably getting axed. *Winning = success. Losing = failure.*

> Team members should not be operating from secret agendas; rather the team agenda should be the operating agenda.

Applied to Business Teams

You have defined what success means to the team, you enjoy success regularly, and have come to expect it. All team members are performing at full capacity, pulling their weight, and contributing to the team and organization's results. You don't want to let the team down, and "showing up" is an important motivator. Team members recognize each other constantly, and you feel delighted in the achievements of other team members as well as your own. Finally, all great teams know how to celebrate.

7. Motivation and fun.

Applied to Sports Teams:

Great teams not only work hard, but they also have fun while doing it. They enjoy being on the field or pitch with their fellow team members. For many, playing together with their teammates is their passion and forms their most powerful and fondest memories.

Applied to Business Teams:

The success of the team brings great joy and meaning to you. You want to win because it brings incredible drive, energy, and passion to the experience. The experience of working with your team provides challenge and fun. You look forward to going to work every day and being with your team members.

8. Coaches (leaders) encourage team commitment.

Applied to Sports Teams:

Great teams usually have great coaches. One of the primary jobs of a coach is to encourage team consciousness and commitment. One example is Nick Saban from his book, *How Good Do You Want to Be?*

> "Teamwork is the key to winning team sports. The best TEAM wins, not the best players. Peer pressure is the best enforcer of the rules. The worry of 'me' destroys a team. Success leads to wanting credit and recognition. Worship of stats is a sign of the 'me' culture."[9]

Nick Saban's team at the University of Alabama won another national championship in 2018! He is less interested in creating stars and more interested in creating a star team. His approach is well documented, and he is certainly one of the greatest college football coaches of all time, having won 210 games out of 272 games for a .774 average over 21 years.[10]

Applied to Business Teams:

The coach in a corporate setting is, in fact, the team leader. Of course, as a part of talent development, coaching and mentoring individuals is critical to performance. However, the role of the leader in High Performance Teams goes much further, encouraging all team members to put the team first and show true commitment to each other and to the success of the team. Once teams taste what it means to engage team consciousness, it's hard to go back. The camaraderie is palpable. Those who are members of great teams express that there is not much in life that can equal it.

Sound too good to be true? If winning sports teams can achieve High TQ, why can't your team? High Performance

> Once team members experience team consciousness, it's hard to go back.

Teams in corporate settings display the above eight characteristics, among others. It's doable and achievable with the right attitude, energy, and perseverance. In the following chapters, you will see how.

> "Best team in the NFL . . . the most incredible men—our players . . . I'm almost speechless about it, because their resilience and love for each other and trust—maybe it's a lesson for the world. It's incredible what you accomplish if you trust each other and work so hard together . . ."[11]

> Jeffrey Lurie, Philadelphia Eagles Owner
> February 4, 2018, after winning the Super Bowl

4

"WORKING TOGETHER" AT FORD

TRANSFORMING TEAM AND COMPANY CULTURE

In the last chapter, we saw how winning sports teams enjoy High TQ. In this chapter, we will witness how High TQ works in a corporate setting. TQ is concerned with team transformation. It's about creating a new or deeper team culture, which is essential for moving to High Performance. Transforming any corporate culture starts with the leader and the leadership team. The leadership team must be the first to embody and demonstrate the new culture for the organization at large to shift. Alan Mulally, Ford's CEO, did just that.

Starting in 2006, Ford began to transform its culture, a process that took four to five years, though it still retained most of the positive cultural aspects that had developed throughout its long history. These included the values of work and accomplishment held by its founder, Henry Ford. Like most U.S. auto companies in 2006, Ford was in the throes of a crisis, losing billions of dollars. Unlike General Motors (GM) or Chrysler however, Ford emerged as a healthy company without needing to rely on a government bailout. It developed a sleek, unified car and truck line under the

"One Ford" identity that extended to the far reaches of the globe; as well as a "One Team" identity that was put in place everywhere from Dearborn to Chennai. In essence, Ford underwent one of the most successful cultural transformations in modern corporate history.

When I first started consulting with Ford in 2014 after its former CEO, Alan Mullaly, had retired, I was struck by the seemingly positive culture that pervaded the walls of any Ford office. That culture was part of Mulally's legacy. During my work with Ford, I had the opportunity to speak with many people on various projects, mostly centered on coaching and coaching training. Without prompting, Alan Mulally's name or the principles he espoused invariably came up. Such was the power of the legacy that the man left with the company.

Mulally was previously credited with turning around Boeing, having spent most of his career, prior to joining Ford, in the aerospace company. There he had worked on or managed the development of most of the Boeing commercial jets that are flying in the skies today. Many of the leadership and management principles that he espoused came out of his work at Boeing. At Ford, he was not only able to apply the best of them, but he also transformed the culture and the company by shifting the culture from an "individual" or "division"-performance mindset to a "One-Team"–performance mindset.

> Mulally shifted the culture from an "individual" or "division"-performance mindset to a "One-Team"– performance mindset.

Prior to Mulally joining the company, Ford's brands were spread out among a plethora of car companies, including Aston Martin, Land Rover, Volvo, Jaguar, and Mazda. While these brands brought an exotic allure to Ford, from a management and operational perspective, they were a distraction. Mulally shed the unessential baggage, selling the other brands (or Ford's stake in them) to other companies. He brought all the remaining brands together under a "OneFord" plan, unifying the company and operations around the Ford brand.

Alan Mulally's reputation as one of the world's best CEO's extended beyond North America. In fact, I first learned of Ford's phenomenal culture and team transformation story in July of 2015 in Shanghai. I had just delivered a keynote address at a leadership conference organized by Mindspan Development entitled, "Building a High Performance Team Through Engagement." Bryce Hoffman, author of the book *American Icon: Alan Mulally and the Fight to Save Ford Motor Company*, also delivered a keynote at the same conference, and we had an inspiring discussion on the topic. (Bryce also generously contributed many ideas to this chapter.)

I was captivated by the Alan Mulally story Bryce told in his address, "Lesson's Learned from Alan Mulally's Turnaround of the Ford Motor Company." More than 300 local and foreign executives attended this speech, despite the fact that Ford had less than a 5 percent market share in China. Mulally had achieved CEO cult status in China.

Even in absentia, Mulally and his penchant for building strong teams and working together were discussed in Ford's offices in China and India. There seemed to be pride that *everyone mattered* to Mulally (as opposed to the insane attention given celebrity CEO's in some companies). One person at Ford said, "Wherever Mulally traveled—China, India, or Europe—employees were impressed with his personal touch. He recognized the importance of pride and identity, and he took time to pose for individual photos with employees he had never met, knowing how much it would mean to them." Mulally met and chatted with as many employees, customers, suppliers, and stakeholders as he could and never gave the impression of

> In Ford offices, there seemed to be pride that "everyone mattered."

being bothered or rushed. The phenomenal goodwill garnered as a result of this attitude went a long way toward establishing his "One Team" success.

"WORKING TOGETHER"

One of Mulally's axioms was "Working Together," which infused his entire management philosophy. His down-to-earth, friendly, and accessible persona belied his cleverness in reading people and his extraordinary business acumen. "Working Together" was all inclusive and pervaded the entire company. One Ford executive posited, "Instead of seeking to change the team players or surround himself with his own handpicked team, Mulally would provide reassurance to the car experts at Ford by saying, 'It's not that we have the wrong players—it's that we just need to get everyone to work together.'"

By 2006, Boeing's commercial jet division was well on its way to record sales, revenue, and earnings. Mulally credited this to a team-based approach he called "Working Together," and it required the top leaders of each discipline and function to meet every week to go over their progress, discuss problems, and figure out how to deal with them as a team. "This is the only way I know how to operate," he said. "We need to have everybody involved."[12]

When Bill Ford, Jr., chairman of Ford Motor Company, interviewed Mulally for the post of CEO in 2006, he asked Mulally some very specific questions:

He asked about Mulally's background, his experiences at Boeing, how he coped with crises. He asked Mulally to describe his management style. Mulally explained how, at Boeing, his entire leadership team was expected to participate in a lightning-fast analysis of the entire business every Thursday morning. Each of his direct reports delivered a brief update on the status of his or her division or function . . .

"This is going to be a culture shock," Ford cautioned.

"What does that mean?" Mulally wondered.[13]

During Ford's search for a new CEO, it was clear that the candidate they would select needed to focus on inclusiveness and on the team. This brought clarity and consistency to the search process. In my own coaching work with senior executives, the subject of "personal branding" often comes up as a key focus. Executives realize the need to have a clear and consistent brand. If anybody had a clear brand, it was Mulally. After conducting extensive interviews and checking references, Ford hired Alan Mulally as only its 12th CEO in its 100-year history.

> "The executives at Ford tried to learn everything they could about their new CEO. Fields (Mark Fields, Ford COO in 2006 and appointed CEO in 2014) started calling friends who knew Mulally or at least knew of him. Everybody told him the same thing: He was an excellent leader who believed strongly in teamwork, execution, data, and delivering on commitments."[14]

Working together also means focusing on others and on the team. One of the ten "rules" that Mulally cited was, *respect, listen, help, and appreciate each other.*" This applied to all Ford employees; it also extended to suppliers and business partners.

I had a personal experience with Mulally's idea of "appreciation." In 2015, having completed a coaching training for a group of senior managers, I was back at Ford's offices in Shanghai. About three months after the coaching program ended, I bumped into one of the participants, a senior executive in purchasing, in the corridor. He said, "Douglas, I just wanted to tell you I got so much out of the coaching training. I am applying it with my coachees with great results." That was one of my best days of the year! For a participant to recognize you months later and go out of his way to show appreciation was the ultimate validation. Upon reflection, I realize it also embodied the Ford spirit, which was to show appreciation in a natural and direct way.

WHO STAYS; WHO GOES?

What is the first thing a new CEO must examine? It's the leadership team, of course, making sure the right "players" are on the team. The new CEO needs to decide who to keep and who to ax, and when the bloodletting should begin. Many leaders will opt to bring in "their own boys" as getting the right talent on the team is imperative, and they will do anything to make it happen.

While having the right talent is imperative to building a High Performance Team, it's more complex than bringing in "their own boys." A leader needs to ask questions around team culture: Will new players get along with the old? What kind of culture do you want to build? To what extent can team players align around the new desired culture? How long will it take for a new player to be productive and gain credibility? Are the players willing to work as a team and put the team first, or will they be strutting around as prima donnas, endeavoring to put forth their own personal agendas? What degree of debate, acrimony, and dissension is permitted or encouraged?

> In building High TQ Teams, culture trumps talent.

Here, I am going to posit a potentially controversial axiom: "*Culture trumps talent.*" No one disagrees that we all want the best talent possible. We would also agree that the right person needs to be in the right job. The tendency is to focus on securing the talent. I believe, however, that the first focus should be on *team culture*. Can the players work together effectively in the culture you want to create? Can they adopt the culture?

In my experience, many high-performing "stars" will naturally fall away if they can't get along in the team culture. Most players, however, adapt and come to understand that working in a strong team culture is beneficial to themselves and to the company.

The other truism is that given a strong team culture, people usually rise to deliver their best work. This is why I usually advise leaders to assume that the requisite skills exist; giving people the chance to rise to the occasion is usually the best call.

Alan Mulally's imperative was to turn the company around. Could he do it with the existing players, or did he need to clean house? It was perhaps the most important decision he faced upon arriving at Ford. He evaluated each player and position in-depth for skills, track record, attitude, and whether they could, indeed, operate under the "One Team" umbrella. His conclusion may surprise you:

> Instead of figuring out whom to get rid of, he was trying to figure out where each of Ford's executives could make the biggest contribution to the company's turnaround effort. He was focused on filling in the blanks on his matrix organization chart. Mulally tried to come up with two or three candidates for each position. He was prepared to look outside Ford if necessary, but he preferred people with deep knowledge of the company and its problems. Mulally looked at who was currently in charge of each function and then tried to identify the best people beneath him or her. That way, if his first choice did not work out, he would be able to quickly fill the position with other, in-house talent. Mulally moved cautiously. He scheduled one-on-one interviews with executives, talking to them about what they had done at Ford, what they were doing now, and where they thought they could help. He looked not only at their qualifications and technical expertise but also at whether they worked well with others. Mulally also needed to know that they had the stomach for the heavy lifting that lay ahead. Most important, they needed to be able to function in the midst of crisis. Mulally sent an email to employees . . . "Working together to make the most of our global talent and resources is critical to our success," he said. "I know I can count on you to join me in supporting the leadership team during this transition. This is a great company. This is a terrific team. We have the right leaders. Together we can do this!"[15]

By and large, Mulally kept the team intact, betting that they could take on the new team culture. He did it methodically, with skill, patience, and aplomb. He bet on existing players. That bet turned out to be a good one.

PEOPLE FIRST

For newly appointed C-level executives, during the first 90 days, a new leader needs to craft a focus and agenda so that the team has clarity on direction. Mulally understood the power of defining the agenda early on. One of his first pieces of communication charted the rules for the senior leadership team.

> ". . . As the executives took their places in black leather chairs around the cherry table, Mulally called their attention to a list of rules posted on the wall. There were ten of them.
>   1. People first.
>   2. Everyone is included.
>   3. Compelling vision
>   4. Clear performance goals
>   5. One plan
>   6. Facts and data
>   7. Propose a plan, "find-a-way" attitude.
>   8. Respect, listen, help, and appreciate each other.
>   9. Emotional resilience . . . trust the process.
>   10. Have fun . . . enjoy the journey and each other.
>
> Like the slide templates, these rules had been imported from Boeing. Yet they seemed tailor-made for Ford. As he went down the list, Mulally added a few specifics to underscore these points. There were to be no side discussions, no jokes at anyone else's expense, and no BlackBerrys."[16]

It is noteworthy that in his new CEO role, Mulally's first rule was "people first." That might seem surprising for an auto company; one might expect "autos first," or "technology and design first," or even "customers first."

Next on his list was "everyone is included." This rule paved the way for his "One Team" concept. Mulally didn't just pay lip service to these ideas; he was dead serious. Mulally was extraordinarily inclusive. That inclusiveness was contagious, and most team members got it, which perhaps accounted for the fact that there was very little turnover, during Mulally's tenure. While some might have thought Mulally's rules were too "fluffy" for an auto

> Mulally's inclusiveness was contagious, and most team members got it.

company, they only had to ponder, "If they weren't too fluffy for Boeing, perhaps we should give them a try." Ultimately it was these "rules" that formed the underpinnings of the culture that led to Ford's transformation and triumph.

MEETINGS THAT WORK

Many team members dread meetings, finding them ineffective, lengthy, and in some cases just plain useless. I have always been surprised that top leaders give so little attention to meeting management. Poorly managed meetings are one of the biggest time wasters for executives. Alan Mulally was acutely aware of the importance of effective meetings and had spent years perfecting his own meeting platform at Boeing, which he instituted at Ford. In the initial days, Mulally laid the new business plan review—the "BPR process"—which was, indeed, a culture shock for his leadership team.

> "There would be only one corporate-level meeting—his BPR." It would be held every week on the same day, at the same time, in the same place. Attendance would be mandatory for all senior executives. All would be expected to personally deliver succinct status reports and updates on their progress toward the company's turnaround goals. This

would not be a forum for discussion or debate. Any issues that required more in-depth consideration by the entire leadership team would be taken up in a "special attention review"—an SAR—immediately following the BPR. This idea was to keep the main meeting focused on the big picture. And Mulally stressed that, when there was discussion and debate in the SAR, it would be based on business realities, not politics or personality.[17]

"The rule on BlackBerrys struck several of the executives as particularly condescending. They all carried them, and most spent the better part of any meeting glued to them—reading emails, checking sports scores, or playing Brick Breaker. This was disrespectful to whoever was speaking, Mulally told them. The whole point of the BPR was to maintain a laser like focus on the facts of the business."[18]

At a Stanford lecture, Alan Mulally described in his own words how he implemented the BPR:

"We started to have a weekly meeting where we review everything associated with the plan. Everybody knows what the plan is, what the status of the plan is. The meeting goes from 7:00 a.m. to 9:30 a.m. So you can imagine how transparent and close you get. When we started this, remember I told you the forecast was we will lose $17 billion. So I start the BPR. The charts were flowing; we even have it color coded red (not done on time or in trouble), yellow (work in progress), and green (completed or in good shape). Any changes on the charts are in blue . . . After about three to four weeks, all the charts were green. He said, "Guys, we are going to lose 17 billion dollars. Is there anything not going well?" Eye contact goes to the floor; nobody says anything. Remember that culture we were talking about? It wasn't okay to bring things up. It was command and control . . . One of the most exciting days of my life was in the following week those charts looked like a rainbow. Now the data says why we are losing 17 billion dollars cause the data sets you free, right? The data tells you everything. Also now it was safe enough where you could share what it was. You weren't red—the issue you were working on was red. You can't manage a secret if people don't know what the real situation is. You can imagine the accountability around an item; can you imagine being red on an item and coming back the following week and being red? The pressure in a positive way is fantastic cause everyone there is trying to figure out how to go forward."[19]

What Mulally was speaking about is transparency around data. "You can't manage a secret if people don't know what the real situation is." He needed to create an atmosphere in which it was safe to be wrong, to make a mistake. He also had to get his team members to begin supporting each other for the good of the team and company. He got his breakthrough, as the team finally embraced his "One Team" philosophy.

Mulally also refers to peer pressure. It is one of the most powerful natural tools on any team. Showing up for the team seems to be almost a primordial instinct. The better the team, the stronger the desire to show up. Therein lies one of the powers of a High Performance Team: People will do almost anything to perform, not to lose face, and be seen as a strong team contributor.

> Peer pressure is one of the most powerful natural tools on any team.

In 2015 at Ford's Asia headquarters in Shanghai, I had the opportunity to observe Mulally's legacy of working together while sitting in on a Ford leader's meeting. Most unit managers had implemented Mulally's famed business plan review in which the manager and key players sat down and reviewed key results and issues with full transparency and with the expectation that everyone was there to support each other. The team I observed was large, consisting of about 15 players. They sat around the table, taking turns presenting, updating, and requesting input. There was no pressure to ensure that all results were green; rather, it was normal to experience red or yellow scores. Working on devices, doing emails, or engaging in other distractions was discouraged at these meetings with the expectation that all team members were fully present. Indeed, I was able to experience the fruits of Ford's cultural transformation all the way across the globe, even after Mulally had retired.

> "The changes Mulally had made to Ford's culture were no longer limited to the upper echelons of the organization. At each level of the company, managers tried to emulate an inclusive and data-driven approach. Every department now held its own weekly BPR meeting, and similar sessions were held regularly at the national and regional level."[20]

CULTURE IS REFLECTED IN BEHAVIOR

What is corporate culture, anyway, and how do you define it? You can describe "culture," but you can't "see" it, although you can witness what culture produces: the behavior. What delights us or annoys us about people is their behavior. Behavior is just as important as results in a corporate context. The right behavior will ultimately produce superior results.

As a leader, the first step in building a new culture begins with the leadership team. Instilling aligned values is a key milestone in creating that culture. Once the team starts absorbing the values and demonstrating behaviors in concert with those values, the culture becomes palpable.

One key behavioral change in Ford's leadership team was the willingness to be transparent about results that had not yet achieved their goals (the red or yellow parts of the BPR). It was this transparency that encouraged team members' willingness to step up and support those whose problems were red or yellow. Mulally's senior leadership team had now absorbed the new culture, but he didn't end there. He needed to find a way to ensure that *all* employees became part of the cultural transformation. He knew a way of simplifying messages that could be disseminated not only to his senior team but companywide:

> "Mulally was struggling to extend his culture revolution deeper into the organization. By the end of 2007, Ford's top executives had embraced his new order. However, lower-level employees reported that the old ways persisted further down inside the bowels of the corporation. Mulally wanted to make sure that everyone understood the aims of his revolution and their role in it. He proceeded to spell it out for them—not in a little red book, but on a small blue card. Wallet cards had long been a favorite tool of Ford's human resources department . . . On the front of the card, beneath Ford's Blue Oval, was the phrase that, to him, summed it all up—"One Ford"—and three other Mulally catchphrases: 'One Team,' 'One Plan,' and 'One Goal.'"[21]

In my work with teams, once we get clarity on aligned values, we spend time identifying the aligned behaviors. In other words, how are we going to show up for each other? Many teams gloss over this all-too-important point, perhaps thinking, "We are all mature adults. We shouldn't be told how to act." This line of thinking misses the key point. Behavior is defined around a context. The context that we all share as a team—our goals, mission, and strategies—will drive our behavior. How we conduct meetings will form the context of how team members behave in them. Are we combative and reclusive, or inclusive? Do we recognize and celebrate, or criticize? These behaviors need to be defined, and teams with great and effective meetings are absolutely clear about what they are.

THE FOUR BEHAVIORS

Alan Mulally was also clear and proscriptive about behavior, both at the senior leadership team level and at Ford as a whole. On the back of the small blue card mentioned above, Mulally listed "Expected Behaviors":

Foster Functional and Technical Excellence
Own Working Together
Role Model Ford Values
Deliver Results[22]

These were the four behaviors he expected all Ford people to embody.

1. **Foster Functional and Technical Expertise.**
   - Know and have a passion for our business and our customers.
   - Demonstrate and build functional and technical excellence.
   - Ensure process discipline.
   - Have a continuous improvement philosophy and practice.[23]

As the former CEO of PepsiCo, Roger Enrico used to say, "Know your business cold." Mulally made it known that every employee should understand this point. It's not surprising that this was the first of his expected behaviors as Mulally was an engineer, himself.

At Ford, you are expected to be really good at your job and become the "expert." I was also struck by this when I coached Ford executives. These executives take great pride in being experts in their respective fields. In a highly technical field such as the automotive industry with its rapidly changing technology, the only way to stay ahead is by ensuring that deep expertise is groomed within the company.

2. **Own Working Together.**
   - Believe in skilled and motivated people working together.
   - Include everyone; respect, listen to, help, and appreciate others.
   - Build strong relationships, be a team player; develop ourselves and others.
   - Communicate clearly, concisely, and candidly.[24]

Mulally was not interested in people paying lip service to working together. He wanted people to really believe in it. Of all the behaviors, this one is probably the unique one.

Working together means several things. First, it means *cooperation*. Ford people go out of their way to cooperate to get things done and find solutions. Remember the example above of people pitching in to support those colleagues who, in the BPR, revealed that their challenges were red? This level of cooperation is exactly what Mulally wanted. He wanted to supplant the stinging criticism of the old Ford culture with support and assistance that exemplified the new culture.

In my own work with Ford, the level of natural cooperation always strikes me. In one case, two parties in Ford discovered the conference room was double booked. Both meetings were important and vital to each of them. Instead of arguing and competing to win the space, the two parties actually worked together to find a solution and another space. These two people were from different functions and didn't really know each other; however there was a natural sense of cooperation and willingness to support each other.

The other area of working together is collaboration. In my own work with Ford involving a companywide coaching project, it became apparent that HR needed advice, opinions, and experience that went beyond their own expertise. They set up a "consultative forum" that enlisted across businesses and functions to act as consultants on the project. This forum was more than just another cross-functional project; it was a venue in which all contributed with the best of intentions and "worked together" to create a successful result.-

3. **Role Model Ford Values.**
  - Show initiative, courage, integrity, and good corporate citizenship.
  - Improve quality, safety, and sustainability.
  - Have a can-do, find-a-way attitude, and emotional resilience.
  - Enjoy the journey and each other; have fun—but never at other's expense."[25]

We have touched on the importance of values in a High Performance Team. Just as behaviors are what we can see, values are those deeply held beliefs that underpin behavior. Most organizations have developed, and perhaps communicated, a set of values, but Mulally went beyond that. He was interested in "role modeling the values."

In the program I worked on with Ford, I remarked upon the importance placed on role modeling. All executives are expected to be the role models, to "walk the talk." They are expected to set an example for others, especially for junior members of the Ford team. Ford is somewhat unique in that executives are expected to "park their egos" for the greater good. The old Ford of the early 2000s with Jacques Nasser at the helm was a different place. It was a Ford of strong command and control and big egos. Nasser had ruled with an iron grip in the nexus of control, alienated some team members, and led to poor results in the early 2000s: "The company has lost 1.5 points of market share . . . quality slipped below General Motors."[26] The Ford of today is completely different, thanks to the example set by Mulally. Everyone is expected to role model the values that have been articulated.

4. **Deliver Results.**
   - Deal positively with our business realities; develop compelling and comprehensive plans while keeping an enterprise view.
   - Set high expectations and inspire others.
   - Make sound decisions using facts and data.
   - Hold ourselves and others responsible and accountable for delivering results and satisfying our customers.

At the end of the day, if leaders embody the first three behaviors but don't focus on the results, the organization won't be around very long. That is why it is incumbent upon Ford employees to exhibit the behavior of delivering results. It reflects a mindset that we are here to produce results and not just report on or talk about them.

Every company culture has its commensurate behavior. Most companies, however, don't spend the time to truly integrate the behaviors in people's daily working lives. Therefore, people's "unconscious behavior" becomes the norm. Mulally did the heavy lifting to ensure that each employee could embody the four behaviors, thereby instilling a level of "conscious behavior." When a company can truly imbue its employees with "conscious behavior," the impact can be the difference between success and failure, as we have seen with Ford.

———

The Ford story is remarkable. It stands in contrast to GM's path during the same period of time when GM endured massive layoffs and declared bankruptcy in April 2009, requiring a $33-billion rescue bailout from the U.S. government. Ford, however, instead of experiencing massive layoffs, found morale soaring to an all-time high as Ford employees saw their work recognized and found managers increasingly willing to listen to their ideas and concerns. At the foundation of this success was a leader who believed in his team and in the power of culture to transform.

5

LEVERAGING THE BURNING PLATFORM

CREATING THE IMPERATIVE FOR HIGH TQ TEAMS

As highlighted in the previous chapter on Ford, Alan Mulally had a gargantuan task: to bring Ford back from the brink. He was faced with a clear burning platform, and accordingly, a mandate for change. The burning platform was so dire that team members had no choice but to embrace the necessary change or leave the company.

The changes Mulally made to his team were substantive. They included everything from meeting formats, reporting, and accountabilities to values and behaviors. In short, he transformed every aspect of the team experience and process. Unless there is a crisis, most leaders don't have the degree of urgency or mandate that Mulally enjoyed. Yet to build TQ, change is essential, and you and your team will need to find strong reasons to make the change.

TAKING OWNERSHIP OF THE TEAM IMPERATIVE

As a team leader, you probably have some clear ideas of the issues concerning your organization or operation and where you want to lead the team. The question is: does everyone share your view? No matter how lofty, grandiose, or compelling your vision for the team is, if your team members don't buy in and take ownership of the goal, you may have difficulty galvanizing them.

I have witnessed many team initiatives peter out for this very reason. The team leader is very clear about what he wants and can articulate it, but not all team members are on board. In fact, it is normal to have some team members who are content to carry on in their usual way. Their attitudes are along the lines of "Hey, I'm so busy delivering results that I don't have time for this stuff" or "Yeah, I'll attend the team meetings but don't expect me to spend much time on team projects and collaboration; I've got a full agenda and can't fit it into my schedule."

A few years back, I was conducting interviews for an upcoming team program at an aviation company. One of the very experienced and key team members had been through lots of team-building exercises, and said, "I'm not really into this 'Kumbaya' stuff." Somehow, he had equated building a High Performance Team with "rah rah" boisterous enthusiasm. He made it quite public that he was more interested in counting the money coming in and building a nice nest egg. It was an attitude of "Leave me alone and let me get on with my job." He was known as the "gray-haired, crusty, hard-nosed task-oriented manager." Interestingly, after he had been through the program and received heaps of feedback on his attitude, he had quite a wake-up call. We even got a few smiles out of him!

The common misperception is that building High Performance Teams follows the traditional team-building approach, which is often associated with "Kumbaya" moments. In fact, creating a great team with High TQ is much more about what happens over the course of one to two years of working to transform the team to High Performance. Ultimately it concerns what happens day-to-day at the office or plant and in the field where the team interacts to create the excellence it desires. To start, aligning the burning platform is essential.

WHAT IS THE BURNING PLATFORM?

Lessons from a Consumer Goods Company

When I was in PepsiCo, the concept of a "burning platform" was top-of-mind for most managers. If Coke is breathing down your neck and gaining market share, you have a burning platform. If you are not able to deliver cans and bottles to the store daily, on time, and well-merchandised, you have a burning platform.

I like the real story of the burning platform because it illustrates graphically the challenge at hand.

> "At nine-thirty on a July evening in 1988, a disastrous explosion and fire occurred on the Piper Alpha oil-drilling platform in the North Sea off the coast of Scotland. One-hundred-and-sixty-six crewmembers and two rescuers lost their lives in what was (and still is) the worst catastrophe in the fifty-year history of North Sea oil exploration. One of the 63 crewmembers who survived was Andy Mochan, a superintendent on the rig.

> From the hospital, he told of being awakened by the explosion and alarms. Badly injured, he escaped from his quarters to the platform edge. Beneath him, oil had surfaced and ignited. Twisted steel and other debris littered the surface of the water. Because of the water's temperature, he knew that he could live a maximum of only 20 minutes if not rescued. Despite all that, Andy jumped 15 stories from the platform to the water.

> When asked why he took that potentially fatal leap, he did not hesitate. He said, 'It was either jump or fry.' He chose possible death over certain death. Andy jumped because he felt he had no choice—the price of staying on the platform was too high."[27]

Fortunately, the man survived the jump from the platform and was rescued shortly thereafter. His philosophy had been "Better probable death than certain death."

The point of the story is that it took a platform fire to cause a major change in behavior. It emphasizes that radical change in people only comes when survival instincts trump the desire to stay in their comfort zone. When making major decisions or solving major problems, an *emergency* attitude is sometimes required.

> Radical change in people only comes only when survival instincts trump the desire to stay in their comfort zone.

Another term for burning platform is "personal inflection point," which is the point at which a decisive moment marks a major change. Sometimes it is a choice; sometimes an inflection point is thrust upon us. The burning platform is often required to begin team transformation by eliciting buy in from the team.

WHAT IS YOUR BURNING PLATFORM?

At PepsiCo in the late 90s in China, it was clear that Coke was, by far, the market leader in the carbonated soft drinks category. We decided to define our goals by "targeted cities." In 1998, Coke was number one in targeted cities. Our goal was to change that and make Pepsi number one in those cities. Our burning platform was distribution: we simply didn't have enough outlet penetration and a strong enough selling system. We identified the imperative to invest in effective third-party distribution, relying on distributors and wholesalers to create outlet penetration at a fraction of the cost of setting up our own distribution system while still maintaining the service quality.

From a team perspective, the missing link was the bottler general managers who employed their own, homegrown distribution methods. We decided to make a strong case for a burning platform and a solution. The only way to succeed was by aligning the team. We couldn't order them to align their goals with ours; rather, we had to show them that they would be successful if they did. We set up several third-party distribution pilot sites and finally succeeded in aligning the general managers' distribution methods. Pepsi achieved its goals and, by the early 2000s, had reached its objective of number one in target cities.

In this case, the burning platform was the lack of outlet penetration required for significant growth, without which Pepsi would not have been able to realize its business objectives. We could achieve success only by getting the team of bottler general managers to buy in and feel ownership of the third-party distribution initiative. Therefore, it was not only my immediate team that needed to work closely together, it was also the larger team of bottler general manager and their teams, who had to collaborate with one another and with us to create the success we enjoyed.

> To embark on the road of a High Performance Team, you need to identify the burning platform and galvanize the team around it.

If you want to embark on the road of leading to a High Performance Team, you need to identify the burning platform and galvanize the team around it. The burning platform may be driven by: 1) dysfunctions, such as conflict, lack of communication, or trust, 2) market exigencies (as in the above PepsiCo example), or 3) shortfall vs. goals and key performance indicators (KPIs). As the team leader, it's your job to communicate and provide meaning to the link between the burning platform and the need for the team to align around the High Performance Team journey.

THE ALIGNMENT MEETING: THE BURNING PLATFORM AND THE PATH FORWARD

We've talked about the need for some kind of burning platform to galvanize the team to move forward. In working with my clients, I've found this can be done as part of a two-day off-site or in a separate session prior to the off-site. Either way, you need to set a clear purpose to this several hour-long meeting, which is to achieve alignment on where the team is and where it wants to go. If there is a clear burning platform, this is the time to align with it. During this meeting, the client will want to have someone to present the findings of the Assess phase (TQ HealthCheck, interviews, etc.). Ideally, this won't be you, the team leader, but a third party or one or several of your team members as you need to involve others to gain ownership.

Prior to the alignment meeting, the team leader should communicate the agenda clearly. One caveat about pre-reading the agenda: I don't suggest sending out the Assess results in advance. It contains sensitive information about the team that, if circulated, has the potential for misuse. Team leaders often will want to dilute anything going out in writing. If you really must send something out, consider distributing the overall themes of the meeting but not the details.

During the alignment meeting, the results of Assess may be presented in any convenient format. Again, I suggest either a third party or a team member do the presentation, not the team leader. What's important is going through the Assess results, or current situation, without getting bogged down on discussion points. These meetings can get derailed when someone has strong opinions about an issue. This can throw the whole thing off track. Set the ground rules up front on this one.

Once the Assess results are communicated, I like to begin by getting general agreement on the overall state of the team. The following example comes from an aviation company's team, which happened to be dysfunctional. I advised that they needed clarity on the "state of team" in order to come to grips with and face their reality. We jointly put together the statement below:

BURNING PLATFORM
[Example State-of-Team Summary]

Lessons from an Aviation Company
"The leadership team is a group of highly competent, seasoned, hard-driving individuals fragmented on the axes of style, culture, geographical location, and continuity. The group operates with silo agendas and is pressured with the complexity of driving a massive change agenda. This has led to turf building and a lack of trust and camaraderie. If we don't change soon, we will lose credibility with key stakeholders."

Figure 5.1

After discussing the state of team, the team seeks alignment on the statement. The team leader should allow the team to evaluate the statement's content and really feel comfortable with it. This should include an open discussion. This important step brings the team to a level of self-honesty and out of denial as the team no longer needs to bicker on all the details. Rather, all will share the same view of where they stand as a team and what needs to change.

> The alignment meeting brings the team to a level of self-honesty and out of denial.

Once the team is aligned with the "State of Team Summary," the next step is to *agree on the key issues.* Here, I get the team members to prioritize issues by having them individually write down what they perceive to be the top three issues on sticky notes and then post them on the board. As a group, the team will move around the sticky notes on the board until they arrive at the top three to five issues.

In the final step, arriving at what the team needs to address going forward is the essential goal of the alignment session. In the case of the aviation company, the aligned direction arrived at the following (figure 5.2).

WHAT OUR TEAM NEEDS TO ADDRESS
[Example]

1. Define compelling *vision* and *agenda* for team and business to pull us forward.
2. What we stand for, live, and die for—*our values*—leading to how we interact as a team
3. Identify and resolve *issues* that need handling and then put the issues behind us.
4. Define *team success* as an imperative.
5. Begin to *trust, respect,* and *appreciate* each other.
6. Identify *imperatives*—the critical things we need to do to be successful.

Figure 5.2

The fourth item on "team success" was an important outcome of the session. In fact, one of the great suggestions that came from the meeting was the point, "We haven't defined what success means for this team." This brilliant thought galvanized the team to consider "How we define success for the team" as something requiring attention going forward. Success is more than just KPIs or satisfaction levels. It inspired me, as a facilitator, to incorporate the definition of success into future engagements.

THE HOLDOUTS

By this point, as you can imagine, the team is really getting aligned as to where they stand and what needs to be done. Yet on some teams, there will be holdouts. These are the members who despite all the discussions and still do not buy into the need to devote time and attention to building a High Performance Team. Perhaps they are complacent and content with the status quo, or they may genuinely not see the need. Perhaps they have a hidden agenda and really don't want the team to go down this track. Ultimately getting all team members' alignment is important. The following are a few keys to get them on track.

Address specific concerns: Everyone has reasons for their positions. In this case, the key is to ferret out the real reasons and objections. It may take some degree of probing to get there, but if you don't understand the basis of team members' concerns, you may never truly be able to help them create a shift in attitude. This can be done at the team meeting or later offline.

Use peer pressure: Done in a healthy way, peer pressure is a positively powerful way to get team members aligned. Ultimately, if the holdout reason is clear, the team consensus will make it easier to create a shift.

> Holdouts who won't get with the program may be on the wrong team.

Highlight the team leader's intent and purpose. If ultimately the team leader declares that this is what he or she wants to do, that will create some pressure to "get with the program." The caveat here is to make sure specific concerns have been properly addressed, as mentioned above.

In certain cases, the holdout still doesn't buy into an agreement of what the group feels. In this case, you might temporarily leave the burning platform alone. At the end of the Culture and Team-Building off-site, the holdout is most likely to shift their attitude. There are just too many positives being created to want to resist it. Having said that, there are situations in which the holdout never gets with the program, which begs the question of whether they are on the right team. I've witnessed several cases where an individual just doesn't want to engage as a true team member. In many of these situations, that individual won't feel a real sense of belonging and ultimately may leave the team. Although no team likes to lose capable talent, it can't afford to carry someone who is unaligned and may hold the team back.

————

Going all the way to a High TQ Team entails a commitment over time, not just for the leader but also for the entire team. All team members have to "get it", otherwise it won't happen. Therefore, ensuring the imperative exists among members is the best way to ensure ultimate success. Finding and acting on your team's "burning platform" will provide the energy, drive, and perseverance to make it a reality.

PART II

THE TQ JOURNEY

YOUR ROAD MAP TO CREATING HIGH PERFORMANCE TEAMS

6

THE HIGH PERFORMANCE TEAM (HPT) JOURNEY

Building a High Performance Team may seem like a daunting task, though it's no more formidable than pursuing personal or talent development. In fact, once you get traction, it takes on a life of its own as team members adopt it willingly. Moreover, it's been my experience that the journey to High Performance is well supported by internal stakeholders. Every company wants High Performance Teams in the company!

Developing Team Intelligence Requires a Road Map

Team intelligence doesn't develop overnight or over a few days of team-building exercises. It is a strategic approach that covers every essential aspect of moving the team to a High Team Quotient. In this chapter, I will introduce the *2-Step High Performance Team Journey*—the road map to increasing TQ and building a strong team culture and

> If you can follow the team prescription effectively, you will be in the top five percentile of teams!

a High Performance Team. *If you follow this prescription effectively, you will be in the top five percent of teams.* You will stand out from the rest of the pack, both in your company and in your industry. Figure 6.1 summarizes the journey, and we will examine each element in more detail later in the chapter.

THE 2-STEP HPT JOURNEY
STEP 1—TRANSFORM: Assess and Develop
STEP 2—INTEGRATE: Embed, Renew, and Certify

Figure 6.1

At the End of the Journey Is a New Team Culture

Culture defines us in our family units, businesses, and organizations. It distinguishes who we are and how we are described. Employees usually find it easy to describe their organizational culture, using such words as *supportive, open, results focused,* etc. Much of that culture is built up over years or even decades. Yet we don't have decades to build a successful team culture; we endeavor to create a strong and powerful culture within one to two years. We do this deliberately and consciously by defining the culture we want and then bringing it to life. When team members start to identify strongly with the team, we know that the team culture has become embedded.

THE "TQ TOP TEN"

Over many years of working with teams, it became evident that defining key characteristics of High Performance Teams became paramount. We embarked on a ten-year study of leadership teams from Fortune 500 companies, inquiring what makes up a High Performance Team. After interviewing 108 leadership teams and more than 1,200 team members, we arrived at the "TQ Top Ten," which leaders feel are the essential attributes in High Performance Teams. In the next chapter, we will see how these are measured to come up a Team Quotient Score. To be sure, *consistently doing these top-ten things well will result in a High Performance Team that consistently wins and gets results.*

1. Aligning a compelling vision, mission or purpose
2. Having the right mix of talent
3. Aligning desired values and behaviors
4. Respecting culture, style, and preferences
5. Demonstrating trust and openness to feedback
6. Conducting effective team meetings
7. Focusing on big things that create results
8. Collaborating on team initiatives
9. Having a powerful team identity
10. Experiencing fun, camaraderie, and recognition

THE EIGHT ELEMENTS OF HIGH TQ TEAMS— "VIVRE FAT"

To make the "TQ Top Ten" manageable for a team, as well as easy to discuss and remember, we have condensed the points into Eight Essential Elements on which teams can focus to get to high performance. These elements can be summarized under the acronym VIVRE FAT!

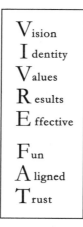

V ision
I dentity
V alues
R esults
E ffective

F un
A ligned
T rust

Figure 6.2: VIVRE FAT

The concept of VIVRE FAT is not to create a group of "bon vivants" or "gourmands." Rather, it's about focusing on the elements that will create a great team capable of fulfilling its mission and realizing its vision. Let's examine each of the eight elements more closely.

VIVRE FAT assumes that the team has addressed the right mix of talent on the team, which is a prerequisite for a High Performance Team. In fact, people come and go, therefore, the acquiring and keeping of the right talent is a never-ending journey for leaders. No matter where a team is on its talent journey, it can start addressing the key elements of VIVRE FAT.

Vision (and/or Mission and Purpose)

High Performance Teams know where they are going and have a keen sense of direction. The vision syncs with the overall company vision yet is distinct to the team. The vision is not something created and communicated by the team leader alone; rather it reflects a core team effort, allowing all to feel ownership. The vision is a motivating factor that propels the team forward. It allows team members to set clear goals, and it targets and measures success. The vision encompasses not only the business but also other aspects, such as team, people, key financial metrics, industry, and stakeholders. Besides vision, we may also want to define the purpose, or mission, of the team, which essentially addresses its raison d'être, or the reason why the team exists.

Identity

High Performance Team members identify with the team and are proud of it. This sense of pride is due, in part, to the personal efforts that each team member has invested in moving toward high performance. Identity forms an important part of one's own self-perception and may even be more powerful than company or industry identity. The concept of identity places the team first and knows that team effort is a key to overall success. The sense of being part of something much bigger drives team members the extra mile. They believe what they are doing has meaning and creates value.

Values

High Performance Teams know what is important to them. They have defined how they want to appear, interact, and be together. Values are not just words on the wall. They are emotional and are packed with meaning. Values drive behavior, and all team members are expected to live the team's values. These values are synced with company values, yet they are specific to the needs of the team. They are easy to communicate, both internally within the team as well as to external stakeholders. The values are top-of-mind, drive the standards, and raise the bar. Just as the core team members are committed to the values, the larger team also has to integrate them.

Results

High Performance Teams drive for consistent results. They are clear about what results they are committed to and realize that a "results focus" needs to be linked to defining team success. They review and measure results frequently and understand that "What gets measured gets done." Team members are not only focused on results themselves, but also on the "big things" or elements that go into achieving the results. All team members feel an obligation to deliver their part of the equation and help others do the same.

Effective

High Performance Teams know that they need more than a maniacal result focus. They need to master the drivers and processes that will create the results. They have clearly established processes for key aspects of the business and interactions. They believe both in doing things right and in doing the right things. They are constantly learning and continuously improving. They understand that team governance is an important part of the team process. Being effective particularly applies to team meetings in which over half of the time is typically spent on "reporting" and "updating" as opposed to making decisions on the truly important issues.

I once interviewed a client who said she enjoyed the monthly team meetings because it gave her time to catch up on her emails!

Don't laugh; that's the state of most team meetings—lots of time wasted being ineffective.

Fun

High Performance Teams know that sustained motivation comes from loving what you do. Team members enjoy being together and interacting in all ways. They also recognize each other, and celebrate successes frequently. *If a team is not highly motivated and having fun, it's probably not a High Performance Team.* That's because the drive required to perform effectively can readily be accessed through the power of emotion, which is generated from the energy of interacting with the team. As we have seen with sports teams, there is little motivation that is equivalent to wanting to show up for your team. That's also why people refer to the power of team spirit, which has the power to overcome obstacles.

> If a team is not highly motivated and having fun, it's probably not a High Performance Team.

Aligned

High Performance Teams are aligned on what to do, and collaborate well to make it happen. They quickly resolve conflicts and move forward. They believe in the power of *support, commitment, communication, collaboration, and agreement,* both within the team and with stakeholders. As a vice president in PepsiCo, one of the key principles I learned was the importance of alignment. For every initiative, we endeavored to get all those involved aligned. Alignment is half the success of an initiative. Once people are aligned, execution is smoother. Conversely, when you don't have alignment, you will have a manifold increase in obstacles.

Trust

High Performance Teams realize that trust is an essential ingredient. They communicate openly and with transparency. They believe in a feedback culture, actively giving and seeking feedback.

To do this effectively, building relationships and earning trust is a priority. Team members have each other's backs. When I survey my clients, they say, *"Trust is the hardest element to build, but it also makes the most powerful impact."*

> "Trust is the hardest of all elements to build; it can also make the most powerful impact."

In the following chapters, we will show you how to build trust quickly and on a sustained basis.

VIVRE FAT is a simple reminder of what really matters in team excellence. Given the eight elements' importance in developing TQ, in Part IV, we will devote one chapter to each element and explore that element in depth. Certainly, mastering these aspects requires focus, energy, and work, but palpable progress can be made if you know how to pursue it.

Now that we have identified the eight essential elements, it's time to embark on the journey.

THE 2-STEP HPT JOURNEY: GETTING FROM HERE TO THERE

Once you understand the elements of VIVRE FAT, the team can benchmark against it. This book will provide you with a TQ HealthCheck tool, which allows you to do just that. When the team self-assesses, the major gaps become evident. The gaps may seem overwhelming, but in my experience, the team can make major progress in a short period of time.

As discussed earlier, building a High Performance Team is a journey and doesn't happen overnight, however you will incorporate all of VIVRE FAT into the 2-Step HPT Journey. The implications of the journey are that now you must start focusing on the team.

Below you will find the framework for the journey; in further chapters, we will drill into the key modules and exercises within each of the processes.

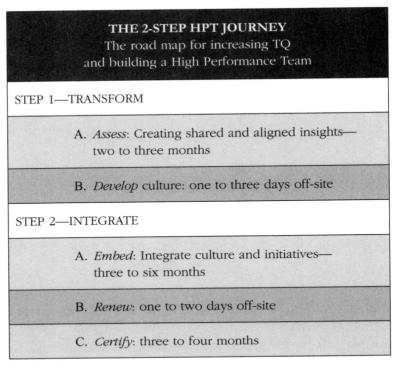

Figure 6.3

The 2-step process usually takes 12 to 24 months. Let's break down the steps.

Step 1—Transform

A. *Assess:* Creating shared and aligned insights—two to three months. This step explores the current situation within the team. It starts by assessing the Team Quotient through the TQ HealthCheck and corresponding TQ tools. It usually requires several team meetings to *understand* the current state of the team and *align* it on the path moving forward. It can also involve one-on-one interviews with team members to drill down into what is going on at the individual level as well as on a team level. As a part of the Assess phase, once the burning platform has been identified and the team is aligned on the need to engage in the High Performance Team journey, then it is ready to move into the Develop phase of the journey. (The Assess phase will be outlined in more detail in the next chapter.)

B. *Develop the culture of the team*—one to three days off-site. During the Develop stage, the team works on all aspects of VIVRE FAT. This is where the transformation begins. The team will feel it ramp up at the end of the off-site.

Figure 6.4 shows the focus areas as indicated in a sample two-day *develop culture* program. All members of the core team should attend this off-site, with no exceptions. I always advise investing in a lovely off-site environment, preferably in a natural setting, in which team members can relax, unwind, and bond with each other. For the meeting, it's best to choose a large room with chairs set up in U-shaped configuration with no tables in the middle. This leaves no barrier to hide behind.

What if teams cannot afford the time or expense to travel to such a setting, or invest 2 days? Where possible they should at least try to get out of the office. I have a few clients who have done the *develop culture* phase by breaking it down into 4 half days. As long as the team members have the right intention and commitment, that also works; in other words you can split the culture building into discrete parts.

In Part IV of this book, we will cover the "how" of each of the essential elements in detail. Some special mention is warranted for "Identity Building Activity" in Figure 6.4. The purpose of this activity is building a sense of team spirit and identity while enjoying and having fun with team members. Teams can choose any activity that serves a specific purpose for the team. It may be as short as a ten-minute icebreaker or something lasting an hour or more. Some teams might even want to spend an extra day engaging the team in just these types of activities. Often, they are the most memorable parts of the program.

DEVELOP CULTURE: TEAM TRANSFORMATION OFF-SITE [Sample]	
DAY ONE	
Morning	Review of key "Assess" areas
	TQ HealthCheck results
	Identify and handle issues
	Identity Building Activity
Afternoon	Awareness, acceptance, appreciation
	Relationship building
	Vision/mission
	Trust
	Identity Building Activity
Evening	Recognition dinner
DAY TWO	
Morning	*Identity Building Activity*
	Define team success
	Values and behaviors
	Collaboration
Afternoon	Meeting effectiveness
	Identity Building Activity
	Commitments, actions, and rituals
	Team charter
Close	Celebration

Figure 6.4

Note that two days is an ideal period for the initial program; however, some teams prefer to invest even more time or mix the meeting with business activities. In this case, I recommend that business be done before or after the team transformation program to allow for the synergy of the elements to do their magic. It should not, however, interrupt the program. If your team cannot afford two days, start with a minimum of one day.

I have witnessed that, after the off-site, the team will experience remarkable shifts, and its sense of closeness and identity will increase considerably. Later in the book, we will cover each of the above in more detail.

Step 2—Integrate

A. *Embed:* Integrate culture and initiatives—six to twelve months. This step takes place back at the office. You have had breakthroughs already, and the team members feel close and cohesive. You have identified initiatives, processes, and loose ends to work on, and you have assigned champions. Now you need to integrate everything throughout the larger team and communicate the changes to stakeholders. The following are aspects of "Embed":
- "Go forward" plan is identified
- Team structures are working smoothly
- Team meetings are effective
- Processes are working
- Initiatives are integrated throughout the larger team
- Communication with stakeholders are executed
- Coach key team members
- Monitor progress
- Feedback
- Course correction

During this step, you will conduct a series of team meetings to arrive at a measure of how things are going. Some meetings will be with the entire team, and some will be with subsets of the team. You will review input from champions on initiatives, processes, communication, and the integration process while considering these questions:
1. Are the vision and values being lived and integrated?
2. What's working well, and what needs to be changed or enhanced?
3. How is the team making progress on the initiatives that were set out?
4. Are any team members holding back or not completely aligned?

5. Are any conflicts brewing or in need of handling?

6. Have all issues been handled, or are there still some that are festering?

7. Is the team committing to its new rituals on a regular basis?

8. Is the team getting together to connect, deepen relationships, and celebrate?

9. Has the team communicated sufficiently with stakeholders?

10. Are the team structures working well, or do they need modification?

11. Stepping back, are we truly becoming a High Performance Team, or are we slipping back into old habits?

12. Are we using feedback to get everyone on track and encouraging openness and transparency?

B. *Renew and enhance*—one to two days off-site. In this step, you will want to conduct another off-site within three to six months of the first one to reconnect and bring the team to the next level. During this program, you will do the following:
   - Review and align how things are progressing and identify the focus going forward.
   - Celebrate what's been achieved both at the business and the team levels.
   - Deepen trust building using feedback.
   - Conduct activities to deepen team skills in identified areas.
   - Schedule fun/meaningful activities to deepen camaraderie.
   - Determine what are next and ongoing focus areas.
   - Augment identified skills.
   - Review commitments and recommit on a team and individual level.

C. *Certify—High-TQ achieved*—three to four months. Assess the team and recommend future direction; certify as a High Performance Team.
   - Perform TQ HealthCheck
   - Diagnose
   - Recommended future needs
   - Certify

Once a High TQ has been achieved leading to High Performance, the team has the option of being certified. In our consulting practice, we certify teams as "High Performance" once they achieve High TQ. This is a time for celebration and review. I recommend a time-lining activity that shows what has transpired and how the team moved to High Performance over the preceding 12 to 24 months. This is a time of reflection when positive attributes are reinforced and the team considers how to move to even higher performance. There are always areas to work on and improve. And importantly, the team needs to reflect on how it will keep its TQ high and not slip back into mediocrity or even dysfunction.

Figure 6.5 shows a summary of the 2-Step HPT journey as applied to a leadership team.

2-Step High Performance Leadership Team Journey

1 Transform

Assess
Interview/
Assessments

Build team and individual awareness, and then create shared and aligned team insights into the team dynamics and team goals.
• Healthcheck
• Interviews
• Gap Analysis

Develop
Leadership
Team
Offsite

Build team culture and create a strong, bonded Leadership Team:
• Vision, Purpose & Values
• Trust building & camaraderie
• Meeting best practices
• Commitment to integrate back at office
• Collaboration
• Team Identity
• Define success

2 Integrate

Embed
Integrating
Into Work/
Championing/
Coaching

Integrate into the larger team / organization and ensure champions are in place to continue momentum with appropriate milestones.
• Initiatives in place
• Communication throughout team
• Coaching to ensure success
• Reviewing and correcting

Renew
Leadership Team
Sessions/
Review/
Skill Enhancement

Come back together as a team to renew commitments and energy and focus on strengthening competencies.
• Review & prescribe
• Renew commitments
• Strengthen team competencies
• Celebrate

Certify
Assessments &
Interviews/
Recommendations

Assess the team and recommend future directions. Certify as a High Performance Leadership Team.
• TQ Healthcheck
• Diagnose
• Recommended future needs
• Certify

Figure 6.5

BUILDING A HIGH PERFORMANCE TEAM
IS AN ONGOING PROCESS

Typically, we consider the High Performance Leadership Team Cycle: Assess—Develop—Embed—Renew below, which may be conducted several times to gain sustained traction. Remember, we are looking for team transformation as opposed to one-off experiences. We are in the business of changing team habits and instilling new behaviors that will create a profound impact.

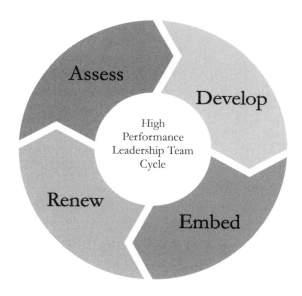

Figure 6.6: High Performance Leadership Team Cycle

Now that we have outlined the 2-Step High Performance Team Journey, it's time to scope out the "who" on the team and "how" the team should go through the journey.

How Large a Team/Which Team?

Who should go through the 2-Step HPT process? When we refer to a team, we are usually referring to a team leader and his/her direct reports or other important players (referred to as the core team). Here we are addressing leadership teams or those teams that manage a company, region, or function. Yet the 2-Step HPT process can be applied to middle management as well. It is this level of a core team (with as few as 6 to as many as 20 team members) that engages in the process.

As long as you lead a team or impact a team in a major way, you can implement the 2-Step High Performance Team Journey. Remember to seek alignment with your management or other key stakeholders, being cognizant of existing company vision/values and culture so as not to contradict existing or overall work being conducted by the company. It's been my experience that the 2-Step HPT process is well supported by internal stakeholders. High Performance Teams are sought after in companies, and there is a recognition that it's a journey; it doesn't happen overnight.

> Our task is to change team habits and create new behaviors that will make a profound impact.

People Come; People Go

One common question is, "How do I know when to conduct a High Performance Team process? Should I wait until my team is completely filled out?" The answer really depends on whether you believe the most important core players are already part of the team.

I had a banking client who was eager to start the 2-Step HPT process but wanted to wait for a couple of key positions to be filled. Given the importance of these positions, I advised her to wait until those people were in place. On the other hand, if you are missing one or two people, or the jobs yet to be filled are not core positions, it's better to go ahead and start the process. People come and go, and waiting until you have the perfect team may mean waiting too long.

Lessons from a Professional Services Client
One of my professional services clients realized that during the Assess phase, a key team member was causing many problems and was the source of much of the pain

encountered by the team. She was a top revenue producer, but she was operating out of a silo fiefdom that was alienating the team. The client realized that she had to go but wondered whether to include her in the upcoming Culture and Team-Building off-site. What happened next was fascinating. After communicating the shared insights from the Assess phase, the problematic manager/core team member realized that she was alienating people and decided to resign. It became clear that she would not sync with the values and atmosphere that the team wanted to create. The team experienced great relief as they didn't need to pull the plug on her and could move forward with a clean slate.

The only problem was that this core member's department was responsible for 40 percent of the team's revenue, and she enjoyed many strong industry relationships. Everyone was justifiably worried that the revenue would disappear overnight. In reality, the opposite occurred. After this team member left, other managers stepped in, and the company didn't miss a beat. Within a year, they had recovered the revenue and began a strong growth trajectory thereafter!

————

The 2-Step HPT process is a comprehensive approach. You may decide to select the parts that are most relevant to your team's situation. For example, some teams may want to focus on a particular aspect first, such as trust. *Even focusing on a single, important aspect can bring great benefits to the team.* You may also decide to go at your own pace. Some teams want to accelerate the process and get to High Performance within a year. Others prefer to take it slowly and more deliberately. Whatever pace you set, the 2-Step HPT process is your road map to High-Team Quotient and team success.

7

WHAT'S YOUR TEAM QUOTIENT?

ASSESSING THE TEAM

ASSESS: THE PRE-WORK

In the last chapter, you will have noted that the first part of the 2–Step HPT process is "Assess." This is the time to use a dipstick to measure where you are as a team and the best way to determine what needs to take place. "Assess" refers to the preliminary work that we do with the team. It's like the "situational analysis" of a business plan. It's an essential piece to start building the team with intelligence and helps to target efforts expediently. Among the Assess tools we will cover in this chapter are these:

1. Collective TQ HealthCheck
2. Personal TQ HealthCheck
3. One-Word Exercise
4. 12-Question Interview

COLLECTIVE TEAM QUOTIENT

As the title of the book suggests, Team Quotient provides a benchmark for the team's current status as well as its journey toward High Performance. The TQ HealthCheck allows the team to assess itself, arriving at a TQ score and landing in one of the five score classifications shown in figure 7.1.

We will highlight more on TQ scoring later, but first it's important to understand why we need a Team Quotient. It's an easy and expedient way to measure the current state of the team and potential future states. It forms a diagnostic for areas to work on and objectifies the process, leaving out the guesswork and subjectivity.

> TQ provides a diagnostic on team areas requiring attention, objectifying the process.

Human nature compels us to measure, track, and score ourselves in all endeavors. Without measurement, we would never know how we are doing. Since we measure everything else, why not measure the team itself? Most teams measure themselves based on key performance indicators (KPIs), yet many leaders believe that High Performance Teams need a more robust measurement than standard KPIs.

COLLECTIVE TQ SCORE GUIDE	
41–50	You are a High Performance Team!
34–40	You are a performing team.
27–33	You are a functioning team.
20–26	You are a barely functioning team.
10–19	You are a dysfunctional team.

Figure 7.1

There are two types of Team Quotient: Collective TQ and Personal TQ. Collective TQ measures the team's ability to function as a High Performance Team. We have developed the TQ HealthCheck to provide a *quotient* or *score* to measure the team's Effectiveness at present and diagnose what areas need improvement.

The TQ measurement takes place at the very beginning of building a High Performance Team. It is administered through an online TQ HealthCheck that can be conducted at www.douglasgerber.com, or it can be taken manually as per below. Ideally, all team members should take the TQ HealthCheck as part of the Assess phase of the 2-Step HPT.

> Doing the "Top-Ten" things well will result in a High Performance Team that consistently wins, and get results.

Collective Team Quotient Is Based on the "TQ Top Ten"

As mentioned in the last chapter, based on our ten-year study, we have arrived at the "TQ Top Ten," which are measurable focus areas for a team. To be sure, *consistently doing these Top-Ten things well will result in a High Performance Team that consistently wins and gets results.* They include:

1. Aligning a compelling vision, mission, or purpose
2. Having the right mix of talent
3. Aligning desired values and behaviors
4. Respecting culture, style, and preferences
5. Demonstrating trust and openness to feedback
6. Conducting effective team meetings
7. Focusing on big things that create results
8. Collaborating on team initiatives
9. Having a powerful team identity
10. Experiencing fun, camaraderie, and recognition

The mix of these factors will make for an unbeatable team. They form the basis for determining the Team Quotient and moving toward high performance. That's why we have formulated the Team Quotient, with a bias toward simplicity, around these ten attributes. There is no need to overcomplicate the measurement of Team Quotient. It should be intuitive and easy to answer, focusing only on the ten questions that matter. Keeping TQ simple will facilitate full participation and provide laser-focused areas that the team can address (see the TQ HeathCheck questions in figure 7.2).

After each team member has taken the TQ HealthCheck, score and total the feedback to determine into which of the following five categories the team falls (see figure 7.3). Achieving a TQ score of 41 or above as a High Performance Team is not easy. It means that for most questions, your team answered "Agree" (4) or "Strongly Agree" (5). Conversely, if team members answered, on average, "Slightly Disagree" (2), your team would be considered dysfunctional.

After compiling the results, we would look at the following:
- average mean and median for each question
- average mean for all questions
- high areas and low areas, which would be highlighted.

When conducting the TQ HealthCheck, some teams enjoy strong unanimity in responses, which is a good indication that people are aware and aligned. On the other hand, some teams have real variances between members. Occasionally members may sugarcoat the answers. This is why the team leader needs to ask up-front for honesty, letting members know that the team is not looking for high scores or low scores, just a reflection of what is. That is also why I advise maintaining answer anonymity; when taken online, the TQ HealthCheck answers remain confidential. The online TQ HealthCheck generates a report that allows for diagnosis of the current state of the team and areas of focus. (See figures 7.4 and 7.5 for TQ HealthCheck report sample.)

COLLECTIVE TEAM QUOTIENT™ HEALTHCHECK						
Check the corresponding box from 1 to 5:	Disagree	Somewhat Disagree	Somewhat Agree	Agree	Strongly Agree	Your Score
	1	2	3	4	5	
1 Our team is aligned around a compelling vision, purpose, or common goals.						
2 Our team is composed of the right mix of capable talent.						
3 Our team is living and putting into action our own "team values and behaviors."						
4 Differences in culture, styles, and preferences are respected and encouraged.						
5 Trust and open feedback are pervasive, deep, and nurtured among team members.						
6 Our team meetings are productive and stimulating, with effective decision making.						
7 We focus on the big things creating results, not dwelling on detail or tasks.						
8 Our team collaborates well and is not stuck in individual or department silos.						
9 We share a strong team identity, and members are committed to team success.						
10 Our team has fun with strong camaraderie, and we recognize and celebrate frequently.						
					Total Score	

Figure 7.2

COLLECTIVE TEAM QUOTIENT™
SCORE GUIDE

TQ Score	Description
41–50	You are a **HIGH PERFORMANCE TEAM. You have achieved Team Brilliance!** The characteristics of your team indicate you consistently achieve high performance and your team members enjoy working together in high camaraderie. Your key objective is to continue this level of effectiveness while seeking ways to take it to improve further.
34–40	**PERFORMING TEAM. Opportunity to move from Good to Great.** Your team performs consistently with a good sense of team spirit. Some alignment will easily take you to brilliant levels. Your team gets results, yet can be put to the test during challenging times, and small issues can easily escalate into big problems if not addressed.
27–33	**FUNCTIONING TEAM. Move from Functioning to Good.** Your team delivers average or good results. With some alignment and awareness, you will readily improve spirit and identity and see improvement. Some team development processes are highly recommended.
20–26	**BARELY FUNCTIONING TEAM. Needs Help.** Your team does not likely achieve consistent results nor withstand major challenges. Action is recommended to identify inherent strengths and priority problem areas and to rebuild the foundation for team effectiveness.
10–19	**DYSFUNCTIONAL TEAM. Needs Urgent Help.** This team is spending excessive energy on feeding the dysfunction, and priority problem areas must be immediately identified to alleviate the dysfunction. Prescriptive options are available if your team, in fact, wants to remain a team.
Total Score	

Figure 7.3

TEAM QUOTIENT ™
HEALTH CHECK FOR HIGH PERFORMANCE LEADERSHIP TEAM

Sample Report
Team Quotient = 35 / 50

TQ Score Guide	
41 – 50	You are a High Performance Team!
34 – 40	You are a Performing Team
27 - 33	You are a Functioning Team
20 – 26	You are a Barely Functioning Team
10 – 19	You are a Dysfunctional Team

TQ Score Description

Performing Team

Your team is very aware of culture, style and preferences. You have a good sense of alignment, vision and purpose. Your team knows how to have fun, recognize each others strengths and celebrate your wins. Your team meetings are overall effective.

By deepening team trust and improving open feedback, you will strengthen your cohesiveness. Through identifying aligned team values and behaviors, you will increase team effectiveness. By increasing your sense of identity you will form a stronger team.

Figure 7.4

TEAM QUOTIENT ™
HEALTH CHECK FOR HIGH PERFORMANCE LEADERSHIP TEAM

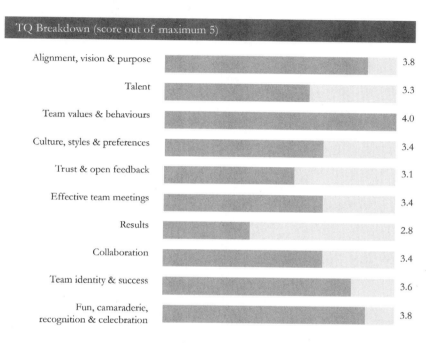

TQ Breakdown (score out of maximum 5)

Alignment, vision & purpose	3.8
Talent	3.3
Team values & behaviours	4.0
Culture, styles & preferences	3.4
Trust & open feedback	3.1
Effective team meetings	3.4
Results	2.8
Collaboration	3.4
Team identity & success	3.6
Fun, camaraderie, recognition & celecbration	3.8

TQ Focus Areas

Relative Team Strengths

- Team values & behaviors
- Alignment, vision & purpose
- Fun, camaraderie, recognition & celecbration

Major Team Development Opportunities

- Results
- Trust and open feedback

Minor Team Development Opportunities

- Collaboration
- Culture, styles & preferences
- Effective team meetings
- Team identity and success
- Talent

Figure 7.5

What Is the Value in Knowing a Team's Collective TQ?

First, it's *aspirational.* Countless teams desire to progress in order to get their Team Quotient up! Arriving at a Team Quotient higher than 40 is a rewarding and satisfying accomplishment, knowing the team has moved to high performance.

Second, the TQ HealthCheck can be taken repeatedly as a way to *track progress.* Teams usually shift from one band to the next (say Functioning to Performing). However, on occasion, when a team is very focused, it may skip a band (for example, moving from Functioning to High Performance). I work with many teams who assess their TQ over a one- to two-year period, taking the HealthCheck several times. Teams find real satisfaction in witnessing progress being made. When High Performance is achieved, that is a cause for celebration.

Finally, *Collective TQ is effective as a diagnostic tool.* It can be a real wake-up call for many teams that may be confused about where they stand. After showing the results, it is useful to spend a couple of hours discussing them and going through each question in some depth. You will find that lots of useful ideas come out of this type of session, and it further propels the team to look at ways to become a great team. The TQ HealthCheck also develops a kind of common platform and language for members to communicate. They start thinking about trust, values, and camaraderie as possibilities that may not have surfaced in the past.

PERSONAL TEAM QUOTIENT

Personal TQ measures the degree to which *each team member* works effectively in the team context. Because a team's progress will be the collective and synergistic result of individual efforts, it is important to reflect on Personal TQ to determine what the team member can individually work on to benefit the team.

The foundation of Personal TQ is based on interviews and interactions with hundreds of team members. In particular, the Personal TQ questions reflect on the shifts in attitude and mind-sets required to become effective team members. Personal TQ focuses on team members' behaviors, mindsets, and beliefs in their relationship to the team. This. provides team members with an opportunity to examine their own actions and beliefs with regards to the team.

The Personal TQ HealthCheck can also be taken online at www.douglasgerber.com or manually (see figure 7.6). It is easy to take, and because it is online, results are instantaneous. Once the Personal TQ test has been taken, it is scored as per figure 7.7.

How to Use Personal TQ

Unlike Collective TQ, which is meant to be shared among team members, Personal TQ is usually kept personal. Whether taken online or manually, the results are kept confidential and only shared voluntarily. Essentially, it is an opportunity for the individual team member to reflect on his or her own propensity to become a strong team member. Often it is a wake-up call for team members to realize the attributes, attitudes, or mind-sets that are useful. As my friend Merle Hinrich, chairman of Global Sources, says, "All work on the team also requires personal work."

> In creating a High Performance Team, focus on *team* needs over *individual* needs.

Some of the questions may be considered confrontational. For example, one statement reads, "I put the team's needs and welfare ahead of my own." This statement is one that some individuals struggle with. Our conditioning ingrains the mind-set of "Looking out for number one." In fact, we all naturally approach the team from an individual and subjective perspective. It is only with reflection and understanding that we realize that treating team needs as paramount will be key to creating a High Performance Team. It is precisely for this reason that Personal TQ is useful. When we realize that team success also depends on personal attitudes, we are willing to consider our own personal role in the process.

Some of the questions are a call to action. For example, the statement, "I am willing to assert my own views and debate where necessary," may require a team member to get out of their comfort zone and consider how to be a more active participant. On the other hand, the statement, "I strive to build strong relationships with team members" may serve as a reminder to move relationships beyond a cherished few and challenge the concept of team cliques, which can be disastrous for TQ.

Of course, it isn't just the individual statements but also the score that is useful to team members. Just as with Collective TQ, increasing Personal TQ is aspirational and allows for team members to monitor their own progress as often as they like.

When using both collective and Personal TQ, I usually start by administering the Collective TQ test and debriefing results. I then introduce Personal TQ as a second stage, once team members are committed to the idea of a High Performance Team.

PERSONAL TEAM QUOTIENT ™ HEALTHCHECK						
Check the corresponding box from 1 to 5:	Disagree	Somewhat Disagree	Somewhat Agree	Agree	Strongly Agree	Your Score
	1	2	3	4	5	
1 I strive to build strong relationships with team members.						
2 I put the team's needs and welfare ahead of my own.						
3 I actively listen to and encourage opinions from other team members.						
4 I am willing to assert my own views and debate where necessary.						
5 I enjoy collaborating with other team members.						
6 I willingly align with final decisions and directions made by the team or team leader.						
7 I am fully present in team meetings and focused on the issue at hand.						
8 I am a strong contributor to team meetings.						
9 We often give and receive feedback and recognize other team members.						
10 I believe teamwork is important in achieving the goals the team has set for itself.						
					Total Score	

Figure 7.6

PERSONAL TEAM QUOTIENT ™ HEALTHCHECK
SCORE GUIDE

Score	Description
41–50	You have **HIGH Personal TQ!** You are a very strong team member and role model. Your commitment and belief in the power of teams will be an inspiration for others. You are very focused on what is best for the team and its members and nurture strong relationships. Through passionately demonstrating your high TQ, you will make a significant impact in helping the team to achieve High Performance.
34–40	You have **GOOD Personal TQ.** You are an active team member who is committed to being in a performing team. You make the effort to work closely with other team members. You have the capacity to make a strong contribution to the team and believe in the power of teamwork. With a bit of focus on certain areas, you can move to high TQ.
27–33	You have **MEDIOCRE Personal TQ.** There are certain areas in which you are actively involved with the team. However, your commitment to the team and its members may be spotty or inconsistent. You tend to co-exist with the team rather than taking an active role to progress the team agenda. You should reflect on how you can increase your involvement and support to the team.
20–26	You have **LIMITED Personal TQ.** You may question the effectiveness or need to operate as a team. You tend to take a more passive role in team interactions. Your relationships with other team members may be limited. You focus on your own area rather than the team. You should examine your fundamental barriers to fully participating in the team.
10–19	You have **LOW Personal TQ.** You don't believe in the power of teams and most likely consider team interactions a waste of time. You tend to operate in a silo environment. Your relationship with other team members may be conflicted. You may be seen as uninvolved or not caring for the team. You should examine your fundamental intentions with regard to team involvement.

Figure 7.7

One-Word Exercise

The TQ HealthCheck provides a benchmark and diagnostic for the team and individual, yet it is sometimes useful to have an "in the moment" sense of the state of the team. During the Assess phase, many people appreciate having a quick and easy way to read the pulse of the team. The One-Word Exercise can be conducted in ten minutes and surprisingly will provide valuable input on the current and desired state of the team. This is how it works:

Explain to your team that it's useful to know where the team is now and where it wants to go. You can tee it up by saying, "This is just a check-in with the team," and ask participants to be as honest as possible.

You then ask each team member for *one word to describe the current state* of the team and *one word to describe the desired state* of the team, ending up with a list of words for both *current* and *desired*. I suggest that you, as the team leader or facilitator, do this together with your team, feeling free to include any other stakeholders or team members who play an important role but may not report directly to you. You simply go around the room and ask each person for their word choices—one describing the current state and one describing the desired state—and record it.

Below is an actual team sample from one of my clients.

CURRENT STATE OF TEAM ONE WORD	DESIRED STATE OF TEAM ONE WORD
• Disjointed • Fragmented • Sigh • Tired • Uncertainty • Inconsistent • Schizophrenic • Forming • Overwhelmed • Pressured	• Unified • Consolidated front • Fun • Energized • Rebuilding • Evolving • Effortless • Spirited • Aligned • Stabilize

Figure 7.8

After this feedback, you will have a good idea of how the team perceives itself and where it wants to go, as well as the size of the gap that needs to be bridged. This exercise also acts as a good discussion provoker.

Through the One-Word exercise, it became patently obvious that the team above was quite dysfunctional. The words *schizophrenic* and *tired* pointed to some real issues that needed to be addressed. On the other hand, the team aspired to something much different and wanted to experience "fun," be "energized," and be "aligned."

One value of the One-Word exercise is that it paints a simple and clear picture to the team in its own words. This can serve as a rallying point for the team to come to terms with itself and act as a starting point on the path toward High Performance. I recommend summarizing it in chart form as shown above and making it available to reiterate whenever needed. Once displayed, it's hard to ignore, and team members coalesce around the desire to make a change. Nobody wants to be part of a "schizophrenic" and "tired" team.

The 12-Question Interview—Drilling Down to the Individual

As a part of the Assess phase, we have been speaking about the importance of the team and putting it first. Why might we also be interested in individual issues and concerns? It is a basic human need to be listened to and heard. There is only so much that individuals are willing to share with the team. Therefore, it is worthwhile, during the Assess stage of the 2-Step HPT process, to spend a little time drilling down to individual thoughts, ideas, concerns, opinions, etc. It is often useful to hear what people are really thinking. Unless there is a high level of trust within the team, members will rarely reveal their true thoughts. It takes a one-on-one session to learn how people really feel.

> One-on-one interviews are important to get team members talking about both the issues and their feelings.

This is best done in an interview process. I recommend about one hour for each team member. Here a critical issue comes up: Who should conduct the interview? This is one case in which a third party is useful. People may be reticent to open up to people with whom they work, and certainly in the beginning of this process, it's more precarious to open up to your boss.

I conduct many individual interviews and find that people will invariably open up to a third party. The key is creating a safe environment by assuring participants that individual comments will not be repeated and that what we are looking for are patterns and themes. This reassures people and often results in an ensuing outpouring of information and frankness. What I have learned about human nature in these sessions is that people need an opportunity to vent and express their true thoughts. One must truly be a good listener.

When conducting these interviews, I use a number of questions that cover the important points (see figure 7.9). People will invariably go off on tangents, which is normal, as long as you can bring them back to this point. The main thing is to *get them to start talking about both the issues and their feelings.* This is why we ask questions such as, "On a scale of 1 to 10 (high), how would you rate the trust level within the team?" This is most useful in obtaining an understanding of how well the team connects and works closely together.

Another important issue the leader: "Describe the leadership style of your manager: What works well, and where are the challenges?" I will align the leader in advance, and inform him or her of the results only as a whole (with no individual comments). Most team leaders appreciate this form of feedback as being about as close to the "truth" as they can get. Another advantage is that team members often appreciate having a chance to answer questions about their manager and to know that someone is listening.

By the way, you may have noticed the One-Word question embedded in statement 3, of figure 7.9 below. Sometimes I like to ask the question up front; then it's easy to present the results during the alignment meeting.

At the end of the process, I produce a report with an Executive Summary. The particular report presented in figure 7.10 happens to be for a regional professional services team that measured as dysfunctional.

―――――

The Executive Summary – State of Team in figure 7.10 will give the team a feel for its TQ and prescribe areas of focus. You can choose to go as deep as you wish. For some leaders, the One-Word Exercise is enough to get started, and you will be surprised how much revealing information can come out of it. That's what I call the "appetizer." The "main course" in the Assess stage is the TQ HealthCheck and resultant Team Quotient.

Ultimately, through the Assess phase, the purpose is to align the team with its current state and galvanize the team to commit to High Performance. It's one thing to review the findings of the Assess phase; it's another to make key decisions that all team members buy into. Your job as the team leader is to create that alignment.

Once the Assess phase is complete, you are ready to move on to the Develop Culture phase of the 2-Step HPT journey.

TEAM CULTURE BUILDING:
THE 12-QUESTION INTERVIEW

The company has undertaken a team culture building journey. As a part of this journey, we are interviewing all key members of the team. The purpose is to find

- where the individuals and team are in terms of a) beliefs, b) behaviors, c) culture, and d) system/structure
- what the desired areas are to strengthen and enhance moving forward.

Feel free to be as honest and as open as you wish. Specific points will not be repeated. We are looking for patterns and themes. Your name will not be ascribed to anything you say.

Questions:

1. Briefly tell me about your background. (Icebreaker)
2. What do you enjoy about working at the company/team?
3. What is one word to describe current state of team and desired state?
4. How would you describe the culture in the team?
5. What are the values with which you identify most at the team, and how are they being lived?
6. What are the behaviors, that work and don't work in the team?
7. Describe the leadership style of your manager: what works well and where are the challenges?
8. On a scale of 1 to 10 (high), how would you rate your experience at the team thus far?
9. What issues and frustrations do you experience at the team?
10. On a scale of 1 to 10 (high), how would you rate the trust level?
11. What does "working as an effective team" mean to you?
12. Do you have any suggestions on how to improve the team?

Figure 7.9

EXECUTIVE SUMMARY – STATE OF TEAM
[Example]

This report is based on interviews with all team members.

Key Messages from Team Members

- The current state of the company regional team is characterized by a group of highly competent team members operating in a silo, with a boutique mentality that has little transparency and a dearth of office- or regional-team identity.
- The underlying company values of generosity, kindness, and collegiality are not uniformly exhibited, and the opposite is often experienced. All are inspired by company values but not all are living them in the regional team.
- Much of the operating culture is communicated via the grapevine subculture, through cliques.
- There is a fundamental lack of trust and transparency.
- The team has now become untenable as the younger generation of team members joined with expectations of working in a culture with distinct company values, and they have been disappointed.
- There appears to be a lack of overall leadership from a visionary or motivational perspective.
- It is clear that all partners need to step up to take a stronger leadership role. Some participants think that selecting champions to take on key initiatives would be effective.

Desired Future

Although the desired future has not yet been articulated, there is a desire to improve along the following lines:

- feedback
- culture building
- ownership of values team-member development
- compelling regional vision
- strengthened leadership
- commitment to a strong team

Figure 7.10

PART III

BUILDING

RIGHT INTENTIONS; RIGHT PLAYERS

8

WHAT KIND OF A
TEAM ARE YOU?

A little self-honesty goes a long way. Many leaders feel that their team is already "good enough," so they focus on individual performers and results. Is having lots of talent on your team most important? As we have seen in sports team examples, individual talent is essential, but it only goes so far. What will make the difference is taking all that individual talent and unleashing it in an unbeatable team environment.

In the TQ HealthCheck, in Chapter 7, we talked about TQ score, landing the team anywhere between high performance to dysfunctional. In this chapter, we will examine characteristics of each kind of team.

THE TQ "MANGO"

One of the best ways to put the team journey in perspective is to break it down in what we will call the TQ "Mango." The TQ Mango allows for easy illustration of the kinds of teams that represent the "state" of the team at any given point.

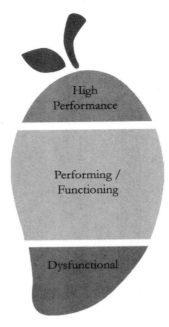

Figure 8.1: TQ "Mango"

A *High Performance Team is not a destination; rather, it's a state.* The implication is that the team never really arrives at a High Performance *point*; it only continues to evolve and improve into a *state* of High Performance.

HIGH PERFORMANCE TEAMS

The top of the TQ Mango is High Performance, or High TQ. Where does your team rank? Are you already a High TQ Team? If you are, you know you can always become better, and you will seek out ways to improve. Occasionally, I witness great teams that want to be just that much better; they constantly seek ways to gain an edge. They strive to keep one step ahead of the competition and to achieve success consistently. There is always something to improve upon. A High Performance Team possesses a High Team Quotient. It has a buzz about it, which is energizing. The team is clear about where it wants to go and why it exists. It delights in being what it is and in the opportunity to excel and make a difference. The High TQ Team has clarity about what's important, its values, and the behaviors necessary to make it work. It is consistently stretching itself to improve and achieve more. Team members enjoy being together, and they often work and play together. Relationships are deep with a high level of trust.

> A High Performance Team is not a destination; rather, it's a state.

High TQ Teams have learned to collaborate effectively with a larger goal in mind. There is transparency and open communication, and all members strive for alignment. Roles, responsibilities, and accountabilities are clear, and team members respect each other's styles. Team members have embraced a feedback culture that allows for mutual improvement and development. The team consistently reaches/exceeds objectives, and where it falls short, it assesses, learns, resets, and acts. It is not satisfied with the status quo, endeavoring to focus an even higher level of performance. Its presence is clearly recognized by others as high performance.

In essence, High TQ teams work on and become proficient in each of the of the essential elements of VIVRE FAT, or Vision / Identity / Values / Results / Effective / Fun / Aligned / Trust.

Lessons from PepsiCo

One of the things I witnessed in my years at PepsiCo was the positive impression left on upper management by those with great teams. I would hear the expression, "He's not only capable; he builds great teams." Why is this so important? Because everyone wants to promote someone who knows how to enter a situation and build a great team, especially when there are major challenges; and a great team often has a good "bench," and the risk of a meltdown is mitigated when it's time for the leader to move on. Great teams require far less classical supervision; rather, they need to build the confidence to self-govern.

> If you want to be considered for promotion faster, build a High Performance Team!

From a personal perspective, the upshot of this is *if you want to be considered for promotion faster, build a High Performance Team!* You and your team will get noticed, and I assure you it's a career enhancer. Conversely, if you just want to stay in your job, building a High TQ Team may not be such a great idea.

PERFORMING TEAMS

One of the characteristics in those teams which have not reached high performance is what we call *silo mentality*. Essentially most teams consist of a group of individuals concerned more about their own agendas and welfare. Without the intention and effort to move to high performance, most team members will naturally operate from a silo perspective. It's a common challenge in most teams, and one which is readily identified by leaders as requiring attention.

Members of performing teams are often 'high performing individuals'. In their own right often they achieve stellar results and are recognized as such. However, unless the team itself consciously has the intention to move to high performance, they will remain high performing individuals in a performing team.

Members of performing teams often operate in what might be called "peaceful or happy coexistence." They may be quite satisfied with the team, engaging in good relationships and/or friendships. They enjoy working with each other and might even have fun outside of work. Getting together is generally a positive experience. Yet members rarely confront or challenge each other. They may be quite task-oriented and spend time talking about accomplishments and reporting. They seldom give feedback to create change or upset the apple cart. The team may exist in a sort of bubble or lull that "all is well." There may be little appetite to seriously consider threats or contingencies.

Performing teams may be very close to high performance; in order to get there, it takes an aligned sense of commitment and intention. An importantly members need to change their mindset to put the team first.

FUNCTIONING TEAMS

Functioning teams, or just functioning teams, cooperate minimally to get along and not raise any doubts. They contribute where needed but don't actually take much initiative. There may be flareups, but these generally don't devolve into warfare. Often a team in this state has a lack of energy or drive; members may only be going through the motions. They're mainly doing their own thing, remaining essentially "siloed" in their approach and protecting their turf should it be threatened. There is a *lack of team identity*, and they may see themselves as a group of professionals or effective managers who only get together when necessary. This type of team often indicates a leader who does not put much energy into the team. Functioning team members often don't see a real need or reason to spend much time on the team or team dynamics, preferring to "get on with their work."

One phenomenon of functioning teams is that they are in a state of "passive coexistence," with the view that "things are as good as they need to be." "Why change much or rock the boat?" The leader and team members may be unaware of the possibilities of achieving a state of high performance. They also may be in denial of threats in the business or the larger team. Or they may lack willingness to address challenges.

Fundamentally, the team in coexistence, while usually clear on goals and objectives, may miss a deeper sense of vision and purpose and lack the drive to be the best or to stretch themselves to a higher level of excellence. They may not have identified what is truly important to them, nor taken it to heart. They most certainly won't have engendered a feedback culture, and while some trust is evident, it may be limited or superficial.

Functioning teams are often the most difficult to move to high performance, given they often lack the imperative or will to do so. It takes a leader who is willing to explore a potential burning platform, and cajole and align team members on the goal.

DYSFUNCTIONAL TEAMS

At the lower end of the TQ Mango are the dysfunctional teams. These are teams that are either partially or completely broken. Some of these teams have enough awareness to make a change. When you can't blame your staff and you know there are major hiccups in your team, you realize you need help and are open to taking a fresh approach.

Some clients state they have a "decent" team but recognize that some areas that "need fixing." Usually, that means they are already broken. At least they are seeking help and admit it.

Lessons from a Dysfunctional Team
One senior director at an aviation company had major team challenges as well as external challenges. The team underwent many diagnoses and blamed its team challenges on their "change agenda," which was causing considerable upheaval within the organization. The fact was that there was real dysfunction in the team: cliques, backbiting, blame games, lack of camaraderie, and little mutual appreciation. These characteristics define a dysfunctional team. Fortunately, the director realized that the team needed to undergo an intense transformation, which we started and

made real headway. Yet in this case, it was "too little, too late," and the director departed without seeing his team's complete transformation.

A few lessons emerge here; If you have or inherit a dysfunctional team, 1) Don't start the High Performance Team journey too late, and 2) Don't blame your team's problems on "change agendas," "external issues," or the like. Be honest and face the music.

A key factor in the dysfunctional team is "negative team energy." Members often retreat into silos. Meetings aren't fun, can often be negative or confrontational, or are, at best, dry and serious. They will often be characterized by withholding information or not sharing openly, with members remaining guarded about their contribution to the group.

Signs that a team already is or is bordering on dysfunctionality:
- infighting and cliques that don't get along
- spotty or poor results
- no joy
- unhealthy competition
- no team identity
- blame and covering yourself (CYA)
- backbiting and being overly critical
- members don't talk to each other or communicate with each other unless necessary
- high turnover
- ineffective meetings that members grumble about
- win/lose attitude

DYSFUNCTION CAN LEAD TO WARFARE

We can also occasionally refer to dysfunctional teams as being in "warfare."

In my Pepsi days, the obvious "enemy" was Coke, and we devoted considerable attention to how to gain market share from Coke. The "cola wars" are all too well known, however occasionally our regional team became just a bit too insular, and there were times when I felt that the enemy was within. When the team was at its lowest point, it seemed like we were busy defending ourselves and jockeying for position—essentially in a warfare state. Yet with the right intentions and efforts, we were able to move the team toward high performance.

The dysfunctional state can be caused by several factors. Sometimes, poor or inadequate results create a blame mentality where team members are in it for their survival and feel the need to cover their rear ends (also known as "CYA"). Impending staff or budget cuts may be another reason for the team to move into a state of warfare. In these circumstances, the team dynamic may shift from defense to offense, and team members may actively try to destroy others to survive.

Warfare may also be precipitated by the leader who may, in fact, believe in a bit of "friendly competition"' on his team. The problem is: how do you draw the line between friendly and unfriendly? Alternatively, the leader may play favorites, leading members to jockey for position or curry favor, producing a cadre of sycophants.

> An autocratic leader who believes in management by fear may breed warfare in his team.

Sometimes leadership style plays a part. An autocratic leader who believes in management by fear may breed warfare in his team, prompting members to engage in subterfuge to gain the upper hand. There are adherents to the warfare mentality who essentially believe that survival of the fittest will produce a superior team. While possibly true in the short term, it is rarely successful in the medium / long term.

Team-member conflicts and cliques may move a team into the warfare state.

I had one client whose team was split into several camps. They were essentially all at war with one another. They could do nothing but criticize and blame each other behind their backs. While cordial in meetings, they were obviously uncooperative. The team became polarized and essentially dysfunctional. My first priority was to point out the state of warfare and then to promote the idea that to move forward the team needed to confront their dysfunctional behaviors. That was a wake-up call that prompted the team to address its situation.

Sometimes a weak leader may feel incapable of dealing with opposing camps. Often there will be strong personalities that lead the camps and continue to propagate a state of warfare. At the heart of this is the idea that there is someone or some camp that is incompetent or untrustworthy or has malicious intent toward the other camp. As long as this conjecture perpetuates, warfare will continue.

> In a dysfunctional team, there is no sense of strong identity.

Finally, a dysfunctional team has no strong sense of identity. Sometimes it may be referred to as "that team." The team has not come together with a shared sense of what's important, and team members have not embraced how they are going to work together to make it happen. Members are not proud of their team, and often they would like to move out. Being part of a team at war does not help one's career, and, on the contrary, it may have a negative effect.

Moving Out of Dysfunction

When dealing with dysfunctional teams, the first step is to look at the behaviors of team members, which will demonstrate the extent of the dysfunction. It's also important to consider what events have led to the problems. Then examine the *team dynamics and social groupings*. In almost every dysfunctional team, you'll find groups of people or individuals who are pitted against one another. Sometimes this occurs due to an event; sometimes there is a chemistry issue between personalities, and other times, *assumptions are made that may not be true.*

Lessons from an Office Supply Company

One of my clients, an office supply company, had a regional president and vice president who were at odds with each other, affecting the entire leadership team. The vice president enjoyed a good relationship with the CEO and often communicated with him directly. The president had reason to believe that they were speaking behind his back. Assumptions were made, and blame and suspicion mounted between the vice president and president.

I was brought in to help them manage the conflict. I got them together to work out differences. It turned out that the president made assumptions without verifying them, and as a result, the relationship had turned sour and bitter. After expressing their views, and the supporting assumptions, they came to realize that many of their views were mere projections. This enabled them to start communicating. While they never became best friends, they were able to work together.

Often, seemingly high-level executives may not get along. It doesn't mean that they are bad managers or leaders. It only means that they haven't worked on the relationship with an open mind and with the right intentions. There certainly are cases that are beyond repair, but again it comes down to self-honesty. Has each person made the effort to understand and verify the issues? Have both parties mutually tried to build a relationship? Are they willing to entertain the possibility of viewing the other as a potential ally rather than an adversary? Have they examined the downside of an adversarial relationship versus the upsides of getting along? Often, these conflicts are reduced to the gut/emotional level, and executives may be incapable of or unwilling to examine them objectively.

THE TQ MANGO IS DYNAMIC

Teams are rarely static in one area. They move up and down the mango based on a few factors, as we saw in Chapter 3 with the Germany World Cup Teams of 2014 and 2018.

A High Performance Team may be affected by poor results, which forces it into warfare. However, if it has done the hard work of feedback, communication, trust building, and so on, it won't remain in warfare long and will be able to climb its way out. Unfortunately, many teams haven't done the heavy lifting to instill and crystallize the key characteristics of a High Performance Team in their members.

Of course, the major factor in this picture involves the leader. Change of leadership means changes in the team. The leader is the crucial factor for moving the team up or down the TQ Mango. I've encountered leaders taking a High Performance Team way down to dysfunction simply due to leadership style and lack of respect for the positive culture of the team. On the other hand, a skillful leader can move the team back up.

A key element in moving to a High Performance Team is "right intention." When we do team interventions, one of the first things we work on is the intention. The leader with the right intention to build TQ will work hard to bring all team members along. As long as the intention is there, the "possibility" of moving to high performance exists. Without intention, it just won't happen. Knowing what kind of team you are and where you want to go is aspirational. It provides your team members with a clear view of the current state and the forward possibilities, creating a stronger intention.

Below is a case study from Cathay Pacific Airways' IT Department, which provides potent lessons on the importance of company culture in a team endeavoring to move up the TQ Mango. It also illustrates the critical role of the leader who may be the cause of dysfunction while also possessing the power to shift the team.

CASE STUDY:
CULTURE AND CHANGE MANAGEMENT
AT CATHAY PACIFIC AIRWAYS IT

In 2008, Cathay Pacific Airways embarked on a long-term strategy to create a world-class information technology infrastructure. Although functional, the IT infrastructure and systems were falling behind peer companies, and investment was required to modernize the systems. Cathay decided to focus on a score of major areas, including an upgraded passenger service system, a new website, mobile apps, customer relationship management, airports of the future, an infrastructure program, a new financial system, handling new electronic devices on planes, and a host of other projects. One key goal was to enhance and simplify the customer experience.

After an extensive search, Cathay management realized they had to acquire the functional leadership and expertise from the outside, and consequently hired a new head of IT. He, in turn, cleaned the IT house and brought in a whole host of high-priced consultants and contract employees with specific expertise in order to build the necessary human capital for this gargantuan undertaking. He believed in "disruptive change" and was personally a driver of the change agenda.

The first step was to sell the grand vision and investment. *The head of IT crafted a comprehensive vision, which not only focused on IT systems and infrastructure but also looked at itself as "a strategic business partner."* This involved a complete revitalization of people, process, and culture in Cathay Pacific's IT department. The price tag would be high, requiring a multi-year commitment, and it would entail extensive change management.

Previously, each department at Cathay had had its own IT team. The new vision moved from an end-to-end, decentralized, small team model, to a centralized, high-expertise approach. Resources became pooled, and matrix teams were set up with project managers and business analysts. In order to get an IT project completed, it was now necessary to pass through various teams and required many processes and significant corporate governance.

These IT changes were disruptive to the long-standing culture, which has made Cathay Pacific the great airline it is today. Cathay people are fiercely loyal and work in a spirit of cooperation, respect, and camaraderie. Decisions are rarely rash; rather, they are painstakingly made through a consensual process that, although effective, is time-consuming. Ultimate decision making lies at the top, and managers are conscientiously considerate of others' opinions throughout the process. The Cathay culture puts a premium on people and is loath to make quick or imprudent people changes or major wholesale changes to the organization. Cathay people operate in a positive, trusting working environment.

The first level of culture clash was therefore with the new IT organization model that centralized decision making. In the past, Cathay units all had their own IT staffs, which allowed for quick action and customized solutions with a high degree of personal touch. All that changed with the new "outsiders" who were intent on driving through the centralized IT vision and solutions to progress their own work agendas. For the first year "honeymoon period," the organization demonstrated a level of patience, an understanding that the new vision would take time to unfold and that change was required. However, by 2010, people started to feel the disruption more than the results. After surveying internal customers, the messages surfacing from the organization were; "IT has morphed into a regulator instead of a business partner," "IT needs to understand Cathay as a business and work culture," and "IT is trying to drive the business when it should be the other way around." Moreover, there was some doubt about the highly paid outsiders who were supposed to be delivering, yet projects were not progressing according to plan and were getting bogged down.

The next level of culture clash was within the IT leadership team, itself. The head of IT was a polarizing figure with strong views who assembled his team consisting of three disparate groups: 1) outsiders with specific expertise, 2) existing Cathay IT managers, and 3) managers from non-IT units. There was also the overlay of overseas and local cultural differences. Needless to say, discord and cliques were prevalent within the team. The state of the team has been summarized below, based on my extensive interviews with the team members.

"The IT leadership team is a group of highly competent, seasoned, hard-driving individuals fragmented in terms of style and culture, operating with silo agendas and pressured with the complexity of driving a massive change agenda, leading to sporadic conflict, with varying degrees of trust and camaraderie."

In due course, the IT head took stock of the situation. He realized that he needed support to rebuild a strong and aligned leadership team as a top priority in order to respond to the challenges with the change agenda. Having done quite a lot of work with the Cathay's parent, Swire, and its human talent and development arm, Ethos International, I was tasked with supporting the head of IT on *revitalizing its leadership team*. During the initial team interview, I was asked how to handle various and opposing cultures on a team. My response was, "The leadership team needs to build its own team culture and identity, which can supersede the existing conflicting cultural elements in the team."

Therefore, at the end of 2011, we worked on building a cohesive *leadership team culture and identity*. The first step was to build trust and dissolve conflict. We engaged in a safe, structured feedback process. It was a first time that all were able to give feedback to others on their contributions to the team. Moreover, the head of IT was open to receiving precious feedback, which he took to heart.

We also identified the *values and behaviors* necessary to realize the IT vision within the Cathay cultural context (see figure 8.1). The key was to craft values around which everyone on the leadership team could feel ownership and align around commensurate behaviors.

Toward the end of 2011, we made real progress within the IT leadership team. A sense of camaraderie and possibility emerged. The three groups within the team began to coalesce around a new leadership-team identity beyond their own cultural biases.

Unfortunately, this proved to be "too little, too late." Despite the progress within the IT leadership team, bigger challenges outside the team were looming. Feedback on IT delivery and its attitudes was not complimentary, and the noise from internal customers was "amping up." Finally, in 2012, it was time for the head of IT to move on.

A new head of IT was brought in to continue the work to move Cathay IT to a world-class provider of information. Although the existing IT projects continued to move forward, the new IT leadership team had to reset the agenda, address the culture question in earnest, and regain credibility. It redefined its purpose, vision, and strategic themes and set a new people initiative to "recruit, engage, and develop."

IT LEADERSHIP-TEAM VALUES AND BEHAVIORS		
	Values	Behaviors
1	*Supportive* Help Each Other Deliver	• Proactively communicating • Co-create • Feedback and help • Respect • Create safe environment
2	*Congruence* Say What You Believe; Do What You Say	• Act with integrity • Provide clarity • Openness
3	*Accountability* Own the Outcome	• Step up • Own it • Create clarity
4	*Learning* Listen, Grow, Respond	• Receptivity • Reflect and review • Applied learning • Responsiveness: fast to fail • Challenging the norm • Feedback
5	*Drive* Courage to Initiate; Energy to Deliver	• Courage • High Energy • Deliver

Figure 8.2

Instead of being viewed as a department outside the organization, IT was integrated back into the Cathay culture while it built credibility with its internal customers. It continues to work on being a trusted partner and earning the vision of "IT: You can count on."

CATHAY PACIFIC AIRWAYS IT
(Takeaways)

- From day one, create a strong, aligned, and effective leadership team that is truly focused on its customers.
- Ensure that outsiders gain credibility and become effective in operating within the company culture before driving the new agenda.
- Treat culture as a fundamental aspect to be addressed in the change agenda.
- While change may be disruptive, it should not be perceived as destructive. Proactively identify the key barriers to change acceptance and adoption and create action plans to address them.
- Place a premium on building trust with internal customers.
- Seek and listen to feedback early on and take rapid action to address it.
- Focus on becoming a strong business partner with stakeholders as opposed to driving one's own agenda at all costs.
- Be willing to diagnose what's working and what's not, and make the commensurate changes in the leadership team.

Figure 8.3

9

THE BEST PEOPLE; THE RIGHT TEAM

I was lucky to join PepsiCo when I did. Given the need to enlarge the sales and distribution function in the Greater China region, I had the luxury of hand selecting over half my team members. This, of course, provides an enormous advantage of being able to select team members based on your own design and those who will be the best players you can find. As our Asia President, Ron McEachern, used to say, "My job is to build a team with the best people I can find and let them get on with their work."

Many leaders are not so lucky. They often inherit entire teams and need to make the best of what they have. Often, there are legacy issues. Therefore, leaders must mold the team in their own image and create a strong sense of team identity. This is why the 2-Step HPT process is so important. As a comprehensive approach, it systematically rewires the way the team thinks about itself, and the way it communicates and collaborates—a surefire way to build TQ.

BUILDING A NEW TEAM

There are many team structures to be considered when designing your own approach. You need to decide, up front, the characteristics of the core team you want to build. In other words, how do you define your team? If you can't do that, it's hard to build a High Performance Team!

Many leaders define a *core leadership team*, which consists of the key team players plus, perhaps, internal business partners, and an *extended leadership team*, which may include a leader's direct report (DR) minus 1 (the DR of the DR), and any other important internal stakeholders.

Let's say you were as lucky as I and were fortunate enough to get to choose a good percentage of your team members. You need to think strategically about your approach. Most executive search firms will view the position in isolation: "Who is the best person for the job?" "Who has both the hard and soft skills and the experience to succeed?" I would agree that is the primary consideration when building a team, but other key considerations are often overlooked.

1. How will the new member fit in with the team? This is not always easy to predict, yet it is important to consider. If your new candidate enjoys a highly successful track record yet is very domineering, you will need to consider how well that person will work with existing team members.

2. Will the new member create diversity, or is he cut from the same mold as existing members? When we consider diversity in the context of a team, it's a comprehensive concept. We are not only looking at age, gender, and multicultural aspects, but we are also considering style and preferences. Generally speaking, diversity and balance in a team are desirable to bring a stronger breadth to the team dynamics.

> Define your team by first determining your core team members.

3. What is the candidate's current Personal TQ? Does the candidate align well with others? Is he or she committed to results while keeping the vision and big picture in mind? What are the candidate's values, and how might they sync in with the team's values? Does he place a premium on relationships and developing trust? Is she a "lone wolf" or does she collaborate effectively? During the interview process, these areas should be considered.

How do you find the answers to the above questions? They can be answered the same way you answer any other queries regarding a new candidate. Ensure that the interview questions are peppered with queries related to TQ. I highly recommend that assessments, including a Personal TQ HealthCheck, be conducted to understand a candidate and his or her profile more broadly.

Onboarding New Team Members

The other question arises when new people join the team. How do you bring them up to speed quickly? The answer begins with the hiring process. During interviews, it's important to communicate the values of the team along with other team aspirations. This is a very strong message to any prospective candidate and will surely be an attractive magnet as it provides candidates an idea of what they are getting themselves into prior to joining. Once the candidate begins the job, I advise clients to put together an onboarding program that outlines key aspects of the team, such as the vision, values, success elements, feedback process, team initiatives, etc. This can easily be done with a Team Charter document (see Sample Team Charter in Chapter 18). Toward the end of this book, we address the Team Charter along with samples, etc.

When You Are the New Team Member

What if *you* are the one being hired to lead a team, to drive the TQ process, and create a High Performance Team? Alternatively, you might be a key team member with the desire to move the team toward high performance. In either case, it's important to vet the company and team you are considering joining to assess them and their existing TQ.

I always recommend that you interview your prospective team members using TQ questions. Try to understand their appetite for building a High Performance Team and where the team currently is on the TQ Mango. Is it already High Performance, mediocre, or even dysfunctional? You need to know where you will be starting. For example, even if the team is dysfunctional, is there an appetite for change and progress? Does the company agree to team off-sites, and does it have a willingness to invest in the team? You might even ask those questions up front and get tacit agreement to pursue the High Performance Team journey.

TAKING ON AN EXISTING TEAM

In Chapter 4, we saw how Alan Mulally at Ford approached his new job as CEO. He was taking on an existing team that had been entrenched for years in both good and bad habits. Essentially, he had to decide whether to clean house or work with what he was given. Mulally's approach was to give each team member the benefit of the doubt and let each person demonstrate whether he or she could adopt the new culture.

As a new leader of a team, you will have a few considerations:

1. Intention. Does the team member have the intention to shift his perspective and adopt the team approach? Does she see the value of working as a team? Is she willing to shift both attitudes and old habits in order to be an effective team member? In other words, you as a leader need to assess the individual's *Personal TQ*. Sometimes Personal TQ can be low or mediocre, yet when the team member starts the TQ journey, she may "get with the program." I often find that smart individuals realize which way the wind is blowing and open their minds to the possibility of putting the team first. You may not know until you are in the Assess phase of the TQ journey where the individual stands. If, through the Assess phase, the team member does not demonstrate the right intentions, it's time to have a conversation with the individual.

2. Team dynamics. Every team has conflicts. Implicit in this are the usual cliques, grudges, personality clashes, and disagreements that naturally occur within any team. The question is: Can they be repaired? Are the team members willing to put aside their own issues with others for the benefit of the team? Sometimes going through feedback and trust-building exercises will do the trick to shift the team's and individuals' attitudes. There may come a time when the individual has the maturity and perspective to let go of personal prejudices and embrace and appreciate other team members. On the other hand, there are situations in which the team member is unwilling or unable the increase their own Personal TQ.

One case in point was my headhunter client whose star performer persisted in taking a "silo" approach. The natural conclusion, which the person reached on his own, was that this team was not for him, and it was time to leave. The good news is that the Pareto Principle (also known as the 80/20 Rule) applies here: When a team decides to move steadfastly toward High Performance, 80 percent of team members will readily put their issues aside, shift, and embrace the vision. The remaining 20 percent will have to "fish or cut bait".

> As a new leader, you need to consider the intentions, team dynamics, and talent of team members.

3. Talent. The second question of the Collective TQ HealthCheck is, "Is our team composed of the right mix of capable talent?" It's a core question for the team leader, however it's also a paramount consideration for all team members. No one wants to be on a team with incapable members or with those who are not pulling their own weight. Alan Mulally had to ask himself that very question. He decided to give his team members the benefit of the doubt, and it paid off. As mentioned in Chapter 3, my axiom here is that "Culture trumps talent." Having the right team culture is much more important than having any individual talent. Nonetheless, a weak link in the chain can break down the team when stressed.

Team talent can be viewed through the lenses of current capability and potential. Does the team member already have the skills, attitudes, and competencies to deliver and contribute as an effective team member? If not, can she acquire them with the right support, coaching, mentoring, and training?

Taking on an existing team is a make-or-break moment for any leader. It is also the perfect time to bring in a fresh approach and galvanize the team to commit to high performance. During the leader's "honeymoon period," it's easy to start the TQ initiative. Once you are already entrenched, the alignment process will require more energy, and you may need a strong "burning platform" to move forward.

CREATING LOYALTY

During my five-year tenure as vice president of sales at PepsiCo, I had a number of direct reports, mostly directors. During that period, I never lost a director. Some were promoted, but none left the company. That was surprising to some of my Pepsi colleagues given the significant turnover at the time. After five years, I was asked how I kept my people.

Those were the formative days of my exploration with High Performance Teams. I worked hard to keep team members engaged, motivated, and satisfied. Many of the VIVRE FAT (vision/identity/values/results/effectiveness/fun/align/trust) aspects were in place at that time, and I realized that one of the keys to maintaining team loyalty was ensuring that people felt they were working in a High Performance Team. People may be able to find higher salaries, promotion opportunities, more interesting jobs, or better bosses, yet it is very difficult to find another High Performance Team.

During that time, I realized that the key to loyalty was building a team with which everyone can identify deeply, a place where people can be proud to work and feel excited every day to be part of the team. Of course, salaries, job fit, career development, and the like also need to be in place. Yet *the most powerful motivating factor is the team.* Rarely do players leave championship sports teams. They relish the opportunity just to play for such a team. The same goes for a High Performance Team in the business world. Not only will you have high employee loyalty, you will also have people clamoring to be part of your team.

Revisiting my executive search client, after building their TQ, the client moved from having a hard time finding "partner material" to being in the enviable position of choosing from among the best. The news of being a High Performance Team travels fast. You won't have to spend an inordinate amount of time looking for people. People will seek you out.

> Strong team identity will breed loyalty.

One of the most significant pieces of research on employee engagement is the Gallup Q12, which consists of 12 key questions that employees answer on a five-point scale (it is available online).[28] According to Louis R. Forbringer, PhD, "The study has produced many important findings, the most powerful of which is that talented employees need great managers."[29] It is the manager who is responsible for building the trust and paying attention to the needs of their people. It is the manager who is going to work with the employee on career development. It is the manager who will listen to people and recognize them for their work. Finally, it's the manager who will set the standards and ensure all members are doing quality work.

Just as it's the manager who will drive employee engagement, it's the team leader who is going to drive high-team engagement. Therefore, the leader is responsible for encouraging team members to show up with High TQ.

> The team leader is responsible for driving high-team engagement.

The team leader needs to be fully committed to the process. If he delegates this responsibility to HR or someone else, the power will be lacking. Team members might go through the motions, but their hearts will be absent. Team members always look for and take their cue from the team leader. If the leader wavers or pulls back, so will team members.

Rogue Team Members?

Ultimately, the team needs to decide if they are going to put up with a rogue team member who doesn't want to fully participate.

Lessons from an Advertising Agency

After one advertising agency client went through the entire 2-Step HPT Process, it became clear that one individual wasn't fully participating; he was not open and refused to commit to being a strong team member. On rare occasions, people will want to continue operating on an island and just "do their job" rather than being a strong team player. Conversation ensued around expectations concerning the lone wolf. It soon became clear that the individual wanted to move into a new job and would never become committed to the team in his current position. The team leader then took steps to find a suitable position for this employee, and there was an amicable parting of ways.

Nobody is forced to "conform." What's important is acting as a strong team member and showing up as such. If the individual isn't committed, most likely he is in the wrong position and team.

WHAT TYPE OF TEAM DO YOU LEAD?

In my work with organizations, I have come to realize that *the nature of the team will impact the approach to building the team.* Increasingly, teams are becoming less straightforward in their structure. It's a luxury to work with a team that has direct-reporting lines to a manager. Given the complexity of the world in which we live, with the advent of globalization and communication technology, teams are becoming more complex, as well. Many managers lament, "Oh, how I wish I could just report to one person, but I am accountable through all sorts of reporting

> Your approach in building the team will depend on what kind of team it is.

lines—straight, dotted, and sometimes no lines at all!" As a team leader, you need to consider *the nature of the team you are leading*.

Further commentary on the "nature of teams" is needed. (See figure 9.1.)

TYPE OF TEAM	CHARACTERISTICS	TQ IMPLICATIONS	CAVEATS
Direct Reporting Teams	Clean org chart High command and control Execution focus	Leadership authority Members follow lead Relationships/ trust critical Clear values and rules	"Group think" Kowtowing to boss Follow orders
Matrixed Teams	Complex reporting Dual/triple roles "Functional business partners"	Clear roles and responsibilities Define "core team" Nurture inclusiveness	Unclear identity Lack of alignment Murky commitment
Project Teams	Finite mission/ endpoint Members with defined expertise Less leader authority	Clear deliverables Stakeholder management Rally around clear mission/ vision Collaboration focus	Silo mentality Commitment essential Alignment challenges
Professional Services Teams	Independent team members Team of professionals Leadership visionary or administrator	Define need for strong team Collaboration focus Align team members	Silo/boutique mentality Teams slow to act Prima donna tendency

Figure 9.1

Direct-Reporting Teams

Although decreasing in frequency, this is the most straightforward team structure with clear lines of reporting to one manager. The organizational chart looks clean, is easy to draw, and is easy to manage. You manage your people directly. As the manager of this team, you are responsible and accountable for the results. Often these teams operate within a distinct geography and can be mission critical. High command and control organizations, such as delivery-service providers, hospital operating rooms, first responders, military teams, certain manufacturing operations, some sales teams, sports teams, and hospitality teams often fall into this category.

TQ implications: As a result of having people reporting directly to you, the sense of hierarchy tends to be stronger and is punctuated by higher control. Team members are often very willing to engage in team activities, and they will follow your lead. You are able to organize off-sites and gain full participation. In this higher hierarchy team, it is much easier to build identity, team spirit, and camaraderie. Parallels to sports teams are the closest examples.

> Direct reporting teams can easily fall into "group think."

Team spirit and morale is especially important as team members often work very closely together. These types of teams need to work on deepening trust and relationships. Having a clear vision and well-developed values are crucial to maximizing the team's potential.

Many sales teams fall into this category: the team operates under closely aligned targets and goals, and a premium is placed on execution. Quality and speed of execution are often paramount, prompting the need for a highly efficient and effective team with clearly defined rules and operating procedures.

Caveats: Direct-reporting teams can easily fall into "group think" and "kowtowing to the boss." It may be harder to foster creativity and think out-of-the-box. The character of the team depends chiefly upon the leader. An overly controlling leader may squash dissension, innovation, and divergent thinking. Such a leader may fall into territorialism and protection.

I consulted with a wine and spirits client in Asia whose team leader even controlled what his people said to colleagues outside the immediate team! His team members were terrified to open up to other stakeholders about business for fear of reproach.

Given the immense pressure many of these teams face to deliver on time-based targets, the stress and pressure can be overwhelming for some team members. It's important to step back, relax, and have fun with fellow team members in an environment outside of the workplace. As a team leader, you need to be sensitive to burnout factors. If you give your team some breathing space and a chance to relax and bond with each other, they will love you for it.

Matrixed Teams
This type of team is the opposite of the direct-reporting team. Most people work under a matrix reporting model, meaning that they often report at multiple levels. The most common reporting is a direct line report to a business owner, with a dotted line to a functional owner, or vice versa, which is becoming more and more common.

As companies re-engineer, consolidate, cut costs, and so on, matrix reporting is a common solution. While highly matrixed teams may seem unrealistic to those who must live under them, from an organizational development perspective, it can look elegant and fancy on paper. As organizations become more complex, they get increasingly matrixed. Moreover, in the endeavor to drive efficiency and cost savings, positions are evolving into dual or triple roles, which further increases complexity. It's common to start off in one role, adding multiple responsibilities to it until the person ends up with three or four responsibilities and at least that many reporting lines.

An arrangement that's becoming more common is the concept of "functional business partners." Many operating teams will have human resources partners or finance functional partners who have a dotted line to the team leader and are considered part of the team. Ultimately, the higher the complexity of the company, industry, or technology, the greater the propensity for a matrix-based organization.

TQ implications: As a leader of a highly matrixed team, it's important that your team members know where their *primary* responsibilities and accountabilities lie. In this vein, clear, well-delineated roles and responsibilities are useful to achieving that clarity. Wherever possible, everyone should be part of a *core team*. If this can be established, that accomplishes half the battle. The question a team leader needs to ask is, "Who are my team members? Are they only those who have a direct-reporting relationship with me, or should I include those who have no direct line?" The answer is simple: To what extent is that individual important in contributing to the team's results? For example, if a manufacturing leader has a dotted-line reporting relationship to a person in a quality function that is important in the overall results, that person should be considered by all to be part of the team, regardless of reporting lines. It implies that he should be invited to most team meetings.

> In a matrixed team, inclusiveness is critical.

TQ caveats: Inclusiveness is critical here. If a dotted-line team member doesn't feel part of the team, team spirit will be harder to create. That person will be seen as and feel like an outsider. This dotted-line staff will usually be relieved and happy to be embraced as part of the team. It's likewise important to communicate to the management of the non-direct team member that you consider this individual to be a part of your team and consequently he should engage in certain team meetings and activities.

Project Teams

These teams usually exist for a particular purpose or for a finite period of time. I consulted with one such team in Hong Kong when I worked for a company called Leighton Asia—an international construction firm. The company put together a team for a hospital construction project that lasted three years. Essentially, they assembled teams of specialists, many of them engineers, from both inside and outside the firm, mostly on a contractual basis.

Project teams are becoming increasingly common. They have clear deliverables and an end point. While they usually designate a lead person, the reporting arrangements may vary. In the Leighton case, there were clear reporting lines to the project manager. In many cases, however, a project leader may have no formal reporting authority. Rather, he may work with specialists who are assigned to the project from both inside and outside the organization.

TQ implications: Given the temporary nature of project teams, it is clear that deliverables must be communicated. In the Leighton Hospital project, there were very specific deliverables regarding time, cost, and quality. Stakeholder management became very important in this project, given the diverse array of non-traditional stakeholders at play; they had to cater to the local community, which would readily contact the press should their needs not be addressed. Project leaders also had to work closely with government bureaus responsible for construction and other stakeholders.

An important rallying point for project teams is "clarity of mission." Why are they there, and why is it important? There is massive pride associated with the successful delivery of a project, and teams need to tap into that as a motivating factor. Visuals, slogans, celebrations are all part of that that rallying point.

Finally, roles and responsibilities are critical for project teams. They need to know clearly whom they can count on and for what. As the team leader often doesn't have much teeth, the team members need to be clear on everyone's roles. The lack of a team leader with positional power highlights the need for good will, cooperation and collaboration, as there may be no one to referee disagreements. The team needs to learn how to work out its differences and be willing to act on them.

TQ caveats: One of the major caveats with project teams is the "silo mentality," which may encourage the attitude "just let me get on with my job and don't bother me about other things." When choosing project team members, it's best to choose those who have a track record of collaboration and working across boundaries, as well as those with a record of stakeholder management.

Often project team members may have other bigger jobs as well, and the project might be an inconvenient distraction. In this case, promoting the project's relevance, making it fun and or interesting, can pique the interest of team members.

As a project team leader, you will want to pay special attention to not drag out meetings and waste time for your team members. Time wasters and inefficiency may turn off busy team members, and they may just not turn up! It's really a battle of "sharing of heart and mind' and how to motivate team members to show up and give their best.

Professional Services Teams

Professional Services firms include executive search, accounting, architectural, engineering, legal, consulting, etc. By nature, these teams consist of specialists in their respective fields. They are often highly educated and respected as subject matter experts. Often, they work in a partnership structure with a managing partner as the head of the group. Unlike clear hierarchy teams with strong command and control, professional teams are just the opposite; the leadership role is often executed either as a visionary or an administrative function as opposed to the strong hands-on, business-driving aspect found in clear hierarchy teams.

> Professional services teams need to be clear on "why" a strong team is important.

TQ implications: As many professional services team members may not have a pressing need to spend much time with the rest of the team, it's imperative that they have a clear understanding of *why* the team is important. This tends to be related to how they can work together to drive business, cooperate on client work, develop practices, drive initiatives across the firm, implement best practices, develop junior partners, etc. Team members need to embrace the benefit of a strong team approach and be aware of the downsides of not working together. Beyond that, they need to find that compelling reason to work together.

During the work with my executive search client, getting alignment on why they needed to spend time on the team was a major effort. Not all team members were convinced. Focusing on both the *downsides* and problems associated with not coming together as a team (dysfunction, backbiting, gossip, lack of alignment, silo mentality) and the *upsides* of coming together (alignment, trust, clear direction, collaboration), finally convinced all partners that it was imperative to pull everyone together.

Lessons from Deloitte

One of my clients is Deloitte, one of the world's top-consulting firms. Working with some of their partners, it became apparent that one of the key benefits to collaborating as a team and bringing people together was the opportunity to "develop the business." This can best be done through a coordinated team effort. The partners not only share goals and information, but they can encourage and push each other for stronger results.

TQ caveats: Just as the high autonomy of professional services team members works well, it can also be their nemesis. Occasionally, partners will build their own practice to the extent that it takes on a life of its own, independent of the firm. A "don't bother me; I don't really care about you" mentality can occur as a result, which can be toxic from a team and even a firm perspective. In this vein, the firm or team identity needs to come into play to mitigate the potential bubble of the individual consultant's personal brand. While being famous or well known in a field is positive for the individual and potentially for the firm, it's a double-edged sword; if it goes too far, it may result in a "prima donna" mentality where the individual's eminence overshadows that of the firm.

As we have seen above, considering the team nature is critical when determining the approach to building TQ. Not being cognizant of the type of team you have can lead to errors or false starts. While the overall 2-Step HPT journey remains the same, the levers you will pull will vary.

10

GSK CHINA

BUILDING A WORLD-CLASS, HIGH PERFORMANCE TEAM AROUND A NEW MARKET MODEL

In the last chapter, we examined how to build, a strong team over time, to arrive at High TQ. Now let's look at a fascinating story of a leadership team with the formidable task of successfully rebuilding after a crisis.

GSK (GlaxoSmithKline) China was faced with rebuilding its pharmaceutical leadership team from scratch and completely transforming the team processes while implementing a new market model. They accomplished this in four stages over two years.

In 2012, GSK in China enjoyed the status of being one of the pharmaceutical powerhouses, with many of its drugs achieving strong penetration with doctors and in hospitals while enjoying high market shares. However, 2013 was the Chinese Year of the Black Snake, which intimated that there would be both turmoil and transformation. Indeed, this year precipitated a major change in how GSK China would operate.

The health-care industry in China is in a state of constant evolution. One of my Chinese clients, a surgeon who now works in the commercial sector, told me that he had to leave his post in 2003 as he couldn't make enough money to feed his family. In fact, many doctors and health-care practitioners have undergone a similar fate, believing that they could leverage their expertise for more prosperous opportunities outside of medicine. Those who remained needed to choose between accepting a low base salary or seeking non-traditional ways to augment their income, such as speaking and educational engagements, all-expense paid trips, endorsements, and the like. My client told me that doctors could increase their income fivefold through these additional income opportunities!

For pharmaceutical firms in China, while paying doctors to speak on behalf of pharmaceutical companies and offering financial support for attending medical congresses around the country are legitimate in intent, there is the potential to abuse the system and become highly transactional in nature. This became more pronounced when the business model linked a medical representative's sales incentives to sales volumes. Doctors also had incentives to prescribe drugs in order to fulfill hospital income targets.

2013, the Year of the Black Snake, precipitated a major change in how GSK would do business in the Middle Kingdom.

In 2014, in a move designed to drive reform of the industry, *Chinese authorities investigated GSK China's operating practices and levied a record fine of £297 million or $465 million.* GSK, however, was allowed to retain its license to operate and trade in China. "Reaching a conclusion in the investigation of our Chinese business is important, but this has been a deeply disappointing matter for GSK," said chief executive Sir Andrew Witty in a statement. "We have and will continue to learn from this. GSK has been in China for close to a hundred years, and we remain fully committed to the country and its people. We will also continue to invest directly in the country to support the government's health-care reform agenda and long-term plans for economic growth."[30]

GSK faced the challenge head on and took immediate action to appoint a new China head, naming Hervé Gisserot as senior VP and general manager of pharmaceuticals. Hervé is a seasoned GSK executive, having headed up GSK's European business. He is known as a commercially savvy executive with a focus on people and a believer in the power of teams. Here's how he did it:

STAGE 1:
BUILD OUT THE TEAM,
VISION, AND STRATEGIES

Hervé's first action was to rebuild the leadership team. Called the China Pharmaceutical Leadership Team, (CPLT), Hervé promoted the best candidates from within China and supplemented their skills by bringing in GSK people from outside of China when specific expertise was required. It was a diverse and well-balanced team, with male and female members from China, France, Canada, Singapore, Belgium, Argentina, and Germany.

Hervé also decided to employ an inclusive team approach at that critical stage, with all key functions having a say in the leadership team for better alignment and internal up-and-down com-

> Essentially, 2014–15 was a new chapter in their history, forcing a change in the old way of doing business and supplanting it with a more global model.

munication. The CPLT consisted of 16 members representing the commercial, finance, HR, medical, government affairs and communication, governance and compliance, legal, IT, procurement, regulatory strategy and planning, and legal and business development departments who met monthly. It was a large, sometimes unwieldy team, but all the participants were necessary for this transition stage.

In 2014, as Hervé was staffing his CPLT, he was also getting clarity on the vision and strategic directions, which had to be commercially viable in a high-compliance mode. This was a tall order considering the Chinese pharmaceutical industry dynamics. There could be no room for cracks. The fiscal year of 2014–15 represented a new chapter in GSK's history, forcing a change from the old way of doing business and replacing it with a more global model, one that fundamentally changed the way a pharmaceutical company engaged and interacted with doctors. China was the second market in the GSK world to implement the model—one that does not have sales-related incentives for its front-line sales representatives and eliminates any transfer of value to a doctor. Essentially, the goal was to prevent any conflicts of interest between GSK and the doctors it interacts with. Implementing such a model presented a challenge for Hervé and the team.

Hervé realized that the new model could only be realized with an aligned and committed leadership team, therefore he and his head of HR, Wang Yi, came up with a plan to create a "World-Class High Performance Team." Wang Yi contacted Gary Wang, head of Mindspan Development, China's largest coaching and leadership development organization. Gary gave me a call saying, "I believe this is a project which requires your experience and approach." As I met with Hervé and Yi in November of 2014, I was struck by their understanding that *building a world-class High Performance Team was a journey, and not a one-off event.* They clearly had the right focus and mind-set, and I sensed their commitment.

> Hervé realized that the new model could only be realized with an aligned and committed Leadership Team.

The first step involved conducting interviews with key CPLT members to understand their perspectives and challenges while building a relationship with them. The idea of creating a "world-class team" was greeted with a mixture of hope and skepticism.

Some participants aspired to the idea, while others were wrapped up in their own departmental or functional challenges and didn't necessarily buy into the team thing. This is a common challenge in the early stages of leadership team development. Many people are skeptical, and it takes time to convert them into believers.

Next on the agenda was observing the CPLT in action for a day-and-a-half during one of their meetings in December 2014. I was pleasantly surprised to see how successfully Hervé and his strategy head, Damien Genestet, had already created real commitment and alignment around the vision and strategic direction. Additionally, all CPLT members seemed to have absorbed the GSK values of "patient focused," "integrity," "transparency," and "respect for people." While these values still needed integration throughout the organization, they were firmly established within the CPLT.

Yet the CPLT was still a bit fragile. There was a sense of self-deprecation and perhaps the feeling they didn't deserve to feel proud of themselves. There was little mutual recognition and a lack of celebration despite the fact they had accomplished much in a short period of time. A healthy, and sometimes unhealthy, tension was present in all functions with some members feeling that the commercial challenges were not fully recognized given the restrictive environment.

Meetings were largely effective, and meeting management ultimately evolved into one of the team's core strengths. Yet there was still too much discussion on details and not enough focus on the major issues. An ongoing challenge was that those with experience and better English-language skills tended to dominate the conversations while, at the same time, cultural norms prevented the team from "challenging the boss." Hervé was excellent at empowering people and being willing to listen to and debate divergent views. And at the end of his meetings, he always recognized others' contributions. Nevertheless, his natural tendency was to arrive at conclusions quickly without allowing time for others to fully participate.

STAGE 2:
START FUNCTIONING AS A HIGH PERFORMANCE TEAM WHILE IMPLEMENTING THE STRATEGIES

At the end of my observation, I came up with the following prescriptions for the CPLT for the coming months in 2015:

- Focus on big decisions and those things that will drive the vision and strategy.
- Need for feedback and trust, and deeper relationships
- Engage in more fun, recognition, and celebration.
- Employ stronger naturally integrated collaboration.
- The team was still too dependent on the leader and needed to build a durable CPLT identity.
- Continue focusing on patients and the commercial challenges.

Over the ensuing months, *the CPLT started to build its identity and feel good about itself.* This had occurred in the face of enormous challenges. I stayed in touch with a number of CPLT members during the first half of 2015. In May 2015, I met Wang Yi for breakfast at the Marco Polo Hotel in Hong Kong. She briefed me on the team's progress and challenges. One major challenge was the integration of the Novartis Vaccine staff. GSK had bought Novartis Vaccines, and Grace Huang, head of GSK Vaccines in China, had the challenge of integrating 550 Novartis staff members into the GSK operation.

> The team started believing in itself; the increase in morale and spirit was palpable.

Along with the personnel additions came some significant organizational reshaping of the business, both quantitatively and qualitatively, to make it fit for the future business model. These changes constituted a massive test for the CPLT: it could either be crushed under the pressure or pull together. To its credit, the CPLT collaborated with each other and pulled together like never before. Wang Yi later commented that she didn't encounter any sense of blame or complaints, and everyone stepped up to help effect the critical transition.

Major challenges can often turn into a rallying point for a team, and for the CPLT, it was a defining moment. The team started to believe in itself, and the increase in morale and spirit was palpable. The team began to *celebrate its success and felt it deserved to do so.* The CPLT was now feeling its identity.

STAGE 3:
TRANSFORMING THE TEAM

In June 2015, it was time for the team to come together for an off-site to begin the next level of transformation. I reminded the team of their desired outcomes, which they had articulated in December of 2014. These came in the form of "My Wish for the CPLT."

TRUST

COLLABORATION

EFFICIENCY

SUPPORTIVE

FUN

ONE GSK

ALIGNMENT

INTEGRATED VALUES

WINNING

BONDING

RESPECT

Based on additional interviews and a gap analysis of where the company was vs. where it wanted to be, we recommended focusing on a few key areas. The first one was to define success. In other words, "How does CPLT know it is successful and a winning High Performance Team?" To answer that question, my co-facilitator, Yvonne Yam, and I utilized a "World Café" approach that focused on defining success in the following five areas:

1. Relationships (trust/feedback/fun)
2. Effectiveness/efficiency (meetings/decisions/communications/ collaboration)
3. Initiatives (strategic programs)
4. Values and behaviors
5. Results (key commercial/functional)

Having the opportunity to define success afforded each member of the CPLT a chance to provide input on each of the five areas. The result was an alignment of how the team would know when it was successful, and the plans it made to get there.

The next major area was trust and deepening relationships. We used our trademark approach called "rear-view feedback" in which everyone takes turns receiving feedback on how they were contributing to the team. In this major exercise, a breakthrough occurs and team members begin to feel closer to each other. Trust deepens. The reassurance that all can give and receive feedback is heartening and brings the relationships to the next level.

We concluded by having each CPLT member highlight his or her commitments to the team. These were all noted and reviewed at a later date. Finally, it was celebration time, at which all team members recognized each other.

Every exercise result required that an action be implemented. For example, the Finance head, Alejandro Monteagudo, felt that in order to make the off-site worthwhile, clear action steps needed to come out of them, and expressed satisfaction that it was happening.

CEO Andrew Witty also weighed in during this period in an interview, saying, "Overall, we are feeling pretty good about where we are in China. We are obviously glad to have put behind us the events of the last year or so, and *we feel that we have a very robust approach to how we now go forward in China,* which is very much in step with what the authorities in China want to see."[31]

In 2015, the CPLT had trimmed its monthly meeting times to half a day. In September of that year, they invited me back to observe their half-day CPLT meeting and provide comments. I was struck by the change in spirit and substance. It felt as if a cloud had been lifted. There were smiles, friendly banter, humor, and a family atmosphere; deeper relationships developed and trust emerged. Participation, although not perfect, had vastly improved, and there were even some healthy challenges to others' statements. There was an alignment of some key areas, such as the strategic deployment of priority initiatives. Decision making had improved. The team was now focusing on the big thing that mattered.

> By mid-2015, the team was focusing on the big things that mattered.

Prior to the meeting, I conducted a TQ HealthCheck, and found that the team was trending well as a performing team, and getting close to achieving High Performance.

One area of core strength was meeting management. Now that the CPLT meeting was cut to half a day, it meant that they were very efficient about time usage. The CPLT had implemented some key GSK processes on meeting management. These included a special "room" in which key results were evaluated and scored. During the meeting, these results were reviewed on an "exception" basis, which saved time and put focus only on areas in which attention was needed. The CPLT had become quite disciplined around the process of meeting management, including rotating roles such as facilitator, timekeeper, observer, rabbit-hole watcher (to keep on track), and scribe. Pre-read materials were sent out in advance so that everyone was prepared to discuss particular topics. The agenda preparation was thorough, with properly allocated time slots. If someone went over time on an agenda item, the timekeeper called it out. Likewise, if someone went off track, someone else called out "rabbit hole" to let that person know that he or she was getting off track. Hervé made it a point to comment after each presentation, providing recognition and feedback where appropriate. As a result, the CPLT had developed a habit of excellent meeting management.

Despite the team's obvious improvement, there were still areas requiring focus. The team was still drilling down to identify areas that it could delegate. The team could also empower those providing input more effectively instead of second-guessing the numbers. Too much time was still spent on presentations, instead of discussing those critical areas that need decisions.

STAGE 4:
MOVING TO HIGH PERFORMANCE

The year 2015 was truly a watershed year for the CPLT. Not only was it transforming and developing a strong identity, but it was also moving through key organizational and external milestones to transform GSK China. The following year, 2016, was when the new operating model would start bearing fruit.

While GSK China was transforming itself, the China healthcare industry, although changing, was moving much more slowly. Though the company's new model was working in certain pockets with certain customers, it would take time and patience. Despite the market challenges, the CPLT was on a firm footing.

The team decided to engage in another off-site day to deepen team members' relationships and take the team to the next level of effectiveness. Based on interviews, it was clear that the team was making good progress. In particular, the different functional departments felt very good about how well the CPLT was operating. Commercial members were also pleased, although they felt that more focus was needed on customers and how to address their legitimate needs while still sticking to the model. This meant that a new level of collaboration was required.

In March 2016, we returned to the City Marriot Shanghai to spend another day with CPLT together. The CPLT had committed itself to spending the time not discussing business, but rather working on its own effectiveness.

The first topic on the agenda was reflection. Over the preceding two years, the team had surmounted some incredible hurdles and achieved significant milestones. We plotted those major milestones on a timeline. Above the line, we listed significant external events, while below the line, we listed milestones reflecting internal events. The team was astonished at what it had been through and accomplished.

The next step was to focus on the future state of the CPLT. We reviewed the "My Wish for the CPLT" list with **changes bolded.** "Winning" was moved to the top, while a few additional "wishes" for CPLT were added:

WINNING

INNOVATIVE

SPACE

CUSTOMER FOCUS

TRUST

COLLABORATION

EFFICIENCY

SUPPORTIVE

FUN

ONE GSK

ALIGNMENT

INTEGRATED VALUES

BONDING

RESPECT

Additionally, the CPLT aligned around the following focus areas:

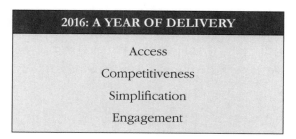

Figure 10.1

The team then identified the gap between where it currently found itself and the challenges in achieving both its 2016 focus areas and its desired state. Using a scouting activity to elicit responses from all team members, it then came around to solutions for those challenges. After discussion, action plans were drawn up and aligned.

The CPLT wanted to further deepen its relationships and trust. Additionally, the team deployed a new form of feedback on contribution to the team: Each team member would provide feedback individually to as many team members as possible about their contributions to the team. This allowed the CPLT to go deeper and strengthen the aspect of one-on-one feedback.

> Moving from a new team with daunting challenges and no real identity, to a High Performance Team in just a year and a half, was a remarkable achievement.

The result of the day was an awareness and celebration of progress made, identification of challenges to achieving CPLT's goals as well as solutions, and a deeper understanding of and commitment to each other through feedback. Added to this were some fun right-brain team activities to ramp up the team spirit and energy.

At the end of the day, we reviewed the TQ HealthCheck that revealed that *the team had just crossed the line into high performance!* Moving from a new team with daunting challenges and no real identity, to a High Performance Team in just a year and a half, was a remarkable achievement. The key was now to move into solid high performance territory so that the CPLT could finally achieve its goal of being a world-class High Performance Team.'

**GSK'S WORLD-CLASS
HIGH PERFORMANCE TEAM INITIATIVE
(Takeaways)**

1. All team members need to be aligned on the possibility of the imperative to move to high performance.

2. An investment of time is required to work on the team in the form of off-sites and reflection periods.

3. The leader needs to be committed for the long term.

4. Moving to high performance is a journey that requires frequent interventions and an ongoing focus.

5. The team can overcome adversity and challenges with the right focus, beliefs, road map, HealthChecks, and reflection.

6. Deepening trust and relationships are essential for moving to high performance.

7. Recognition, celebration, and fun need to become a part of the team experience.

8. The power of building team identity cannot be underestimated.

9. Meeting management is a core enabler in increasing TQ.

Figure 10.2

PART IV

THE LEADER'S OPERATING MANUAL

INTEGRATING THE EIGHT ESSENTIAL ELEMENTS OF A HIGH-TQ TEAM

INTRODUCTION

The first three parts of this book have dealt with the imperative, the journey, and examples of companies with teams that moved to High TQ. The remainder of the book is a manual for the team leader and provides specific tools for transitioning your team toward high performance.

Chapter 6 introduces the eight essential elements of High-TQ Teams, which are summarized from the "TQ Top Ten," as derived from our research. They are represented by the acronym VIVRE FAT, which stands for:

Figure 11.1: VIVRE FAT

Yet there is another meaning to the acronym. In French, VIVRE means "to live." And the sense of "living FAT" implies a fullness to the team and a big presence. A High Performance Team is visible, and the results it creates are noticeable. Its vision (or its mission), as well as the team's behaviors and what it stands for, are transparent and obvious to its stakeholders. Whether it walks or runs, its presence in the company is felt.

Now in Part IV, we are devoting a chapter to each of the essential elements of VIVRE FAT because each deserves its due focus. In the chapters that follow, you'll find explanations, processes, tools, cases, and stories that illustrate the role that these elements play. Each of the chapters will provide you with more than enough tools to engage the team. You can decide to employ all eight elements to move all the way to high performance quickly, or yon can cherry pick the ones that you believe are most important to your team.

Once you have identified the burning platform and are clear on the need to move to a High Performance Team, you will outline your road map according to the 2-Step HPT Journey. Each of the eight essential elements is addressed in the 2-Step HPT Journey (figure 11.2).

The eight essential elements form the core of High TQ. In this leader's manual, we offer many tools and practices. Just choose what suits you and focus on what you need to accomplish, based on diagnosis from the TQ HealthCheck. Don't overcomplicate; keep it simple.

THE 2-STEP HPT JOURNEY	
Addressing the Eight Essential Elements	
STEP 1—TRANSFORM	**ADDRESSING ESSENTIAL ELEMENTS**
A. *Assess*: two-to-three months	Where is the team relative to each of the eight essential elements? Conduct TQ HealthCheck.
B. *Develop Culture*: one-to-three days offsite	*Align* around the *vision, values*. Clarity around *results*. Build *trust, fun*, and *camaraderie*. Determine *effective* team processes. Nurture a team *identity*. Have *fun!*
STEP 2—INTEGRATE	**ADDRESSING ESSENTIAL ELEMENTS**
A. *Embed*: three to six months back at office	Execute the *vision*. Live the *values*. Operate with a *results* focus, *effective* processes, and team *identity*. Practice feedback and *trust'* enjoy the team!
B. *Renewal*: one-to-two days off-site	*Re-align* around all eight elements: what's working, what's not. Focus on areas to strengthen. Fortify the *Identity*. Recommit to High Performance.
C. *Certify*: three-to-four months	TQ HealthCheck review with team. Certify as High Performance Team and identify areas to further strengthen.

Figure 11.2

11

ELEMENT #1

A COMPELLING VISION OR MISSION/PURPOSE

Lessons from Integra Telecom

Dudley Slater, author of recent best seller *Fusion Leader*ship and founder of Integra Telecom, believes that the leadership team needs to start with an aligned shared vision or mission/purpose. Dudley states, "Any member of the team should be able to articulate in clear terms the vision and mission of the organization and be able to inspire others with that vision. I'm looking for team members who have a passion for the vision and mission, which, at Integra Telecom, was 'to lead the industry by providing a quality, user-friendly customer experience.'"

As Dudley emphasizes, one of the first things on the agenda when building a High Performance Team is crafting a meaningful vision, or mission/purpose. This is usually done at an off-site meeting. Many teams rely on the *company* vision or mission to pull the team together. That is acceptable for a mediocre team, but it's not good enough for a High Performance Team that realizes that a *team* vision or mission is essential as the galvanizing force to propel it into action.

THE FALLACIES

I worked with one leader at a pharmaceutical company who, in fact, wondered if they "had the right" to have a team vision, thinking somehow it was sacrilegious to do so. "After all, shouldn't I be submitting to the company vision? Our department primarily executes the vision and gets results." He missed the point. "Executing and getting results" is only one aspect of being a High Performance Team. Furthermore, the company vision is very general and broad. Knowing exactly where the team is going is essential to being an effective and High Performance Team.

Another common fallacy is thinking that KPIs or even a "dashboard" is all that a team needs to measure performance. After all, "What gets measured gets done." While it's true that performance measures are essential, without a longer-term vision, teams will be mired in "hitting or exceeding short-term targets." Overreliance on KPIs creates a short-term focus, which obviates striving for a much bigger aim. It also reinforces the "task focus" that plagues so many teams. How many times does someone ask, "How are we doing on the things that really matter?" The question is: Has the team defined what really matters in *this* team?

WHO NEEDS A TEAM VISION, ANYWAY?

Team vision defines a bigger game beyond the day-to-day production at the office and in the field. It's about stepping up to play that bigger game. Your team needs to know the rules of the game and how to scope it out in an accurate and compelling fashion.

When I work with teams on crafting their vision, it's usually in combination with mission and purpose (Why are we here?), together with an overall direction (Where are we going?). That gives it meaning and relevance. It also makes it more comprehensive. The problem is that defining all three—vision, mission, and purpose—can be overwhelming in a team context. That's why I like to think of the vision and mission/purpose components rolled into one broad "vision exercise."

Vision defines the larger game, the team's role in the game, and importantly, the team's aspirations. The vision then creates meaning for team members and can be very motivating.

Lessons from a European Bank
One of my clients was a team at a European bank responsible for "transaction banking." Transaction banking handles the safe and efficient movement of cash and securities around the global financial system. It is the business of facilitating the transactions that affect money flow, whether it is cash management, trade and supply-chain finance, or correspondence banking.

This bank was a medium-size player in transaction banking and realized that it couldn't strive for leadership in all products. This had translated into a "ho-hum" sentiment within the team, leaving the members feeling that the bank was very "average" in many respects.

After much discussion, the breakthrough was the "Vision for Leadership in Selected Products," which was challenging but within the bank's grasp. This created the necessary aspirational drive to break the team members out of their doldrums and coalesce around a worthy goal. It made all the difference in the world. Suddenly, the team felt that its existence had meaning. Essentially, the team vision gave them purpose, drive, and meaning. It also gave the team clear targets and focus as well as a road map for success. Strategy, tactics, and KPIs were then geared toward the selected products as identified in the vision.

The vision also became a useful tool for communications. Whenever someone asked team members what they were working on, they could clearly cite the vision and then talk about the targets and focus areas. When they made presentations to other stakeholders, they could always refer to the vision, which allowed for more contextually rich and focused discussions. During its own staff meetings, focus on the vision was very useful in decision making.

The vision also created a much-needed sense of confidence and feeling of reassurance that the team was moving forward rather than people "just doing their jobs." It gave them a reason to go the extra mile and strive for excellence. It was one of the factors that made members proud to be part of the team. It also reinforced the sense of being a winning team as opposed to being just an execution team.

FIRST SET THE DIRECTIONS FOR THE TEAM

Prior to the visioning meeting, the leader must have done her homework. She must have identified the industry/company dynamics, scoped out the opportunities and challenges, and arrived at some clear directions with which to engage the entire leadership team. The better prepared the leader, the higher the overall quality of vision.

Something magical happens when a team aligns around its forward direction. Psychologically, team members start to actualize the vision in their minds, and this puts them on the path to creating the success they want. In order to arrive at team directions, the following are key questions to address;

- What business are we truly in, and how do we define it?
- What are the areas in which we want to be a serious player?
- What are the areas in which we don't want to compete?
- In what market segments do we want to create leadership?
- What quantifiable benefits do we offer our customers?
- How do we contribute to the company overall?

The above questions will help identify the *external* view of the company—how others see it. The following questions will help identify the *internal* view—how the company sees itself:

- Who are our key stakeholders?
- How do we engage them?

- What are the organizational and personal dynamics?
- What are the company expectations and KPIs?

During the direction-setting process, it's useful to set a time frame for executing the vision. This will depend upon the industry, team focus, and function. The range will usually be somewhere within three to five years, but I've been involved with groups that accomplished this with shorter-term visions of one year, as well as longer ones that would take up to ten years to accomplish.

The directions that the leader identifies may focus on several markets, areas, and functions. The key is to come up with prescriptive statements in those areas of focus.

For example, directions for a bank might be:

- Become a top-tier player in cash management.
- Lead the industry in product innovation.
- Be recognized as a provider of cross-border solutions.

These statements do not yet constitute the vision, itself; rather they provide the input to the team in crafting the overall vision.

Once the directions are set forth, it's time to communicate them to the leadership team members via a directions-alignment meeting. This is the time for the fundamental debate about the direction for the team. I suggest holding this meeting two to four weeks before getting together for the formal vision session. This allows the group time to digest and clarify the directions, and perhaps conduct some useful internal jockeying on positions ahead of time.

NOW THE FUN PART:
THE TEAM CRAFTS THE VISION

How often does a group of people have the chance to get together and truly create their future, destiny, and the possibility of who they want to become and where they want to go? That's exactly what a team must do to become a High Performance Team. It's especially liberating to know that a team has the power to collectively envision the future and set the mechanisms in place to get there.

The visioning work is best conducted as part of an off-site meeting with plenty of time to work on it—typically between a half day and a full day. As mentioned previously, the alignment on directions should have already taken place, so there should be no surprises. It's best that the team leader present and review the team directions to be executed within the next three to five years, as the case may be. Allow time for some discussion and clarification on the direction even though most issues will have been ferreted out during the alignment session.

Once the directions are clear and most of the issues have been addressed, it's time to break the vision into meaningful aspirational visions. These typically include:

1. Product/service vision
2. Market/industry/customer/stakeholder vision
3. Financial/operational vision
4. Employee/people vision

In this case, you would divide the team into four groups, and each group would be responsible for brainstorming on one of the four visions. Questions to answer for each of the visions may include the following:

1. Product/service vision:
   - On what products/services do we want to focus?
   - What position in the market do we want to occupy?
   - What image do we desire to project for our product/service?
   - What are the product/service advantages we will offer?
   - What are our core competencies with respect to our product service?
2. Market/industry/stakeholder/customer (internal/external) vision:
   - What which markets/customers/stakeholders do we want to engage?
   - What position do we aspire to occupy in each key market/industry or with each key customer?
   - What image do we want to project to the market/customers/stakeholders?

3. Financial/operational vision:
   - What will be our financial/operational benchmarks?
   - What milestones do we want to achieve?
   - What value do we desire to create?
4. Employee/people vision:
   - What kind of team and workplace do we desire to create?
   - How do we want our people engaged?
   - What is our desired vision for our team/company/leaders?
   - What personal benchmarks should we create?

The way you break down the vision depends on your team's nature, responsibilities, customers, and stakeholders. For example, one project team for a construction client had the mission of building a hospital. Instead of the four categories above, their directions were divided into aspirational visions:

1. Department vision
2. Project vision
3. People vision
4. Client vision

Once each of your groups has answered the questions for their vision areas, they will come up with a vision statement for each area. For example, the group that addressed the product/service vision will summarize their work through a specific vision statement that they will present to the full team for discussion and buy in.

The vision statement that the construction firm produced is shown in figure 11.3.

After the aspirational visions have been produced and shared, it's time to pull them all together in an overall vision for the team. The overall team vision for the construction team project is an amalgamation of the aspirational visions.

You'll note that there is an overall vision, and a vision for each of the four aspirational areas.

Once the overall vision is agreed upon, I suggest breaking it down into meaningful and actionable strategies and plans, along with KPIs and milestones.

VISION STATEMENTS FOR CONSTRUCTION FIRM

Department Vision
Build a superior reputation with our clients and earn
a reasonable profit while being accident free,
thereby paving the way for future work.

Project Vision
Achieve a safe, quality project on time and on budget.

People Vision
Be self-motivated, proud to be a team member,
and work as a family.

Client Vision
Become the preferred and long-term partner of our client.

OVERALL TEAM VISION
Our vision is to pave the way for the future by working as a
High Performance Team to deliver a safe, high-quality, and
profitable project to our client, making us their preferred and
most reliable long-term partner.

Figure 11.3

WHAT ABOUT MISSION AND PURPOSE?

Mission or purpose-based organizations are motivated by different goals, as in the case of non-government organizations NGOs and government institutions. I remember working with Ivy Ning, an accomplished coach and mentor, who taught me many lessons in facilitation and executive coaching. Ivy was leading a training program at the Hospital Authority in Hong Kong, the quasi-government agency that regulates and manages the health-care system. Many of the top managers were doctors who had moved into hospital administration. I was struck by how many of them were not motivated by results or goals but rather by *doing what was right by patients* with the overall mission of "Helping People Stay Healthy."[32] In NGOs, there is less emphasis on achieving and accomplishing and more focus on serving and caring.

> In NGO's, there is less emphasis on achieving and accomplishing, and more focus on serving and caring.

For NGOs, mission and purpose form the crux of their existence. NGO teams are not necessarily motivated by commercial or financial goals; rather they contribute to a larger mission or purpose.

I did some pro-bono work with Hands on Hong Kong, a locally based charity. They state their mission right up front: "Our mission is to mobilize and empower our community to meet pressing social needs in Hong Kong through volunteer services."[33]

The mission of NGOs is the most important statement of who they are and their key motivating factor. Once you have a compelling mission, it's much easier to motivate team members. This is why NGOs may spend days or months coming up with a compelling mission that is easy to understand and motivational. After all, it's not the financial or self-oriented approach that works with NGOs; rather it's the contribution and participation factors that will create the motivation. NGOs are "other oriented" and supported through the goodwill of members and stakeholders.

Beyond NGOs and government institutions, what is the purpose-based motivation in the corporate and business sector?

Many corporations have their mission clearly identified. Starbucks, for example, has this: "Our mission is to inspire and nurture the human spirit—one person, one cup, and one neighborhood at a time."[34]

I particularly like Virgin Atlantic's mission, which is: "to embrace the human spirit and let it fly."[35] In fact, I would characterize Virgin's mission as sort of a hybrid mission/vision statement.

For some key industries, purpose is quite critical. Roche, a

Swiss-based Global Pharmaceutical firm and key client, places a big premium on the concept of purpose for their employees. In their corporate website, this statement is front and center. (See figure 11.4.) Moreover, Roche demonstrates the power of purpose through lots of individual videos of employees who express their own purpose and why they work at Roche. This is very inspiring for both staff and external stakeholders.

Lessons from Roche

Roche is very committed to developing people and teams. I was fortunate to be able to support some of their units in building High Performance Teams. One of the exercises we engaged in was identifying each team member's purpose, as well as the overall team purpose. It was easy to key in on the corporate information on purpose, which was front and center. It made a difference to the team, and gave credence to the "why" part of their existence.

For an organization with primary focus on commercial results, having an expression of purpose can be a powerful motivating factor for team members. Not all teams are able to find a purpose that is meaningful, but for those who can, it brings a deeper level of meaning to the team's existence.

Doing Now What Patients Need Next . . .

We believe it's urgent to deliver medical solutions right now—even as we develop innovations for the future. We are passionate about transforming patients' lives. We are courageous in both decision and action. And we believe that good business means a better world.

That is why we come to work each day. We commit ourselves to scientific rigor, unassailable ethics, and access to medical innovations for all. We do this today to build a better tomorrow.

We are proud of who we are, what we do, and how we do it. We are many, working as one across functions, across companies, and across the world.

We are Roche.[36]

Figure 11.4

STEPS TO CREATE MISSION/PURPOSE

Mission/purpose statements are great at the corporate level, but how do you make the mission or purpose relevant at the team level? It's one thing to know your purpose and role as a team and whom you're supporting (i.e., your stakeholders); it's quite another to turn that purpose into a powerful motivating factor, which is why strong leadership is required. The key is finding those hot buttons that people can latch onto.

It's up to the team members to decide how much time to spend identifying their purpose. It may or may not be a critical motivating factor. So how does a High Performance Team go about creating its mission or purpose? I advise companies to start with the stakeholders, asking themselves questions like these:

1. "Who are the critical stakeholders I serve?" (These may be internal or external customers.) The key for the team to focus on is: "Who are the key stakeholders?" (As opposed to all stakeholders).
2. "What needs do these key stakeholders have that our team can fulfill?"
3. "What are my prioritized deliverables to the key stakeholders?"

Once you have answered these questions, you are in a position to create your purpose or mission statement. The idea is to make it as compelling as possible so it can serve as a motivating factor for the team.

When implementing the purpose or mission statement, it's a good idea to ensure that all the department and relevant employees are also on board. It's also advisable to let key stakeholders know the role of your team and how you may be there to serve them.

Figure 11.5 demonstrates an example of one purpose process we did with a client.

The Defining Team Purpose exercise can usually be done in a half to a full day, ideally in an off-site environment.

Depending upon your company and team nature, you will decide whether to define a vision or mission/purpose, or take a hybrid approach. The key is to create something of relevance to your team members that will motivate and inspire them while achieving clarity and a sense of direction. As the first step of VIVRE FAT, *vision* is a fundamental building block for the other aspects of creating a High Performance Team. It will galvanize the team to move forward with energy and meaning.

DEFINING TEAM PURPOSE
(Exercise)

STEP 1

Discuss the importance of purpose. Purpose is important because it answers:

- What drives us to succeed?
- What motivates us?
- Why we are here?

STEP 2

Answer:

- What is your purpose in your job at the company? What are you here to do?
- Write in your notebooks: "My purpose is . . ."
- Discuss your purpose with a partner.

STEP 3

Review:

- sample purpose statements from other companies.

STEP 4

Review:

- purpose of the company as a whole (any aspirational or motivational aspects are useful).

STEP 5

Come up with the team purpose, considering:

- the business vision
- your own purpose.

Each of you should come up with a simple, one-line purpose statement for the team. Write it on a sticky note and place it on the board:

- "Our team purpose is . . ."

STEP 6

- Discuss and consolidate the inputs into ONE team purpose.

Figure 11.5

Below is an interview with Chris Geary, an entrepreneur with multiple businesses. For Chris, the mission is the critical element to instill in all his people, as it is the guiding force upon which all else rests.

CASE STUDY:
CHRIS GEARY AT BSD –
AN ENTREPRENEUR'S APPROACH TO TEAMS:
THE IMPORTANCE OF MISSION

Chris Geary is an entrepreneur based in Hong Kong with businesses extending throughout Asia, Europe, and North America. He runs a number of companies, including BSD Code and Design Academy, Hatton Studios, Melville Fine Jewelry, and a number of others. He also runs the Fargo Foundation, and is a founding curator in Global Shapers Community of the World Economic Forum. I got to know Chris as he was speaking at a Leadership Program for Swire.

I found Chris to have a novel approach to engaging his teams and companies. As a business owner with a hand in all his ventures, the human aspect is particularly important to him. There is no doubt that he encourages his successful teams in large part through his effusive personality and the culture that he engenders in his companies. Each of his businesses resides in a different industry and is managed quite independently from the rest. For example, Melville Jewelry trades in fair trade jewelry, whereas BSD Code and Design Academy is a cutting-edge educational institution focused on providing technology education in Asia. Each has a clear mission/purpose. What is unique is the level of passion and engagement that his people share in the business. They have fun, are highly motivated, and work hard, assuming extraordinary accountability for doing good business.

Chris forms his teams and leaders, often promoting quickly from within. For example, he promoted his executive assistant directly to general manager and partner of one of his business. He likes to work through observing behavior. In the case of his executive assistant, she was smart, took loads of initiative, was commercially savvy, and really put herself out for the business. He recognized her potential and trusted his gut that she could actually *run* one of his businesses. In all of this, there is total transparency with a balance sheet; everyone knows what's doing well or badly. The imperative is to show trust.

This is a recurring theme with Chris; he believes it's all about people. The people drive what to do with the business. Instead of a top-down approach, he prefers to work organically to allow the businesses to evolve and develop based on the people, their creativity, and their ideas.

The underlying thread through Chris's approach is ensuring that all of his teams operate from a strong sense of mission. The question he asks is, "Are you willing to prioritize the mission, and where does it sit on the list of priorities?" Mission is one area on which Chris is very focused with all of his teams. He believes companies are a hugely important part of society. Even if companies are there to make money, his main purpose is not to create profit for himself; it's to pay the payroll every month—that's the number-one job. Most of his people spend more time working than in any other aspect of their lives; therefore Chris feels it is his personal mission to ensure that their basic needs are taken care of.

> "Every company needs to nurture its own culture organically, developing a distinct personality."

Chris had previously spent some years working for a recruiting company. Despite the size of the check he received, he ultimately got tired of the industry because he didn't really care about that particular business. He constantly talks about doing "good business," which relates to a core purpose. Education technology (BSD Code and Design Academy) has a definite purpose. The company works with teenagers, teaching them how to write innovative code that they can actually use and apply. For example, one of his courses teaches, "Real Code . . . Your child can soon become an expert in making websites, games, mobile apps, or even robots."[37] They are doing "good business."

Chris constantly talks about doing "good business," which relates to having a core purpose.

At Melville Fine Jewelry, they're also doing "good business." There is a purpose for beauty and fair trade. It's an ethical company that buys gems from identifiable mines. Melville Fine Jewelry is the first company in Asia to deal in fair-trade metals. "Creative Director, Nathalie Melville, is an advocate for sustainable sourcing, covering everything from gemstones to metal. For Melville, it's not just a trend; it's a way of life."[38] The company operates a design studio where people can come and learn. Jewelers on Melville's platform rent a space and run their business from there. They can display their jewelry, and Melville promotes them. It allows young, talented, and new jewelers to get into the business with very little capital

Chris believes that every company needs to nurture its own culture organically, developing a distinct personality. Each business stands on its own and works independently, yet they will cross-pollinate between businesses, getting together a couple of times a year to provide the necessary synergy. He likes to see "people bringing their own unique stuff, forming their own culture, and doing their own things together." They allow the culture to be driven from within, with each company deciding on its desired working environment. Chris believes that his companies' rock-solid retention rate is due to how they form their individual cultures and the passion for the mission they all share. People join and fit very nicely into a culture of their own creation. The company has frequent events, and the individual teams organize their own off-sites. It all happens organically and naturally.

> Chris's focus on mission is a key driver and the glue to keep his teams operating in alignment.

He doesn't believe that culture should be top-down; rather the company should absorb the culture that develops from the team, itself.

Culture is paramount to Chris. His companies don't pay that well, but people are treated as smart individuals. Chris is very direct, but people don't seem to take it personally. "I rip the piss out of everyone in the business, yet people keep the humor. From day one, there is quite a bit of friendly hazing . . . People know that I don't take business too seriously. Business is business, and one may win or lose. If something is not being done properly, I will immediately give feedback, like, 'Dude, that's not cool.'" Everyone is constantly giving each other feedback, therefore people enjoy a good level of trust. Chris believes, "It's not possible to operate without a lot of trust. People start on day one, and they are trusted. They can choose the title they wish, fostering a sense of ownership in their work."

Alignment is imperative in Chris's teams. He starts with an open forum in which anyone can agree, disagree, and put forth suggestions and opinions publicly. He doesn't encourage a sense of hierarchy and doesn't like the notion of "I work for Chris." Anyone can criticize anyone, and if they don't agree, they can challenge each other in public. In the end, people know it's Chris's job to make key decisions. Once a decision is made, he expects people to back it.

Given Chris's entrepreneurial style, his teams benefit from strong autonomy, the ability to create their own culture and to chart their destiny. Chris's focus on mission is a key driver and the glue to keep his teams operating in alignment. The high degree of trust in an environment with less structure and hierarchy works well in small and medium environment settings.

CHRIS GEARY'S TEAM APPROACH
(Takeaways)

1. Teams embody and operate from a sense of mission/ purpose that underlies everything they do.

2. The mission of "doing good business" is core in all of his companies.

3. Taking care of his people is the number-one purpose.

4. Allowing teams to grow their own organic culture fosters ownership and loyalty.

5. Trust and transparency is a core operating principle in his teams.

6. Mutual feedback without a sense of hierarchy is expected.

7. Team members are encouraged to speak up and offer suggestions and ideas. Once Chris makes the final decision, full alignment is expected.[39]

12

ELEMENT #2

IDENTITY, BONDING, AND RELATIONSHIPS, A-A-A TEAMS

You may have a talented team with a clear vision; perhaps you have even identified core values and behaviors. Yet, the soft, intangible side of the team—the connections, relationships, bonding, and identity—often makes the difference between good and great teams. This chapter will focus on those intangibles and how to develop and nurture them.

RELATIONSHIPS, AND PUTTING THE TEAM FIRST

Lessons from Germany's 2014 World Cup Team
Becoming a team of the highest level is a special feat. Think of Germany's "Die Mannschaft" in the 2014 World Cup (Chapter 3). Many reasons can be cited for the team's greatness, but watching them play, fans were struck by the team's synchronicity. To achieve that sense of fluidity, they had to develop strong, deep, and trusting mutual relationships, knowing how each player responds, as

well as knowing each player's strengths, weakness, styles, and chemistry. They needed to execute the playbook to the T. They had to communicate and interact at the highest level of the game.

The 2014 German National Team also possessed massive pride and a sense of identity as the best in the globe. Certainly, they had very High TQ. They had but one goal: to win. All other goals were subordinate to winning. In the process, they understood it was a team goal, and *putting the team first* was what really mattered. Individual aspirations were subordinated to team aspirations. Moreover, each team player knew that if Germany was successful, their careers would get a boost.

This led to the axiom: *Team success = Individual success*. After Germany's convincing victory in the World Cup, the players were avidly recruited with contracts that were among the highest in the sport.

It does not, however, necessarily work the other way around: *Individual success ≠ Team success.*

In the 2014 World Cup, the best-recognized players—Neymar (Brazil), Ronaldo (Portugal), Messi (Argentina), and the like—were unable to translate their individual genius to the team. The question is this: "How much time did each of these stars spend building relationships with team members of their national teams?" What we know is that the intensity of relationships that the German National Team built throughout weeks of focus was not evident in the Argentine, Brazilian, or Portuguese national teams. Individual stars don't necessarily make a team successful.

That brings up one of the key points for a team to keep in mind: every member of the team must have the *intention* to deepen their relationships and the willingness to invest in them. When I work with clients, there are always team members who balk at spending more time with the team. The attitude may be, "Everyone is busy, and why spend the time?" or "Let's finish the meetings and get on with our work." This attitude tells me immediately that this team member has not experienced the power of being part of a High Performance Team, which brings with it satisfaction, pride, and purpose.

The implication for High Performance Teams in business is that they are not just spending endless hours in meetings; they actually enjoy the challenge of working together towards success. They have fun together. Yes, High Performance Team members do, indeed, enjoy each other's company and look forward to their interactions.

Creating strong relationships takes forethought, planning, and clear intent. Just as Germany intentionally invested in its special training camp, you will need to invest in building your relationships as a team in a very tangible manner.

IDENTITY

Strong team identity is an intangible element present in all High Performance Teams. The Germans knew this well:

> Just as the German team had built a phenomenal team identity for the World Cup 2014, it appears that Brazil lost theirs. Brazil used to be the epitome of the "beautiful game," which was characterized by strong offense with swift and nifty passing. But the team of 2014 had completely lost the "beautiful game" thanks, in part, to the philosophy of their coach, Luis Scolari. Scolari preferred to play with bigger players who were willing to foul and defend with vigor. Fast-paced passing was replaced with many attempts to move the ball a long distance.
>
> In addition, Brazil became a "European team" (as opposed to a Brazilian team) with 19 of its players on the national team squad contracted with European teams. This resulted in little consequent opportunity to build relationships or a team identity. There was lots of "talent" on the Brazil squad

with the likes of Neymar, César, Silva, and others, yet the talent never seemed to gel. Notwithstanding the clobbering by Germany, Brazil looked anemic in its other matches. Even their fellow countrymen heaped on criticism throughout the World Cup. Brazil never established a true identity with their 2014 National Team, which appeared to be a mere shadow of its former great teams.

Unfortunately for Germany, they lost the sense of strong relationships and identity by the time 2018 rolled around. Having two camps within the team precluded a 'one team' identity. Relationships were fragmented and the closeness of four years prior was lost. The lack of identity and relationships was the perfect storm for crashing out of the first round.

As in sports, identity is fundamental in High Performance Teams, and a key part of TQ. One of the questions I ask team members is to rank their sense of identity with their a) industry, b) company, and c) team. This tells me something about the strength of the team. Most members of a High Performance Team identify first with their team. It's a given that you spend the most time with your team. If the team identity is not ranked first, it is unlikely to be a High Performance Team.

> The strongest form of team identity comes from an unyielding commitment to success.

If identity is so important, what does it consist of? Strong identity is a by-product of being able to relate to and feel good about the team, what it stands for, and the success it creates, as well as the relationships and camaraderie experienced by its members. Essentially, teams need something to be proud of and strive toward.

The strongest form of team identity comes from an unyielding commitment to success based on the goals the team has set for itself. All team members must be committed to contributing to success.

This creates a palpable "buzz" about the team. Everyone wants to be part of a winning team and the sense of identity that ensues.

Lessons from a Global Ad Agency

One example of a turnaround team was my ad agency client, a Regional Leadership Team based in Singapore that was part of one of the world's largest advertising groups. The regional office ranked in the lowest quartile in customer satisfaction and employee engagement scores. Team identity was almost nonexistent. A new general manager resolved to correct the situation, and I was brought in to support a turnaround exercise.

We implemented the core principles of the High Performance Team by conducting an off-site to address the main issues, and building trust, identity, vision, values, and feedback. The result generated the internal mantra, "We buzz." That mantra represented the energy the team wanted to instill in the organization.

After much effort to integrate the new culture and identity throughout the organization, the team conducted a further survey a year later. The results were astounding. Customer satisfaction and employee engagement moved from the bottom quartile to the top quartile. And the turnaround was not isolated to the leadership team itself. The entire regional office was positively impacted.

The team had employed their new mantra, "We buzz," to generate a whole new feeling in the team, and the sense of identity completely shifted from almost nil to very strong. Moreover, employee turnover dropped considerably. The Southeast Asian team became known in New York as a great and High Performance Team within the space of only one year.

DEFINING IDENTITY

Such is the power of identity. Team identity is the outcome of many factors. It is strengthened by defining the team vision, mission, purpose, and values, and by nurturing relationships and enjoying success.

Below is one of the exercises we use to set and boost identity.

WHO ARE WE?

This is a simple exercise that describes who the team aspires to be in current terms, which is accomplished by answering the following questions:

1. What are our strengths, capabilities, and core competencies?
2. What is special and unique about our team?
3. What are we capable of?
4. What motivates us?

An example of this from one pharmaceutical team is: "We are a highly ambitious team with particular strengths in research and development, and are adept at converting new concepts into a successful reality, providing us with a strong desire to deliver for our patients and clients."

Figure 12.1

RITUALS: BOOSTING IDENTITY OVER TIME

Toward the end of a team-transformation program, the team will work on rituals, things they will do differently and consistently to change behavior and absorb positive change into the team. Many of the rituals involve continuing team bonding and keeping relationships and energy at the desired level.

One company that keeps consistent rituals is "Pret A Manger," the fresh food outlet. The company encourages employees to socialize regularly. Once a month, they fund Friday night drinks. Likewise, Pret has large parties several times a year. Pret people work hard and play hard together. This contributes to the positive atmosphere one feels in their shops and how its employees interact with each other in a very upbeat manner. In any given store, Pret employees "have each other's backs" and are very supportive of each other, as highlighted by Richard Preston in *The Telegraph*.

Lessons from Pret A Manger

With Clive Schlee, Pret's chief executive since 2003, I take a tour of five shops within half a mile of the company's London HQ, near Victoria station. It's a walk-through, at high speed that he must have conducted many times before, but that doesn't make him any less observant of detail. "The first thing I look at," he says, "is whether staff are touching each other—are they smiling, reacting to each other, happy, engaged? Look; she's just touched her colleague—squeezed her arm. If I see hands going up in the air, that's a good sign. I can almost predict sales on body language, alone."[40]

Schlee's "walk-through" ritual reveals the essence of good sales—engagement and interaction. Again we can witness the power of relationships here. And there are plenty of other incentives, too: if the mystery shopper has had outstanding service from an individual and names that person on the questionnaire, that employee gets an extra cash bonus; and any shop recognized to have a "Star Team" gets a wad of cash to spend on a team outing. That is in addition to Friday night drinks once a month, quarterly events for groups of shops, and two enormous parties a year for the entire company. As Andrea Wareham, Pret's director of people, says, "If you can't dress up in costume twice a year for a party, Pret's not for you."[41]

Pret has many rituals to promote team spirit. Team energy can be felt and is a key objective for any Pret manager. The supportive team atmosphere is part of the "scene" at Pret.

There are also three core behaviors at Pret: passion, clear talking, and team working. "Team working" is a core behavior that underlies the camaraderie at Pret.

EIGHT RITUALS FOR BOOSTING IDENTITY

Rituals are an important part of Pret A Manger's success, whether it's parties, outings, or drinks. In my own work with clients, the following are a few noteworthy rituals that have come out of different company programs:

1. Drinks. Friday afternoon/evening or on regular basis. This keeps the informal aspects of relationships alive and well. It also provides a venue to unwind and vent when necessary at the end of the week. One of my client departments at Cathay Pacific Airways regularly designates Friday at 5:30 p.m. for "drinks with the team."

2. Lunches. Regular team lunches are great. Once or twice a month, they mix breaking bread with good informal banter. The key is to schedule them as regular events.

3. Outings. One company I know schedules quarterly outings to new and fun places. It's up to the team to decide if these take place during work hours or on the weekend, and are half-day or full-day activities. The key is to make them regular and try interesting and new ideas. In any given city, you can find a plethora of ideas for group engagement, including paintball, theme parks, dance studios, voice lessons, golf, rock climbing, kayaking, rafting, or other sport outings; the list goes on and on.

4. Trips. Our leadership team at PepsiCo used to schedule annual trips to exotic places combining meetings and fun, and attended with spouses or partners. These were most memorable and created a strong sense of identity.

5. Meeting rituals. Why do meetings have to be serious, dull, and long? Some clients include icebreakers in every meeting.

Others share "What has been a success and failure over the past month?" One innovative concept is the "team governance index," which rates the state of the team over the past month: to what extent is it operating as a High Performance Team? Remembering, "What gets measured gets done," is a great way to focus on team health. Another ritual is keeping track of recognition; during team meetings, any form of recognition, positive comments about another person or idea, or applause, was counted as recognition. One person was tasked with keeping track of how many instances of recognition were demonstrated and tallied it up at the end of the meeting.

6. Team feedback sessions. Later in the book, you will be introduced to "RearView Feedback," a team-feedback exercise. One team liked it so much that they instituted it once a quarter.

7. TQ HealthChecks. Constantly measuring how the team is performing is a useful way to keep awareness on the team's progress. One way to do this is for team members to take a team assessment on a regular basis and spend time discussing it.

8. Round-Robin Meet-ups. Outside of formal meetings, most team members meet with a handful of other members on a regular basis. This may be due to natural collaboration on projects, functional dependencies, or just plain chemistry. It's important to consciously build relationships over time. We have devised a ritual called Round-Robin Meet-ups that encourages each team member to meet informally with each of the other members at least once a year (see figure 12.2). This is best done outside the office over coffee or lunch, but where and how members meet is purely up to them. I suggest that each meeting last a minimum of 30 minutes. The key is to conduct no formal business. It's just a chance to "shoot the breeze," reconnect, and deepen the relationship. Some teams prefer to do this twice a year instead of once, but it really depends on the size of the team. As

> By committing to team rituals, you will ensure that your team stays on the track to high performance.

simple as it seems, this exercise is a very powerful way to deepen relationships. It can look something like this (assuming there are ten team members). Note that the actual meeting date and time should be specified.

ROUND-ROBIN MEET-UPS									
	Mary	Royce	Ming	Edna	Flavio	Jerry	Pierre	Dawa	Thianna
John	Jan	Feb	Mar	Apr	May	Jun	Jul	Aug	Sep
Mary		Mar	Apr	May	Jun	Jul	Aug	Sep	Oct
Royce			May	Jun	Jul	Aug	Sept	Oct	Nov
Ming				Jul	Aug	Sep	Oct	Nov	Dec
Edna					Sep	Oct	Nov	Dec	Jan
Flavio						Nov	Dec	Jan	Feb
Jerry							Jan	Feb	Mar
Pierre								Mar	Apr
Dawa									May

Figure 12.2

By committing to rituals, you will ensure that your team stays on track to high performance. You will also deepen and strengthen relationships and the sense of identity and bonding necessary for team brilliance.

To demonstrate the power of team identity, I interviewed Dudley Slater, author of the book *Fusion Leadership* and founder of Integra Telecom.

CASE STUDY:
DUDLEY SLATER AT INTEGRA TELECOM
THE POWER OF TEAM IDENTITY

Dudley Slater founded and led Integra Telecom since its inception in 1996 to become, within 15 years, one of the ten largest landline telecom companies in the United States. Dudley and his team at Integra changed the telecom industry, moving the customer relationship to a high-touch model focusing on business and shifting from a centralized model to customer-focused model.

Although Dudley retired from his CEO post in 2011, he is proud of the 15-person core leadership team that he built. His team has mostly disbanded, but the key members have gone on to assume major leadership roles in the C-suites of major competitors such as Comcast and Century Link. They have risen to the top with influential roles in the industry.

Dudley articulates an interesting way to define a High Performance Team: "If the team ends up creating a competitive advantage, and the functioning of the team causes it to perform at a higher level than its peer group, then it's a High Performance Team. That can be measured by the extent to which key team members are sought out by competitors." Dudley's team members were consistently put on the "A list" of potential executives by executive-search firms in the sector.

Dudley considers team identity paramount, stating "Building a sense of identity is hugely important because people want to be part of a winning team. It's never fun to introduce yourself to people and describe yourself as working for a losing team. The way we built Integra started with a shared vision—we were all about providing the best customer experience in the industry. Any member of the team should be able to articulate in clear terms the mission and vision of the organization and be able to inspire others with that vision. All leadership-team members, and all employees for that matter, need to embody the passion for the Integra vision and mission: to lead the industry in providing a quality, user-friendly customer experience. It was the core of what we were trying to achieve at Integra. Everyone on the team shared that identity. Corporate politics were discouraged and

> "Building a sense of identity is hugely important because people want to be part of a winning team."

not tolerated. When you are clear about what's important, it has an amazing ability to drive politics out of the team."

How do you build identity over time? Dudley believes it's exceedingly important to celebrate successes and have a reward system that works. That might involve calling out individual or team performances, or providing stock options, recognition awards, or other incentives. The leadership team at Integra also invested in off-site retreats at stunning beach and mountain resorts twice a year to set annual goals and revisit the strategy and their competitive position. They would mix business with fun, including recreational activities, from hiking to scuba and skydiving. All of this contributed to an identity that the team deserved to work and play together in meaningful, interesting, and fascinating settings. These unique and memorable experiences contributed to a special sense of belonging for the Integra "A team."

That identity extended into the role of the leadership team, which was to serve the organization as opposed to serving its own interests. Dudley felt, "This is very much a servant-leadership principle. The role of the leaders is to serve the organization, not to empower themselves. From a tangible perspective, this meant sharing the ownership structure deeply within the workforce." Dudley would ask his board to approve stock option awards broadly across and deep within the organization, pushing his investors beyond the more traditional model limited to the C-suite. Dudley believed it was important to be able to look his colleagues in the eye and say, "If we succeed in creating value, you will have a tangible opportunity to participate in that wealth creation. We are in this together."

At Integra, all ideas were welcome, and there is nothing better than a good debate.

How did Dudley instill and encourage the servant-leadership behaviors and values in the leadership team? Modeling was immensely important—the need to walk one's talk. Dudley himself invested time traveling and talking to the frontline and serving the organization, saying,

"I would get out in the field and work with the frontline to figure out how we can help them be more successful. Then I could justify demanding that others on the leadership team do the same thing!"

Dudley had high expectations for leadership-team meetings: come prepared and create ownership and an environment of safety. Anything was fair game, and there were no sacred cows. To avoid domination by certain members, he would assign topics to those who might be surprised to lead that topic discussion. Dudley viewed his role as getting all the opinions on the table. It meant coming to meetings with a sense of urgency and resolving any problems then and there. High participation and energy level was mandatory in leadership-team meetings.

The other key behavior was mutual respect—being more cultural than strategic. When it comes to human behavior, Dudley believed that "People want to work for a cause, not just for the advancement of their boss's initiatives." Mutual respect means that everybody is treated with a high degree of respect in the belief that each of their roles is fundamental to the organization. At Integra, all ideas were welcomed, and there was nothing better than a good debate. Often the question would come up: "Do we, as a team, do a good enough job of holding each other accountable?" The leadership team was open to those types of discussions. It all came down to a culture of mutual respect.

The other way to drive respect was by mining for golden nuggets. Dudley would often meet with employees and ask, "What can I do to make you more effective in your job?" That question helped drive change in the organization. When Dudley heard a good idea, one that would help the company operate more effectively, he would implement it, giving credit to the frontline workers for driving tangible change in the company's operating capability. It encouraged people to operate more effectively, fostered mutual respect, rewarded people for working outside the limits of their job description, and focused on the success of the company's mission.

Collaboration was an operating principle for Integra's leadership team, and the team members actively nurtured it. Dudley intimated, "It was an environment that welcomed debate. All questions were welcome, and people shouldn't be afraid to ask anything. People need to feel safe collaborating." They addressed it organizationally by physically avoiding silos. The six geographic regions each had all the various functions: the call center, engineering, repair, and other departments were all located next to each other. In doing so, they created a modular operating structure in each region, pushing out service so it was closer to the customer, in contrast to the centralized model employed by its competitors. It was highly controversial due to cost concerns, but it ended up paying off with the highest profit margins in the industry. All functions took joint ownership of total financial results. The model worked phenomenally well, however it only works in a high-collaboration environment.

Alignment is fundamentally important and is the metric to measure whether you have a successful organization that is collaborating and executing effectively. Dudley put alignment into action; whenever he went out to one of the regions, he would sit down privately with key individual leaders and ask, "What are your regions' most important three priorities?" If the responses were not aligned among the key leaders, he would come unglued and come down on them hard. Dudley believed that "A company is nothing more than a group of people working together, and alignment is how you measure whether people are truly working together."

The strong identity at Integra engendered a powerful team spirit over time. Team members would say things like, "I would have worked for free." "I so enjoyed being a part of that team." "It has been the best role in my career." The Integra team developed a swagger and was recognized nationally as providing the best customer experience. Integra also achieved the highest profit margins in the sector, generating loads of third-party recognition.

Ultimately, a true measure of the leadership team is continuity. Regional media reports noted the long tenure and stability of the Integra leadership team, spanning two recessions and dramatic changes in telecom technology. Dudley remarked, "The team was so stable with very little turnover. Largely the same people were on the team from beginning to end."[42]

> ## DUDLEY SLATER'S APPROACH TO
> ## BUILDING HIGH PERFORMANCE TEAMS[13]
> ### (Takeaways)
>
> 1. Building a sense of identity is hugely important because people want to be part of a winning team.
> 2. Any member of the team should be able to articulate in clear terms the mission and vision of the organization, and be able to inspire others with that vision.
> 3. Celebrate successes and have a reward system that works
> 4. Model servant-leadership values and behaviors.
> 5. In leadership-team meetings, anything is fair game, and there are no sacred cows.
> 6. Mutual respect is a key leadership-team behavior.
> 7. Alignment is fundamentally important and is a metric to measure whether you have a successful organization.
> 8. Collaboration is an operating principle of the leadership team that must be nurtured.
>
> Ultimately, a true measure of the leadership team is continuity.

Figure 12.3

A-A-A TEAMS:
AWARENESS, ACCEPTANCE, APPRECIATION

A-A-A is a process we devised to bond, deepen relationships, create identity, and move rapidly up the trust curve.

It begins with the premise that we are all human. That means we all have various degrees of credibility and intentions. Moreover, at a deep level, we all recognize that no one is perfect or totally trustworthy all the time. Even though human beings are imperfect, we can "strive for perfection."

Where have you heard that before? Of course, all the great religions refer to it. All sports strive for it. And businesses work toward it, as well. What is "zero defects" or "accident free"? It's simply striving for perfection, knowing that although we may never get there, we can always improve and excel. The same goes for building relationships and trust; we are where we are, but we can always improve.

A-A-A is a process, meaning that we move from awareness to acceptance and then to appreciation. Awareness is the critical first step. After all, how can you accept and appreciate if you don't know what you are appreciating?

1. Awareness. During our daily routines, we really only become aware of colleagues in certain work contexts. Getting to know each other as individuals is not a given. Yet awareness is critical for knowing the capacities and limitations that fellow team members possess. The following are several key areas for gaining awareness.

> A-A-A is a process for team members to bond, deepen relationships, create identity, and move rapidly up the trust curve.

- *Leadership/management styles:* Really knowing each other starts by getting to know others' leadership or management styles. Knowing the tendencies and predilections of team members helps enormously when dealing with problems or opportunities.
- *Preferences:* It always amazes me how little we really know about each other's work preferences, meaning how we want to be treated. Do we want lots of information or broad-brush direction? Do we want to talk more strategically or tactically? Do we want a more macro or micro approach? How do we want to be recognized? Developing an awareness of preferences is a sign of respect and care. We care about each other enough to get to know how everyone wants to be treated, and then we make an effort to follow through. By doing so, we develop more effective communication and relationships. The new golden rule should be, *"Treat others as they would like to be treated."*

- *Personal:* How much of the basic stuff do you know about your co-workers—family, hobbies, lifestyle, exercise, diet, and so on? As simple as it seems, this knowledge is important in developing relationships, connections, and

> Understanding others' preferences means "treating others as *they* would like to be treated."

trust. The more we disclose about our own personal characteristics, the more others begin to open up, too.

If you can develop awareness of styles, preferences, and personal tastes, you are well on your way to moving to the next level: acceptance.

2. Acceptance. Once you have expended the effort to become *aware* of fellow team members, you begin to *accept* your colleagues' diversity of styles, preferences, and personal tendencies. Then you begin to comprehend how people differ in these areas. You develop an acceptance of the larger aspects of your teammates. This is critical because our normal, context-driven awareness is very narrow, leading us to make conclusions and judgments about each other in a black-and-white manner.

> Team members *want* to be accepted; yet they *love* to be appreciated.

For example, suppose you are involved in a meeting with a team member who has just nixed one of your proposals. You might conclude that he is too simplistic or has poor judgment and then form a black-and-white conclusion about him. However, if you have developed awareness about his styles, preferences, and personal tendencies, you may have a more informed understanding of why this teammate decided the way he did. Moreover, you may realize that if you change your approach in interacting with this individual, the outcome might change. Then you would be better equipped to interpret the decision based on the added information.

After enduring some criticism for my presentation style at PepsiCo, I realized that I needed to modify it based on the individual to whom I was presenting. It took me a while to figure this out. I finally realized that the Asian Region president responded well to a more strategic or macro approach, whereas the Greater China president responded better to a numbers or action-oriented approach. Had I invested upfront in developing awareness of their respective styles, I could have adjusted much more quickly and would have accepted their styles without cursing them under my breath.

In the end, you begin to accept that the diversities of styles, preferences, and personal tendencies are, indeed, important for optimal team functioning. If we were all alike, teams and outputs would be very one dimensional.

3. Appreciation. If acceptance is an *internal* process, appreciation is an *external* process. Team members want to be accepted, yet they *love* to be appreciated. After all, appreciation is a form of recognition.

During a team session with a large European insurance provider, I asked team members about their highest form of motivation. Stuart, the regional director, said that being recognized by his peer group in the industry was the greatest form of appreciation. I had mistakenly assumed that for leaders at the C-suite level, recognition was less important. I couldn't have been more wrong; recognition is equally powerful at all levels.

There are dozens of ways to appreciate fellow team members. In the context of the team, members want to be appreciated for who they are and for the unique aspects they bring to the team: their strengths, capabilities, and contributions. The more they are recognized, the more they are willing to show up, contribute, and perform for the team.

ACTIVITIES TO CREATE A-A-A TEAMS

There are many ways to build awareness, acceptance, and appreciation. The following work well when facilitating groups:

1. "What is your secret?" I often use this or a variation of this question when kicking off a program. It always gets the group going, creates laughs, and has some real value in getting to know people at a different level.

a. I will ask participants to think of but not share one secret that no one on the team knows about them (reminding that this information must be kept in the room; before running this exercise, I ask participants to agree to confidentiality). This should be something personal, not a work secret. It should be something interesting, fun, and if they are willing, juicy. It's useful to give examples of what is and is not an "interesting" secret. For example, some people will take the safe route and cite mundane things such as, "I attended the Kellogg Executive Program," or, "I have a half-brother." While these may be noteworthy facts, they are not particularly interesting. You will need to give participants time to think of something. Some people can immediately think of something while others won't. Others may have several secrets, but they need to decide which one to reveal.

b. Ask them then to mingle, and share as many secrets as possible, if possible, with each member of the team.

c. Once finished, ask the group to form a large circle. Ask one person to start by picking someone in the circle and proceeding to tell the group that person's secret. Then the person who was picked chooses someone else and does the same. The process continues until the last person chosen was the first to speak.

d. If someone can't remember the secret of the person they have chosen, they may "confer" with that person, if necessary.

"What is your secret?" is a fun and lively way to kick off any program, and it provides some real information about people, as well. Some astonishing facts are revealed, and there tends to be lots of laughter.

I sometimes use a variation on this exercise: When you are pressed for time or have too many people, skip the initial mingling and just pick a partner—preferably someone you don't know well. Each set of partners will then share their partner's secret with the larger group.

2. "My Preferences" exercise. Over the years, I realized that executives, given their differences in style, approach, and personality, have very specific ways of thinking and communicating, and want others to communicate with them in a manner that is most like how they operate. Yet rarely do executives share this information with others. This leads to lots of "guesswork" and an enormous amount of wasted time. It was clear that I needed to address this problem.

This exercise addresses that issue. See figure 12.4 to see how it works.

Provide a handout (like the one below; you may modify it however you wish) to all participants. Once you have distributed this handout, ask people to spend five minutes considering and answering the questions. It's then time to reveal the responses. Ask everyone to gather in a circle and share their preferences with the rest of their team. Each person takes a turn revealing their preferences. Participants are advised to keep their sheets and even share them with others on their own teams after the program.

As simple an exercise as it is, it's very powerful. The ability to tell others how you want to be treated and other preferences doesn't happen very often. This provides a safe and structured way to do it, which won't come across as overly focused on one's own needs.

HOW TO GET THE BEST FROM ME? (My Preferences Exercise)		
Area	Detail	Comments
Communication	Receiving feedback: Direct OR diplomatic?	
Structure	When assigning me projects/work: Structured and detailed OR broad and general?	
Information	When giving me information: Detailed OR key points?	
Recognition	How do I like to be recognized? (Open ended)	
Other	Other comments about how I like to be treated and my style. (Open ended)	
Pet Peeves	What are the things that annoy me? How not to treat me? (Open ended)	

Figure 12.4

When I tee this up, I mention that "Part of teamwork is about respect—respect for each other and what everyone wants and doesn't want." Participants feel good about being able to share their preferences and learn others' to avoid second-guessing. This contributes to awareness, acceptance, and appreciation (A-A-A). Participants say that this exercise allows them to truly appreciate the needs of others.

3. "What I Appreciate about You" exercise. This is a simple yet powerful exercise that goes to the heart of appreciation. It's about recognizing others for their strengths and contributions. We all know how potent recognition is. Many of us live for varying degrees of recognition. Sometimes, if nothing else, a bit of appreciation and recognition is all that is necessary to shift the team toward a positive mind-set

Participants form a circle. Someone volunteers to be appreciated. Each team member begins with the following:

"(Name), what I appreciate about you is . . ."

After each person has had a chance to recognize the team member, the next team member receives recognition until everyone has given and received recognition.

With the What I Appreciate about You exercise, it is important to stick to the time allotted. This exercise can easily run long as people love to heap praise and tell stories. Therefore, you may want to limit the stories and the elaboration. Team member should address their comments to the person being appreciated by name or by saying "you." Stay away from "we." This is not a collective appreciation exercise but a personal what "I" appreciate about "you."

4. Assessment tools. There are many great assessment tools for getting to know respective personalities, leadership, and management styles, and building awareness and acceptance. I usually will pick one that the organization uses most and feels most comfortable with.

One of the oldest and most-widely used personality tests is the Myers-Briggs Type Indicator (MBTI). The great thing about MBTI is that it's easy to take and relate to, and it offers lots of opportunities to run different team-variation exercises. You can group people in a myriad of ways and come up with notable contrasts.

Another great assessment tool is Harrison Assessments™.[44] This tool creates a "Paradox Report" that leads to a deeper understanding of one's self but can also be used for teams. Essentially, it plots the team along a variety of dimensions. This is useful for identifying a team's strengths and gaps. Harrison Assessments is based on Paradox Theory. A paradox is a seemingly contradictory statement that may nonetheless be true. According to Paradox Theory, a trait can be either constructive or destructive depending upon other complementary traits. For example, when frankness is complemented by diplomacy, it takes the constructive form of being forthright and truthful. However, without the complementary trait of diplomacy, frankness becomes bluntness. While frankness and diplomacy appear to be contradictory, they paradoxically co-exist, complementing and fulfilling each other."[45]

The individual reports are combined into a Team Paradox Graph, in figure 12.5.

In this particular client's case, 12 team members are indicated by the letters A through L, each of which is plotted on the graph. This brings to the surface interesting team dynamics: The entire team is on the higher end of "FRANK," though on the "DIPLOMATIC" axis, individuals range from high to low. Through understanding where each team member is located on these axes, we note their relative contribution to the team, e.g. which team members would be good for certain tasks. For example, the team leader in this case happens to be "B," who is in the "BLUNT" quadrant. Would this leader be the best to deliver sensitive messages? Probably not. To compensate, the team leader might empower "K" or "H" to handle this task. Likewise, the leader's bluntness could be off putting to some, yet with the recognition of the leader's profile, team members may be able to view the dynamic more comprehensively. There is a richness of understanding that can come out of discussions using the Paradox Team Report.

Harrison Assessments'

Team Paradox Graph "Communication"

(Alphabetic letters refer to individual team members.)

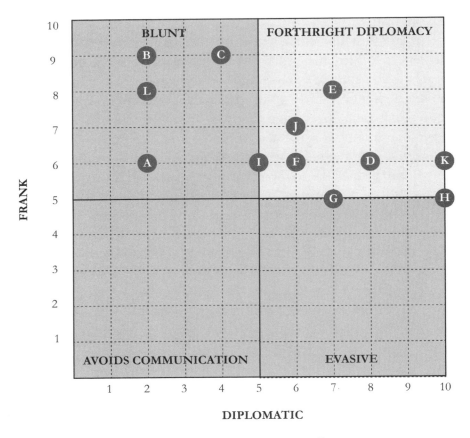

Figure 12.5: Team Paradox Graph—Communication[46]

There are a host of other assessment tools such as DiSC, Hogan, FIRO-B, and others that are very useful and can provide insight and awareness into individual styles and team dynamics.

One of the advantages of using assessments is the adoption of the "assessment language" in relating as a team. People start to feel comfortable in explaining certain behaviors of individuals and teams through the assessment language. It provides a new platform for communication and readily facilitates acceptance of self and others.

In order to conduct assessment processes, internal or external facilitators should be certified in facilitating both individual feedback as well as team dynamics.

5. Specific team activities. Under the guise of "team building," you will find specific team activities. In fact, you will find hundreds of exercises and activities that can assist in developing awareness, acceptance, and appreciation. These include the following:

a. Outdoor activities: These range from nature programs, to outdoor challenge/survival programs, to ropes courses, climbing, and others. These activities often have a role to play in helping team members discover, in a natural setting, how much more capable of accomplishing a task they are than they might have believed.

b. Event-based activities: These involve a program around a theme or event, and can include competitive situations, problem solving, music and rhythm, innovation games, creative challenges, or community activities. Many of these have a specific purpose. For example, during community-activity events, the purpose may be to work collaboratively to "do good."

c. Games and simulations: There are a myriad of games and simulations created for various purposes, including business simulations, communication, trust, goal setting, creative processes, and so on.

The proliferation of specific team activities allows teams to be very targeted around their needs and learning new skills. When using specific team activities, be sure to be clear about exactly what you want. Don't expect that a day or two spent in one of these exercises will create a High Performance Team. The exercises are very useful in situational and purpose contexts, e.g. trust building, collaboration, etc. The challenge is in how to take the knowledge gained and create transformation-based work. For that you will need to take a long-term holistic view with an end goal in mind to build a High Performance Team.

Many other exercises establish an initial degree of awareness, acceptance, and appreciation. The key is to find the exercise that is specific to your purpose and use it at the right time.

———

The A-A-A process is very powerful in building relationships, strengthening the bonds of the team, and developing trust. It also will make the team more effective while functioning at a higher level, increasing both individual and Collective TQ.

13

ELEMENT #3
VALUES

WHAT REALLY MATTERS?

Lessons from PepsiCo Greater China Leadership Team

At PepsiCo, our Greater China Leadership Team met monthly. One of the earlier members was the general manager of a bottling plant in China whom we'll refer to as "Madame." Often she came late to these meetings, and sometimes did not even show up. When she did attend the meetings, she was quite combative and fought hard for her positions, which tended to polarize the group and make it difficult to have reasonable and effective meetings. Many team members thought that her behavior was out of line. The problem was that we had never done the work as a whole team to articulate the team's values. Every member of the team interpreted the team's values from their own perspective. From Madame's perspective, she was operating out of her own sense of values. She was standing up for her bottler operation with little regard for the regional leadership team. Had we agreed on and aligned our values (assuming that Madame had been a part of that process), it would have been easier to point out to her when she was out of line and perhaps her behavior would have changed.

As discussed in the previous chapter, if you don't know where you are going, you'll never get there. Likewise, if you don't determine what's important to the team, members will not buy into its power.

All teams have values in some form, whether conscious or unconscious. Unfortunately, many teams haven't articulated and aligned their values, so you never know what kind of behavior will appear. And unless you have done the values work, it's hard to blame other team members for behaviors that may seem out of line.

What's the Value in Values?

Most parents are very clear about the values they want to impart to their children and willingly talk about it. Values are the most deeply held beliefs that we carry, and our guiding principles are derived from them. Without Values, the direction and education of our children would be rudderless.

Interestingly, when it comes to work, we don't tend to share our values with each other; we have our own sense of what's important, and often we assume that others share some of our basic values. If not, it may lead to misunderstanding.

Taken to the next level, the *alignment of team values* is a core principle in High Performance Teams. Values form the glue that holds the team together. They compose an essential part of the *team culture*. Once the team creates, shares, and aligns its values, those values become a key driver of *behavior* and the way changes are implemented.

THE GENESIS OF OUR VALUES

Values come from three sources: education, society, and experience.

Values from the first source, *education*, come in large measure from parents who are always, consciously or unconsciously, projecting their values upon us. The "chip off the old block" refers, in part, to the values we learn from our parents. We naturally embody them until we rebel against them. The process of questioning or rebelling becomes a necessary part of achieving individualism.

> *Lessons from Human Resources at a Multinational Company*
> Education of values comes at any age. I was astonished by a statement made by Stephanie, the Regional Head of Human Resources at a large, multinational company. Stephanie was from mainland China but had worked with several global firms. She confessed, "I learned my sense of values from working in multinational companies!" Apparently, Stephanie's formative education instilled in her the value of survival, but right or wrong, her corporate education taught her the values required for successful interaction with people in the workplace. Education of values can come from any source or at any time in one's life.

The next source is *society*. Like the values projected onto us by our parents, we are bombarded with societal values that are constantly reinforced, whether consciously or unconsciously. Anyone who has worked in another country will experience, firsthand, societal values. As a student in Japan, I was impressed by how polite the Japanese were in most contexts. However, when it came to getting into the crowded subway car, all politeness vanished. The old lady gouging the umbrella in my rear was a vivid reminder of that. I couldn't reconcile the observation that, given that the Japanese were arguably the politest people on Earth, they could also be quite rude in the busy subway or in crowds in general. I finally came to realize the key difference lay in values. In Japan, the "context" of politeness was important in direct or personal interactions. If there is no "face," the value of politeness can disappear.

Finally, values are influenced by *experience*. As we progress through our working lives, many of us develop values based on experience. In my early career, Joe, a general manager at Kodak, told me that he believed in the following axiom by the astronaut

Jim Lovell: "There are people who make things happen, there are people who watch things happen, and there are people who wonder what happened. To be successful, you need to be a person who makes things happen."

Joe often referred to the quote and said that based on his experience in managing teams and companies, he could classify people into those three buckets. Joe attributed the greatest value to "people who make things happen."

DEFAULT VALUES

When a team doesn't articulate and align its values, it ends up with what I call default values, which can exist in a team or a company.

> At PepsiCo, we didn't spend a lot of time discussing values. Fortunately, given the company's long history, the values were clear. The company valued hard work, creative solutions, taking initiative, a results focus, and a bias for action. These values were not discussed much, but they were clear to most and have made PepsiCo a great company. On the other hand, since they were not discussed, there were a few implicit values as well. These included a strong individual survival instinct. Sometimes that meant throwing someone else under the bus. The other was that if you don't perform within a year or two, you're out. PepsiCo tended to hire the best talent in the market and had high, short-term expectations.

> Thus, while PepsiCo engendered a passion for performance, it also resulted in a strong focus on self-preservation rather than preservation of the firm or team. The behaviors associated with this sometimes manifested in a focus on short-term, individual achievements, and sound bites, all within the context of a relatively political environment. The focus

tended toward "High performance individuals" as opposed to High Performance Teams.

The other phenomenon was the "revolving door," which meant relatively high executive turnover. Executives are well compensated with the expectation that they will deliver performance quickly. When I joined PepsiCo as vice president of sales, I realized that high turnover was not commensurate with strong, long-term customer relationships. We served a multitude of large customers, such as Wal-Mart, Carrefour, 7-Eleven, Tesco, Metro, Yum! Brands, and others for whom long-term relationships were crucial. Thus, I decided that for my team, I would focus on creating a strong team of which members could be proud and wanted to stay. I had a number of capable directors reporting to me who handled critical customer and bottler relationships. One of my crowning achievements as a manager was that in five years I never lost a director. Some were promoted, but none resigned.

People would ask, "Douglas, how do you keep and motivate people in the revolving-door context at PepsiCo?" I replied simply, "Build a strong team with strong values and a team environment in which people love to work."

It's important to remember that regardless of what the company values may be, the team values are more relevant to team members, as they provide a tangible, immediate, and compelling reason to stay and perform.

PERSONAL VALUES SHOWING UP

It is essential to articulate and align team values so you can minimize conflicts among team members' personal value systems.

Default values show up when individuals or teams have not

aligned or articulated their values. Personal values are those that are present for every individual, independent of company or team values, whether we like it or not. Personal values are sometimes in conflict with team values or even the manager's values:

Lessons from a Legal Firm

> Articulating and aligning values will minimize conflicts stemming from team members' personal value systems.

I was coaching a client named Andrew, a lawyer who worked for a legal firm that valued hard work as a priority. His team leader, John, also valued hard work, but higher on his list of values for his team members was business development. He wanted Andrew to reorder his values and focus on going out and developing clients, networking, and making new contacts. It was a struggle for Andrew who felt an internal conflict of values.

Therefore, it is essential to articulate and align team values so you can minimize conflicts stemming from all the team members' personal value systems. Values are the most deeply held beliefs. If yours and mine are in conflict, there is a good chance we will ultimately be in conflict.

The conflict in values is also easily illustrated in contrasting cultures. I deal with a few Swiss companies that work in China and Asia. Many Swiss, as individuals, value "Doing things the right way"; however, some Chinese may value "Getting things done in the most expedient way." The Chinese get the job done using many creative ways, some of which may involve short cuts or circumventing the rules. This is seemingly in conflict with Swiss values. If you have two or more nationalities on the same team whose values are not aligned, conflicts may arise.

The conflict of personal values in a team is not reserved to differing nationalities. As all team members possess different personal values, conflicts are natural if values are not aligned. The default values will be the operative norm in this case.

CORPORATE VS. TEAM VALUES

Often the question arises: "We already have our corporate values; how do we create team values that are not in conflict?" It's a valid point given that corporate values do represent what's deeply important to the team. While corporate values articulate general principles, they may not reflect the existential needs of the team. Individuals may not feel an immediate sense of ownership with corporate values ("Not invented here" syndrome) and may be content to let them hang on the wall without bringing them to life. Team values, however, reflect with immediacy the needs of the team and form a code by which team members show up and interact with each other.

Team values should not conflict with corporate values; they should complement them. At this stage in the team-value creation process, I often recommend reviewing corporate values first and answering the question, "What is most relevant to us as a team within the corporate values?" Then ask, "What else do we need to embody to be successful in realizing our vision?" Most teams naturally feel a comfort level with this kind of exercise. In fact, I have never encountered a team that got stuck on the conflict between corporate and team values once they went through that exercise.

Lessons from a Global Executive Search Firm
A great example of this process is a top global executive-search client. This client was founded on the concept of operating from strong values. In fact, the founder himself espoused the concept that "Values form the underpinnings of culture."

These values touch on the firm's operating principles—how they charge, the interaction with clients, and the role of consultants.

As we worked together, the question became: "How do we translate these values to the team in Greater China (China/Hong Kong/Taiwan) to make their work more relevant? Which of these values should be emphasized? What else is important given the operating environment in Greater China? How do we ensure that our values correspond with our vision?

After going through the values exercise, we established the following values for the Greater China Leadership Team:

- integrity
- generosity
- professionalism
- clients first
- fulfillment

These values were created by the entire team and reflected imperatives for how the team would handle existing challenges and realize their vision. The team's values synced well with the firm's global values. Most importantly, they served as a foundation for determining what behaviors would work for the team.

Do You Own Your Team Values?

Most of us have worked in organizations that have "published values"; often they are on the wall for all to see. Corporate values are important, and it's useful to articulate them and have them visible. However the more powerful values are those that the team has created together. *The very act of creating, aligning, and articulating values as a team results in a sense of ownership.* They become something that the team can stand behind and be proud of. Indeed, this collective process of creation can be magical, as it opens the space for the team to shift into a higher gear.

VALUES FORM CULTURE
AND UNDERLIE BEHAVIOR

Ultimately, peoples' values form the underpinnings of a culture. That's why, when I speak to clients who want to strengthen their culture, I invariably suggest working on their collective and aligned values. *Culture* is essentially the characteristics that distinguish a group of people. It is a larger concept that involves habits, rituals, behaviors, and ways of being and operating. In a strong culture, you know what to expect and can rely on the firm to act in a certain way. Culture also refers to how the team interacts and behaves, and its collective beliefs and values.

As teams and companies, we need to learn to move quickly to build our culture as people come and go, and organizations change. *The fastest and surest way to build team culture is to establish jointly aligned values with full commitment from team members.*

How to Change Team Behavior

When teams seek to form or strengthen culture, they are really seeking to identify behaviors that are conducive to an effective team operation. Team members want to know what kind of behaviors they can count on through interactions. Here is a secret: You can't form lasting change in behavior by focusing on behavior, alone. You may be able to do it initially, but people usually revert to their old patterns of behavior.

Another way to change behavior involves altering the beliefs of the individuals. A deeply held belief is, in fact, a value. So the best way to change behavior is through changing beliefs or values. Likewise, in order to extract consistent and desired behavior from team members, it is important to align their collective team values with their beliefs.

Looking at it another way, team values are what we collectively believe are important, and *team behavior is how we demonstrate our values.* Changing only a team's values is meaningless unless they connect to actions and behaviors. I always recommend that teams identify and commit to behaviors that reflect their aligned values. Once the team is clear about its values and behaviors, the key to bringing the values to life depends on how we hold each other accountable as team members. This can be accomplished through a feedback exercise.

ALIGNING TEAM VALUES: EXPERIENCE THE MAGIC

We have considered the "who" "what," and "why" of values. Now it's time to consider the "when," "where," and "how." Teams that go through the values alignment process start to experience some magic. The process coalesces the team around the essential ways of being and showing up.

One frequent question from clients is: "Should we construct values or vision first?"

I ask them: "During the genesis of your business, what came first?" It almost always starts with the vision—the vision of what is possible, the opportunities, niches, business model, and so on that will work based on customer needs, desires, or aspirations. The vision is the "what" and "where" of your business, and the values represent the "how." The question I pose is: *How* do we need to show up, interact, and work together (our values), to realize our vision?" Connecting values to vision creates relevance and urgency. The connection is also directly related to how a business achieves success. The best time to start on your values is after finalizing your vision.

The Venue for Values Creation

Given the importance of the values process, I always suggest going off-site to allow for absolute focus without interruptions or distractions. Creating values requires fresh thinking unencumbered by reminders of day-to-day work.

At the off-site, I recommend assembling the chairs in a "U" shape, with no tables to hide behind. This sense of opening makes a huge difference to the whole process. If possible, the offsite can involve the team spending the night at the off-site location. Having an overnight in conjunction with the process means that it is something special, something worthy of a time commitment. It also allows participants to "sleep on" all that has been gleaned from the day.

Facilitating the Values Discussion

When facilitating a values-creation process, it's important to set the tone. After initial icebreakers, I find that a good way to start off is by using "values cards." These are photos or images that attract participants in some form or another because they connect directly to the deep subconscious. Ask team members to choose a card that they feel drawn to. Then ask them to write in a notebook, responding to these questions: "What attracts you to this image?" and next, "What value does it represent?" In this way, participants begin to understand what values are and how our values can be revealed through images.

I then will ask those participants who have children, "What values do you want to impart to your children?" This is an easy way to get them to start thinking about what's important in their lives, and what we mean when we refer to "values." What's interesting about this exercise is that if you ask this of five different people, invariably you will get five different answers. We all have distinct ideas of what we want to teach our children. In fact, a good friend of mine, Ed Sanchez, founder of one of the leading companies in the quality-control business, ProQc, has interesting thoughts on values. He posited, "The most important thing you can give your children is not education, opportunity, money, or material things. Rather, the biggest contribution to your kids is good values." Strong values will take you where you want to go and allow you to survive in any environment. Solid values help you do the "right thing" even under tenuous circumstances.

After discussing the values that participants want to give to their children, I follow up with another question: "What happens if you and your spouse are not aligned on these values?" The answers can be quite disconcerting, ranging from "divorce" to "confusion" to "family conflict." Even in a family unit, aligning values is essential for its health and well-being.

Then, on a PowerPoint slide or flip chart, I define the team values in terms of:

1. What team values do we need to embody to realize our team vision?
2. Our team values: What's important to us in terms of the following:
   - how we show up
   - how we communicate
   - how we interact
   - what we stand for
   - what energy we want
   - what we live and die for

I ask everyone if they clearly understand the meaning of what team values are and what they mean.

At this juncture, you might use what is called a "decreasing options technique" (DOT), which is a process that helps groups reduce and refine large numbers of suggestions into a manageable number of ideas. It works like this:

1. Ask participants to individually brainstorm and list in a notebook: "What team values are most important to me?" They end up with a list of values. I ask them to circle the three most important.
2. Then I ask participants to write on three sticky notes each of the top three team values they circled.
3. They then place the sticky notes on a board or flip chart.
4. Next, the whole group starts the process of consolidating values inputs into themes. The themes essentially become the values that the team will embrace. For example, the team may have identified three similar values: honesty, truthfulness, and integrity. The group may then decide to consolidate all of these under the heading of "integrity." Integrity then becomes one of the top values. The group goes through this process until it has identified three to five themes, and one value to represent each of the themes. The

great thing about this process is the interaction that ensues. The group experiences lots of discussion, cooperation, creativity, and bargaining.

5. When the group decides on the top three to five values, they write them on a separate page of a flip chart. (Note that I discourage the participants from coming up with more than five values because that becomes unwieldy.) As a final check, the group should ask itself if anything is missing in the context of the vision or mission/purpose. During one client interaction process, the team felt good about their values but then sensed some drive or energy was missing. They decided to add a value that represented the energy, calling it "passion."

6. As a final step of the DOT process, I ask the participants to shout out each of the values as a team to emotionally connect. I then ask, "How did that feel? Do you feel ownership? Do you feel excited? Is it compelling?"

BRINGING VALUES TO LIFE

Your team now has identified three to five values, which have been collectively created and aligned. Now what? Well, it doesn't stop there. Words do not make a culture. Three steps are required to bring the values to life.

I usually break up the team into three groups that will work separately and then bring them back together. The groups work on the following:

1. The first group works on *defining the meaning of each value and indicating related behaviors*. This is borne out of the need to communicate with clarity, lest the value be understood differently by different people. Take the earlier example of "integrity." What does it mean? Is it "walk your talk," "honesty," or something else? In fact, many of the articulated values can mean different things depending on the individual;

> Jointly aligned values are the glue that forms team culture.

therefore prescribing exactly what is meant by integrity is essential. The way to do this is to simply describe, in the most specific way possible, what is meant by the value at hand.

During this process, it is useful to *indicate not only the desired behaviors, but also the behaviors to stop.* This addresses upfront many of the poor habitual behaviors in which team member frequently engage. It brings them to consciousness and is a deliberate attempt to address them in the team context.

Figure 13.1 shows an example from my executive-search client, with bullet points expanding on each of the five values.

2. The second group's focus is on *visual representation* of the values. This can be in the form of a logo, drawing, or anything that can, in some way, capture the essence of the values. It's amazing how creative groups can be. The visual representation may incorporate the value words or simply be a visual. It really doesn't matter as long as the group feels in some way proud to share and integrate it throughout the organization.

3. The third group will focus on creating a *mantra* or slogan that represents the values, condensing it into a meaningful, impactful phrase that can be communicated. I tee up the mantra as follows:

- "Come up with a mantra or internal slogan that represents the values with power and emotion and is easy to communicate and recall. It should be done with three to five words."
- Examples of successful mantras are: "We Are One," "Up, Up, Up," "Growth Through Collaboration," "The A Team," "Move Beyond Ordinary," and "Power of One."

The creation of a mantra need not include the verbatim values as identified by the team. More importantly, the mantra needs to capture the essence and feeling of the values and be something that can be cascaded and integrated throughout the larger team.

After the three small groups have worked on their respective areas for about one hour, they return to present their work, seek alignment of their work with the entire team, and ask the larger team to buy into them. The team should have the opportunity to tweak and change the suggestions. For the mantra, I suggest that the whole team shout it out and feel the energy.

Once the team has gone through the values alignment exercise, the final part of the process will be a discussion regarding how to integrate the values into the rest of the team or organization. A plan should be drawn up to do just that, with designated milestones and champions.

After going through the values alignment process, your team will experience a definite shift; team spirit, and identity will be noticeably improved.

Overall, the values alignment process is a fun and essential exercise. At a fundamental level, it's simply figuring out what's most important to the team. It forms the underpinning of team culture and serves as a guide to team behavior. Every High Performance Team is clear about its values.

VALUES	BEHAVIORS
Generosity	• Give and share unconditionally. • Want the best for others. • Include a "generosity" moment at office meetings .
Integrity	• With clients • As a firm—honesty and truthfulness • With candidates

Professionalism	• Internally and externally, professionalism is:
	  a. An attitude
	  b. A process

Clients First	• Put self-interest aside. • Do not use as an excuse to do something for self-interest. • Treat everyone as a client.
Fulfillment	• Enjoy and seek fun. • Be the best. • Discover the joy of giving. • Embrace individuality. • Seek collegiality and common interest. • Celebrate team success.

Figure 13.1

Lessons from The Bayer Group

A good example of an organization that brought its values together is my client, Bayer Group, which uses the mantra "L.I.F.E.: Leadership, Integrity, Flexibility, Efficiency." All of this is captured in a very attractive visual (figure 13.2). Each of these four values is illustrated with seven examples of behaviors that reflect each value.[47]

A great example of the power of values is the Environment and Sustainability Team at MTR Corporation. I interviewed Dr. Glenn Frommer, sustainability and development manager, on the subject.

L.I.F.E
"Leadership, Integrity, Flexibility, Efficiency"

Leadership

- Be passionate for people and performance.
- Show personal drive, inspire, and motivate others.
- Be accountable for actions and results, successes and failures.
- Treat others fairly and with respect.
- Give clear, candid, and timely feedback.
- Manage conflicts constructively.
- Create value for all our stakeholders.

Integrity

- Be a role model and be honest and reliable.
- Comply with laws, regulations, and good business practice.
- Trust others and build trustful relationships.
- Listen attentively and communicate appropriately.
- Ensure sustainability: balance short-term results with long-term requirements.
- Care about people, safety, and the environment.

Flexibility

- Drive change actively.
- Be ready to adapt to future trends and needs.
- Challenge the status quo.
- Think and act with customers in mind.
- Seek out opportunities and take calculated risks.
- Be open-minded; embrace lifelong learning.

Efficiency

- Manage resources smartly.
- Focus on activities that create value.
- Do things simply and effectively.
- Deliver with appropriate costs, speed, and quality.
- Speed up good decision making and be accountable for consistent execution.
- Collaborate for better solutions.

Figure 13.2 (previous page)

CASE STUDY:
DR. GLENN FROMMER'S ENVIRONMENT AND
SUSTAINABILITY TEAM AT MTR CORPORATION

Strong Values Create Sustained Performance

MTR Corporation Limited (MTR) runs Hong Kong's metro and rail systems, with an average weekday patronage of more than 5.4 million passengers, and owns and manages many selected properties in conjunction with its railway stations. It is regarded as one of the world's leading railway operators for safety, reliability, customer service, and cost efficiency.[48]

They also protect the flora and fauna and ensured that environmental contractual specifications were implemented as specified. The nature of the work was both routine and ad hoc. In 21 years at MTR, Glenn undertook and implemented more than 28 environmental impact initiatives for railway projects consisting of hundreds of civil and electrical and mechanical contracts.

Glenn's team was almost entirely educated overseas in the disciplines of ecology, noise, air, water, and waste. The skill sets and centers of excellence at MTR mirrored the air, noise, water, and waste sections of Environmental Protection Department, while the ecology issues mirrored those of the Agricultures and Fisheries Conservation Department. This allowed a direct read across expertise and experience between individuals and groups as well as across projects. The total team size under Glenn was 57 staff members, with 7 to 8 of them attached to different divisions. He had a second-in-command who made most of the day-to-day reports.

Team values formed the underpinning of behavior. Glenn and core team members aligned on the team values to be exhibited in their daily work:

1. Environmental focus
2. Trust
3. Problem solving

4. Accuracy
5. Self-motivation
6. Dedication and commitment

Glenn displayed a unique team leadership style at MTR, which produced high camaraderie and loyalty. He served as a role model and allowed team members to learn from his experience and knowledge in the environmental and sustainable-development areas. One day a week, they all spent time together trading war stories and sharing. This was the opportunity for Glenn to be a mentor and coach. Ultimately, team members were proud to be a part of the team, with an ensuing strong sense of identity. These weekly sessions built a strong camaraderie in the team.

To build a sense of collaboration and communication, "centers of excellence" were set up, and those who were interested joined in. This provided a chance to educate themselves and each other. Glenn built a sense of transparency, in that everything was done as a team. People would see each other's reports. Members talked to each other a lot. Having access to reports meant that all were on the same page and feedback was shared. Glenn purposely allowed and encouraged disruptive elements into the teams, allowing team members who did not necessarily fit well together to work together. This seemingly unsettling action actually enhanced other members' transparency and made them more flexible and tolerant of others' views, encouraging them to ultimately take the "team view."

Glenn believed in catering to team needs to create fulfillment and exterior recognition and innovation. In one case, the "team's tree specialist" created a database program so that the public could log in and follow what was happening to the trees. This was of benefit to MTR and its image, as well as being a service to the community. In another case, he allowed space for a team member to set up an initiative for a web-based noise-monitoring and alarm system, using closed-circuit cameras that filmed project construction over time. This unique initiative won the company several awards for its innovative nature and assisted the supplier in developing a new business.

Glenn's brand of recognition was unique. He arranged work schedules based on the needs of the individual, making sure it met their personal and family needs. One of the ways Glenn showed personal care and concern about people was quite novel. He instituted a separate interview twice a year; this was a not performance review. He modeled the idea on the book, *Be Your Own Guru*. He would sit down with each staff member and ask them to grade themselves on where they were and where they wanted to be a year from then. If a team member was newly married, he would not keep them late at night. If money was an object, he would move them into the right positions within or outside of the corporation. The goal was to use the corporation's assets to provide benefits in lieu of cash rewards.

At the end of the day, there was a gentleman's agreement to help members achieve what they wanted in both work and life. Glenn used a "radar plot"[49] (figure 13.3) to get people to understand where they were and where more balance was needed.

Glenn also tried to shield team members from broader organizational challenges. He avoided the "blame culture" by focusing on the resolution of issues. Because this eliminated reproach for doing things differently, it thereby fostered a willingness to make a mistake. Furthermore, he would shield his team members from any criticism from above: team members always got the strokes and never the whip; for mistakes made in the department, Glenn personally took the blame. Whenever Glenn had the opportunity, he promoted the efforts of the team and gave credit to its members.

Over the years, Glenn built a highly successful team with strong support from the projects director, board, and chairman. This was evidenced by team achievements, including:

- Based on internal surveys, Glenn's team had one of the highest happiness indices in the projects division.
- Staff turnover was extremely low, holding at less than 1 percent per year for more than 20 years.

The sustainability projects and their success resulted in good press and goodwill throughout the community.

Radar Plot

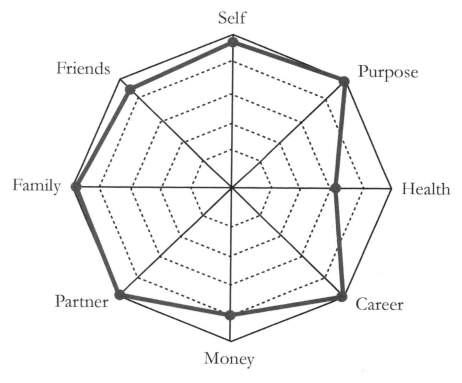

Figure 13.3

DR. GLENN FROMMER'S PHILOSOPHY
Building and Growing a High Performance Team[50]

- One person can't do it all, so you need a team.
- Employ the best people. Get out of their way and let them do their jobs.
- Recognize team members by scheduling flexible work agreements.
- Give the team space to innovate, make mistakes, and gain recognition both internally and externally.
- Foster a sense of transparency with lots of sharing, discussion, and feedback on projects.
- Show personal care and concern so that both life and work goals are being met.
- The leader should take any whipping from above—not the team.
- Be a mentor and coach and set fixed times for this purpose.
- Provide team members with an opportunity to grow through sponsoring pet projects.
- Make sure team members live the values of the team and absorb them as part of the culture.
- Family comes first.
- Make the work enjoyable and rewarding.

Figure 13.4

14

ELEMENT #4
RESULTS

THE PROOF IS IN THE PUDDING

Teams with a High-TQ focus on results. These are measurable and visible, and the main indicators of performance. In the world of free enterprise, results equal success. One leader who has mastered the art of incorporating results into his team's focus is Achal Agarwal, president, Asia Pacific Region, Kimberly-Clark.

CASE STUDY:
ACHAL AGARWAL AT KIMBERLY-CLARK
TEAM PRINCIPLES TO CREATE STELLAR RESULTS

Achal Agarwal is President of Kimberly-Clark's Asia Pacific Region. He has a reputation for delivering results and creating phenomenal teams. In his eight years in that role, his region has consistently delivered results and exceeded expectations. Asia Pacific is the largest revenue generator and the most profitable region in the International Division. It has also earned the "Wal-Mart Supplier of the Year" distinction in China four years in a row. The team is gaining market share and increasing revenues in all of their categories, and Kimberly-Clark is among the top consumer companies across the Asia Pacific Region (excluding Japan). Not surprisingly, turnover on his team is extremely low.

For Achal, the definition of a High Performance Team is simple: "It's all about results vs. the competition. Put up an aggressive Vision and move towards it with no excuses. Market share is key. As long as the team is gaining share, you are winners. It's not so much about hitting annual targets; rather the key is gaining share profitably and building a sustainable business. The defining feature is getting it done with no fuss."[51]

To realize this vision, you have to find phenomenal people and build a winning team. Achal's imperative is to get the right people on board quickly. His core principle is to empower his leaders, but he believes that you cannot empower the incapable. He doesn't want the pain of developing a relationship with leaders who are unable to perform. Achal assesses people very quickly, stating, "There are great guys, there are problem guys, and there are guys who will work."[52]

When Achal came into his position, he moved quickly and had a new team on board within a year. Despite his speed in hiring, when it comes to releasing people, he does so humanely and with dignity by helping them land on their feet elsewhere.

For Achal, his team is so important that he spends an inordinate amount of time on their career development, exploring and creating different assignments for his employees. His management principle is, "Make everyone's dreams come true" by helping people reach their full potential. He says to his team members: "Tell me what job you want, and I will find it for you." He recruits the best people, and one of the first things he asks of them is, "What do you want out of life ten years from now?" Achal adds, "If you deliver for me, you will be in the job of your choice within two years." He also creates roles with a view to nurturing the right talent.

For example, he created a strategy function that reported to him with an objective of elevating the successful individual to a new general manager function. Someone from his corporate strategy team aspired to earn that role. In less than two years, Achal supported him in assuming a general manager role in Europe. Now that individual occupies a key role for Kimberly-Clark in the United States. Achal subsequently took another individual from the corporate strategy group as a replacement and soon made him a managing director of a country in the Asia Pacific Region. In another case, he recruited an outside consultant who became managing director in another country while another individual is being groomed for that role. That strategy role that Achal created in 2008 when he joined Kimberly-Clark has since yielded three managing directors who have performed very well.

Achal likes to pluck people from consulting firms and train them to become managing directors because they provide some diversity of experience to an operating team. He can give them a well-rounded experience and turn them into operational guys.

But he obviously doesn't only recruit consultants. In one instance, he hired an executive from Unilever and assigned him to a regional marketing role. The individual was keen to become a general manager, and Achal supported his development. Now he is general manager of a big business in the company's North America operations. As a result of this track record, Kimberly-Clark Asia has developed a strong employer brand and is able to attract the best talent.

Achal believes in developing local talent in the Asia Pacific Region. He emphasizes having local leadership, and not just in line functions. Kimberly-Clark is one of the only multinational companies that employs a 100 percent local leadership team in China. Moreover, Asia Pacific has been a net exporter of talent.

The defining feature of Achal's management style is the level of empowerment he gives his employees who are all highly capable people. One of his managers exclaimed, "I wouldn't contemplate leaving; you have given me such freedom." In the end, Achal is proud of his people-development strategy, claiming, "We make lives; not a single person will

"Use your power for the development of your people and team."

lose in their development, and we don't lose them. You need to use your power for the development of your people and team. It's such a pleasure to see them progress."

Building a Winning Team Culture Focused on Results

Once team members are on board, they need to acclimate to the very distinct team culture. They must adapt fast or leave. Achal subscribes to several team operating principles, which are essential to success.

Results are measured against the competition, and decisions are consumer centric. As a consumer products company, Kimberly-Clark must have a consumer-centric culture. Achal believes that the interests of the consumer should be the determining factor in making decisions. Key considerations are: Will the consumer benefit? Will the consumer notice? Will the product gain share? Will it build our brand? Will we progress versus the competition?

Leaders are empowered to run their businesses. Team members need to learn to think quickly and act and decide independently. Once they have demonstrated this capability, Achal will get out of their way and trust them to run their businesses. He doesn't want information for information's sake, only on a need-to-know basis. He is happy to sit on the sidelines and let them perform while actively supporting them where necessary. Achal prefers that they not just sit comfortably in the regional office; they need to be actively engaged in creating results. His team members have maximum flexibility and manage their time as they wish. Yet this hands-off approach doesn't mean abnegating his leadership role; Achal gives his team members immediate and constant feedback so that they can glean fresh perspectives on how to achieve even better results.

Simplicity, speed, and relevance. Achal is hell bent on destroying the bureaucracy and time wasters who get in the way of creating results. There are very few formal meetings, and in principle, most meetings do not last more than an hour. He usually calls for small meetings and only engages the relevant members of the team. He makes sure that all discussions are relevant and doesn't bring up unnecessary topics. The ultimate test is the relevance to the market and the consumer. Achal asserts, "Keep it simple and don't overcomplicate it. Focus on the big things and add value based on consumer needs."

The two-conversation rule. When Achal learns of, say, a market issue, he might contact the pertinent country managing director for his perspective, then speak with the relevant functional head. He will get the whole story from both sides and then resolve it fast. The rule is to have no more than two conversations to make a decision. The same goes for all management levels; everyone is expected to resolve issues within two interactions. It forces speed, breaks down hierarchy, and puts a premium on cooperating to make the right decision. As a result, no one would be caught dead discussing issues ad nauseam. Arguing for the sake of protecting one's position is discouraged.

Encourage disagreement. Most leaders don't like conflict in their teams, which can cause decisions to gravitate to the lowest common denominator and produce average decisions and results. Achal encourages disagreement and debate, positing, "Dissent is healthy. In this age of compliance, transparency is key. I am completely transparent in my dissent. One of the roles of a leader is to create a new campaign with accompanying slogan and philosophy when necessary. One that I created was 'dissent transparently.'" He will employ a new philosophy when fighting something dangerous. For example, at one point he was concerned with cost cutting and eliminating products with the objective of standardization. But this came at the expense of innovation and market focus. He countered that with the new philosophy: "Winning products in every geography," which implied that standardization is great, but having the right products in the right geography is more important.

> Team leaders not only empower—they also play the all-important role of connector.

The role of the leader is connectivity. Team leaders not only empower people but they play the all-important role of connector.

> "I only want good human beings on my team who care about each other, the environment, and doing the right thing."

They are the glue that brings team members together to focus on the right agenda and make key decisions. They also connect talent with other parts of the organization to move things along.

I asked Achal what he is most proud of with regards to his leadership team. He states, "It's the quality of team and culture that has been created. I only want good human beings on my team who care about each other, the environment, and doing the right thing. We have been able to build a culture that delivers results and beats the competition. We have a High Performance Team with good values."

Achal confides that his unique philosophy only works with the right leadership, and some have asked him "What will happen when you leave?" His response is simple: "The most important thing I can leave behind is a phenomenal team and a great business."

THE TEAM SUCCESS IMPERATIVE

We can only succeed as a team by defining success. *Success* is more than just goals or KPIs; it's a robust view of all the important aspects of our team and business. Ultimately, we are not here just to realize a goal or a vision, or hit a number. We are also here because we want to succeed both as a team and individually, which may in some small or large way contribute to overall company success. Therefore, as a High Performance Team, we need to look at results holistically as part of being successful.

Hervé Gisserot, general Manager of GSK China, and I were having a conversation on results and success. I asked him, "Is it possible to reach all your key performance indicators and *not* be successful as a High Performance Team?" After some discussion, he concluded that, "You may hit all your numbers, but that doesn't mean you are completely successful." Success is more than reaching

KPIs; success is essentially whatever, we, as a team, decide it is. As a leader, you need to come to terms with this point. For example, if you hit your KPIs this year, ask yourself these questions:

- Is this performance sustainable: Will the team be able to do this consistently?
- What if you hit your numbers but morale is low?
- What if your team members are burned out and leave?
- What if the pressure on numbers leads to major conflicts?

Numbers are only one indicator of success. Defining success deserves some time and energy.

HOW TO DEFINE SUCCESS

One of my clients in the transportation business came to the realization that something was missing in the leadership team. The management team realized that they hadn't defined what success meant for them. In other words, how do you know if you are

> To know if our team is succeeding, we first have to define success.

successful if you haven't figured out what success is. As the famous baseball player Yogi Berra said, "If you don't know where you are going, you might wind up someplace else."[53]

This team decided it was time to define success. They asked themselves: "What does success look like for us as a team?" Together we came up with the following to examine and consider:

1. What are the elements of success we need to consider and define? (e.g., our team/people/stakeholders/internal and external customers)
2. How would you describe a successful team?
   - What does a successful team do well?
   - What does it feel like to be on a successful team?
3. How do we know we are successful?
   - Achieve internal validation within leadership team?
   - Obtain external validation outside of leadership team?

4. Why is it critical to be a successful team?
   - What happens if we are not successful?
   - What are the payoffs for being successful?
5. How do we measure success?
   - What are the tangible measurements across all areas?
   - What are the intangible measurements across all areas?

One company created the following definition of success:

Defining Success for Our Leadership Team

Our successful leadership team clearly understands roles.
We are supportive, with clarity of outcomes.
We realign quickly as required within a team context.
Being part of a successful team provides a sense of belief
and achievement, leading to motivation and energy.

We know we are successful internally and
externally by delivery to promise.
We thereby experience a sense of achievement,
feeling empowered with a clear direction.

The payoffs of our successful team are:
People: feeling motivated
Customers: strong delivery
Consequences: reward and recognition

Once the team has gotten some traction on the vision/values/ trust building, it's time to examine the definition of success. This can take two to three hours of focused discussion and brainstorming, again usually in an off-site environment. Teams find it rewarding to get clarity on how they define success.

MEASURING SUCCESS

The concept of measuring everything has become a core management practice for many companies. Wal-Mart, for example, measures everything. As the vice president of sales with PepsiCo, I called on Wal-Mart regionally at least once a year. In meetings, they would bring reams of information about our product and their performance. For any given product, they would share with us sales, facings, profit margin, inventory turns, pricing, promotion—the list goes on and on. All this information was very useful in optimizing our product performance. In their outlets, they knew even more about our in-store product performance than we did! Some may consider it overkill, yet I learned a lot from this experience. The discipline of measuring creates focus, clarity, and action, and ultimately translates into a stronger likelihood of success.

> As a team, once we have clearly defined our success formula, we need to measure it.

As a team, once we have clearly defined our success formula; we need to measure its outcome. Most teams and companies will use some form of KPIs to evaluate their work internally. Here we will include some of the critical KPIs that get reported to upper management; however we will also include other measurements that are essential for team health and lead to a higher TQ.

Below is a sample team dashboard that we created at my company, Focus One, which we share with clients who want to measure team performance. It looks at the factors related to the definition of success. It highlights the importance of the non-KPI factors. Note that some of them are qualitative and require a judgment call.

In the figure that follows, you will see that the team decided to measure three areas:

1. **Key performance indicators.** This happens to be a business unit team, so typical KPIs of sales, Earnings before Income Taxes EBIT, market share, staff retention, outlet penetration, are measured and updated. On the left side is the actual

performance for the period, and on the right is the percentage vs. target for the period.

2. **Initiatives.** These are key projects or initiatives that are critical for team success. They happen to be measured by level of completion, with a name for the "champion" indicated as well as the target date of completion.

3. **Team culture.** This team wanted to measure other factors under the category of "Team Culture." Each member scores him- or herself for collaboration both individually as well as relative to the team. For example, let's say "Jane" rated her own collaboration level as a 6 and her overall observation of the team collaboration level as an 8. The average score submitted by Jane would be 7. Each team member provides the same set of scores, which are summarized with the resulting average put on the chart Any factor could be measured, but this team wanted to measure six items: collaboration, camaraderie, energy, values, meetings, and communication. Note that comments regarding team culture are also submitted, using both "kudos" (done well) and "cultivate" (improve).

Figure 14.1 is just a sample dashboard, and teams can define any measures and formats they wish.

I find it best to review the team dashboard monthly. During the monthly meeting, a short discussion can be held regarding which reports on what factor is working and what is not working, whether there are any "showstoppers" or major hurdles, and what it will take for continuous improvement. The key function of the dashboard is not just to "report" but also to use the information as a platform for meaningful discussions.

For example, if the team is measuring values, it could review each of the values and the mantra to confirm how they are being lived and integrated into the immediate and larger team. The function of the team leader or facilitator would be to sense the overall progress on values, as well as seek individual comments and material to share on the topic.

Teams can get into ruts. Sometimes these are energy ruts in

which everyone is running around, busy and stressed, and they forget about having fun and keeping a positive energy—a value to which they committed. Review of the dashboard and discussions can uncover these types of obstacles and help the team address them. The remedy can be a brief activity to shift the energy and move through the obstacle.

The major concern is team members reverting to habitual patterns of behavior. As people are creatures of habits, it may take a sustained period to establish firmly the desired team habits. One of the

> Be on the lookout for team members reverting to habitual patterns of behavior.

principle challenges to resist is the reversion to the "silo mentality." Encouraging team members to consider the team as important as the individual is a critical part of TQ. Team members are constantly moving back and forth along the self/team continuum. The key is getting people to skew habitually toward the team. One effective way is to reinforce aligned team behavior. When team members show up in the best interests of the team, they should be recognized.

TEAM DASHBOARD

KEY PERFORMANCE INDICATORS

SALES	EBIT	RETENTION	MARKET SHARE	PENETRATION
112m 95%	12m 110%	95% 105%	22% 100%	72,000 98%

INITIATIVES

% COMPLETED	ALPHA	MINA	KONA	REBECCA	OPEX
TARGET DATE / CHAMPION	JUL 1 JERRY	AUG 31 MINA	JUNE 20 ARNOLD	DEC 12 REBECCA	NOV 30 NATASHA

TEAM CULTURE

COLLABORATION

KUDOS
-
-
-

CULTIVATE
-
-
-

ENERGY

KUDOS
-
-
-

CULTIVATE
-
-
-

MEETINGS

KUDOS
-
-
-

CULTIVATE
-
-
-

VALUES

KUDOS
-
-
-

CULTIVATE
-
-
-

CAMARADERIE

KUDOS
-
-
-

CULTIVATE
-
-
-

COMMUNICATION

KUDOS
-
-
-

CULTIVATE
-
-
-

Figure 14.1

OWNERSHIP AND SUPPORT

At the end of the day, a team can be called High Performance only if it consistently creates the success it defined. The High Performance Team knows that the synergy of the team will be a major factor in realizing the success it wants. Mutual support, collaboration, and ownership are keys to that end.

Ultimately, all team members need to feel ownership of the team's goals because they affect the entire team. Therefore, the concept that "Ownership of the goal lies beyond individual responsibility of the goal" needs to be understood and embraced. The implication is that mutual support kicks in where necessary.

A just functioning or dysfunctional team often views ownership this way: "Joe is not reaching his goal; he will sink or swim accordingly. It will only reflect on his performance."

The High Performance Team looks at it still differently: "Joe is not reaching his goal. We are committed to supporting both Joe's success and helping the team reach its goal. Moreover, Joe's inability to reach his goal will reflect poorly on the team."

The major difference lies in *support*. As team members, we are there not only to deliver on our own goals but also to support other members because we know how important it is for the team. Note that this is not based on altruism; it's based on a clear understanding of the definition of success for the team. If some members are not reaching their goals, the team may not be successful. Again, a sports example is apt. If a key player excels in a particular skill but is weak in another area, we don't trash the player; we *coach* the player to success.

One recent example is NFL quarterback Marcus Mariota, 2014 Heisman Trophy winner.

Lessons from an NFL Quarterback

Mariota played college football for the Oregon Ducks in the hurry-up/no-huddle offense, which differs from the professional, NFL approach of huddling and operating from the pocket. The pundits say that he needed time to convert from college to the pro approach. It's a matter of transition and learning the new system. It's also a matter of coaching. Ultimately Mariota has made the transition well, leading his team, the Tennessee Titans to the division championship round in 2018.

We expect our executives to be highly proficient once they reach the leadership-team level. Just as with Marcus Mariota, however, they need support and coaching to help them adapt to a new environment. The High Performance Team recognizes this and provides support, or helps get support, if required.

TEAM INITIATIVES

A results focus goes beyond KPIs or individual goals. Results from team initiatives form an important part of the team's raison d'être. As distinct from critical individual goals where the individual is responsible for achieving the goal with team support, team initiatives are those that cut across the team and usually don't reside in any one functional area. As team leader, it's important to identify team initiatives where team members can be involved in creating success. These initiatives become critical to engage the team on substantive work at a team or sub-team level.

Examples of team initiatives that I have seen include:
- developing compensation and talent programs
- integrating values into the organization
- ensuring that the vision is well integrated
- arriving at ways to measure and monitor team success
- examining industry game changers in the future
- pursuing potential synergies across business units
- establishing plans or challenges with external stakeholders
- leveraging core competencies to create new business opportunities
- creating meeting formats for the leadership team

The most effective way I have found to accomplish this is by creating initiative teams. Each initiative team will have a "champion" who is responsible for keeping the team on track. Champions are usually those who have more vested interest or passion in the initiative; other team members will also be assigned to work on the initiative. The initiative team needs to obtain clarity on its charter and deliverables, and do what's necessary to make it happen, occasionally bringing in other members who are not in the leadership team.

To work effectively on initiative teams, members must learn some essentials of collaboration. Collaboration is a skill that is not always easily understood or achieved. Team members need to learn to reach out beyond their own areas of responsibility to support larger initiatives. It requires a mindset that "I will support others even though there is no personal benefit or recognition."

> Team initiatives are a powerful way to create engagement and collaboration within the leadership team.

Ultimately, team initiatives are a powerful way to create engagement within the leadership team and to leverage the brainpower of the team members.

15

ELEMENT #5
EFFECTIVENESS

Lessons from a French Luxury Brand

My client Pierre was the head of the leadership team for a French luxury brand,. He had a great leadership team. They worked hard and played hard. They drank the best French wines together and, after their monthly leadership-team meetings would dine at restaurants that were gastronomic delights. The team enjoyed lots of friendly banter and got along well. Team members had mutual respect for the enormous talent on the team.

By all accounts, a High Performance Team? Think again. Pierre confessed that despite the stimulating team ambiance, they were ineffective. During their monthly meetings, presentations and discussions would drone on, and often important decisions were hastily made at the end of meetings. I sat in on one of their meetings and found Pierre was right; there was a lack of structure, and although the team felt good together, the lengthy discussion around topics meant the agenda was never more than half covered.

With Pierre's team we had a singular focus; institute-effective meetings and decision-making practices. We reviewed and committed to meeting practices that you will find in this chapter. That was all it took. The team started plowing through the entire agenda and made informed decisions.

The lesson here is that High Team Quotient is much more than team ambiance, relationships, and camaraderie. The team needs to be effective. *Effectiveness includes the way the team conducts meetings, communicates, collaborates, and chooses its focus—in short, how the team spends its time.* In essence, team effectiveness concerns *how the team will structure the success it desires.*

EIGHT TIPS FOR EFFECTIVE TEAM MEETINGS

Surveys have shown that more than half of all meetings are viewed as a waste of time. Many people complain that meetings last too long and are poorly organized. All of us have experienced lame meetings and may have come to assume that they are the norm. When meetings waste time or are poorly run, do people speak up? Rarely; instead they grin and bear it and pretend to be engaged.

Most people (myself included) have coping mechanisms to put up with half-baked meetings. Some of the most common are: reading emails, texting, working on the computer, or playing with devices. Some people doodle, and others have side conversations during the meeting. How do you cope with ineffective meetings?

Given that over 80 percent of the full team's interaction takes place during meetings, it's imperative to get them right to be effective

> It's imperative to get meetings right to be an effective and High Performance Team.

as a High Performance Team. I never understood how, as smart and brilliant as many leaders are, they rarely get meeting effectiveness right.

A leadership team spends most of its time together in the meeting environment. High Performance Teams treat meetings as a precious investment of time and energy.

There is no single "right way" to run a meeting, but a few guidelines can go a long way toward achieving success.

1. Preparation

Creating and focusing on the right agenda is fundamental. Sending the agenda out in advance is important so people can come prepared to the meeting. Otherwise, members will show up not knowing the specific areas for discussion.

Many fine teams realize that pre-reading is a very efficient way to make meetings more effective. How many presentations have you attended where lots of background information is presented that is not germane to making the decisions at hand? If team members send out key materials for pre-reading in advance, that information doesn't need to be presented during the meeting. Discussions can focus on the important areas that need consideration as a team as opposed to being an information dump. Instilling the discipline of pre-reading sounds perfunctory but it can save lots of time and frustration.

The other part of preparation is asking team members to *prepare* and *be ready to discuss certain topics.* The outdated way of conducting meetings involved presenting all the information and having team members passively listen and comment. A more efficient way is to ask team members to pre-read and "Be prepared to discuss." Sometimes it's just a matter of getting participants to spend some thinking time in advance.

The preparation part of effective meetings can be tedious and is not always high on people's priority list, yet preparation leads to more effective meetings, allowing participants to focus on discussing key issues and making decisions as opposed to reporting and informing.

2. Agenda

Stepping back, what are the right agenda items to focus on? Much meeting time consists of reporting on results. While some reporting is necessary, much of it can be emailed or communicated outside of the meeting environment. In your leadership-team meetings, you've got all the brains of the team in one place. Are you truly involving them and unleashing their creative potential, or are you underutilizing your resources?

When considering regular weekly, monthly, or quarterly meetings, structure is crucial. I like to think of meeting agendas as covering the following areas:

a. *Important issues driving of the success of the business:* This refers to the WIG concept and may involve brainstorming, planning, reviewing and reporting on status or results.

b. *Decisions that require group discussion:* Decision making plays an important role in the leadership team, and it is best to focus in meetings on those areas that affect most team members and where discussion is required. If it involves one or two people, the topic can be handled separately. What are the major issues or challenges facing the team that require decisions by the team?

c. *Information and reporting:* If it's a functional or regional issue that affects only a few people, why spend team time on it? Focus on the important matters, such as key initiatives, projects, KPIs, policies, and trends. Most teams spend more than half their time reporting and updating. With pre-reads, preparation, and discipline, much of this can be avoided.

d. *TQ areas:* This refers to keeping the keeping the team focused on those areas that will drive a High Performance Team. This may be the TQ dashboard items, team governance areas and team initiatives, sharing, and icebreakers. It's an opportunity to reflect, correct, and commit.

MEETING FOCUS	TIME SPENT BY MOST LEADERSHIP TEAMS	TIME SPENT BY BEST-PRACTICE LEADERSHIP TEAMS
Decisions	10%	40%
Important issues	20%	30%
Information/ reporting	70%	20%
TQ— Team Quotient	Negligible	10%

Figure 15.2

If you revise the content of your meetings to focus on important issues that contribute to success, people will be much more engaged and involved. You can expect them to contribute more and show up prepared and ready to engage.

3. Sharing Lessons, Thoughts, and Wisdom

Most meetings launch right into the presentations without stepping back to reflect. Of course, everyone is busy, and the agenda is packed. How can we find time for anything else? Yet if you structure your content as mentioned above, you will have time to address more than the basic content.

There are many ways to share important information in team meetings, and you can come up with your own. Consider the following thoughts and questions as a way to approach sharing:

- Success and failures: Have executives share one success and one failure and what they learned.
- What lessons were learned over the past week or month?
- What has been done to enhance contribution to the leadership team?
- What has each team member learned about being a better executive?
- What have they needed to discontinue or to let go of?

- You might consider allocating one minute per person at the beginning of the meeting for sharing. This way there will be no long-winded monologues, and you'll only be investing only 10 to 15 minutes in "TQ areas." You'll be surprised how this little change brings the group closer together and creates mutual inspiration and learning. Try it and see what happens.

4. Meeting Logistics

An often-overlooked area that is critical to a meeting's success relates to how you organize and control the meeting. For each meeting, try appointing different individuals to take on the following roles:

a. *Scribe:* The scribe's role is to take notes and circulate them. The scribe's role is to highlight decisions made and actions planned.

b. *Timekeeper:* Keeping meetings on track is a perennial issue, and the timekeeper's role is to alert the group when a discussion has gone on for too long. This implies that the agenda has allotted time for each topic. One less intrusive way to do this is to hold up a note when five minutes remain and then again when time is up.

c. *"Rabbit Hole" Watcher:* Often, discussions get off track or get lost in an endless rabbit hole of details. When this happens, the person in charge of watching out for the rabbit hole needs to call out "Rabbit hole!" and get the group back on track.

d. *Facilitator:* This is the person in charge of the overall meeting, which may or may not be the team leader. The facilitator moves the meeting from topic to topic, introduces agenda item, and lets people know that it's time to move on to another subject.

e. *Observer:* The observer maintains overall meeting discipline and plays a key role in helping the team reflect. He or she will observe how often team members are recognizing each other and celebrating success, and to what extent people are showing up and contributing. Some observers are quite active and even give a short summary at the end of the meeting.

In essence, the observer also plays the role of the meeting coach. Documenting and tracking progress is also valuable.

You'll be surprised how effective and efficient your meetings will become when participants have clearly assigned roles. After getting used to them, you will wonder how you ever did without them.

5. Presentations

Meetings often involve some type of presentation. In fact, presentations consume a lot of time, and team members may experience "PowerPoint fatigue." Some standards and guidelines are necessary to ensure that presentations are a means to an end and not an end it itself. What is the purpose of the presentation? Presentations are best used to inform, drive decisions, and gain support. Beware that the sub-agenda for many presentations is often to impress. While I won't discuss presentation skills here, keep the following in mind:

   a. *Purpose of the presentation:* Too many presentations have no clear purpose.

   b. *Main messages and decisions:* The presenter needs to be clear on this. Research has shown that people remember only three things from a presentation. What are the three messages that you want people to remember?

   c. *Showing only what needs to be shown:* Showing anything more than what is necessary is a distraction and a waste of time. Too many facts and figures will lose the audience or force the meeting down a rabbit hole. Standardization of format may be helpful.

   d. *Keep to the timetable:* Enforcing this discipline will keep the meeting on track.

6. Participation

Participation takes two forms. The first requires that everyone attends the regular meetings. This is a non-negotiable and should be kept that way except in extenuating circumstances.

The second form of participation is who "shows up" in the meeting discussions. Based on my observations of many teams, most talking is done by 30 to 40 percent of the team members. If a team consists of 12 members, 4 or 5 of them will do most of the talking. Those talkative ones tend to dominate the meeting. Another 40 to 50 percent of attendees contribute sometimes, usually only when something concerns them. Finally, the remaining 10 to 20 percent rarely say much. They speak only if they are called on or if they need to discuss something related to their area.

Lessons from GSK China

Hervey Gisserot, general manager of GSK China, was highly engaged in meetings and tended to weigh in on every subject during his monthly team meetings. While the team appreciated his passion and interest, it had the effect of muting of the quieter team members. After receiving feedback on his style in meetings, he realized that a change was necessary. He established a goal of listening first and speaking second. After he made this change, he asked the meeting observer, at the end of every meeting, to comment on his progress, so that he could learn and self-correct.

> It's important to set the team expectation that you want everyone to participate in meetings.

The phenomenon of having both more and less participative members in a team is inescapable. What can and needs to change are the participation percentages. I often point this out when I observe teams. Many of them "get it," and work hard on it, and I have witnessed teams improve to the point that 50 to 60 percent of team members are participating actively. I am equally pleased to witness the percentage of quiet ones dwindles to fewer than 10 percent. This shift in participation will completely change the dynamic of the team interaction and result in much more lively and robust discussions. It will force team members to show up, have a point of view, and stand up for what is important to them. It will also mitigate the dominance of those talkative members. As a leader, you will find that this change will make your meetings much livelier and encourage a more robust input into key decisions.

The ways to do this are manifold. First, it's important, as a team, to set the expectation that everyone participates. Second, the leader, coach, or mentor can have one-on-one conversations with the quieter team members to understand their challenges. They will appreciate it, and it will create stronger expectations and help them break through their barriers.

7. Humor

Some may find it odd that I mention humor in the context of meetings. This refers to the concept of keeping "good humor" during the meeting and making it a positive experience. Too often, meetings are so serious that people dread them. To interject some positivity into your meetings, consider the following:

a. *Tone:* I worked with a pharmaceutical leadership team that had significant regulatory challenges. These meetings were somber, and the participants were quite hard on themselves. It's almost as if they didn't feel they deserved to be positive. Three months after I pointed this out, I returned to observe the team. The tone had changed dramatically, and the meeting now included some levity and laughter. While the issues were just as serious as before, the team was no longer letting that affect the mood.

b. *Fun:* Yes, meetings can be fun, especially if you interject some icebreakers. Part of the function of icebreakers—short, sometimes silly, activities—is to create physical movement and activate the "right brain." Injecting some fun into your meetings unleashes creativity and refreshes the team.

c. *Celebration and recognition:* The practice of including some celebration and moments of recognition is useful when working on team identity and building camaraderie and relationships. While some people may think that celebration and recognition are organized affairs and only done on designated occasions, successful teams find that the practice is part of creating good humor during meetings.

Recognition can be done frequently, as a habit, simply by referring to what has been presented or mentioned. It's part of changing how thoughts are expressed. For example, instead of directly injecting a point as most people do, you might first say, "You made a clear point about . . . ", "That's a good idea . . .", "I liked what Jane said about . . .", "John correctly referenced . . ." or "While you provided some good analysis about X, I have a different view about . . .". Even when you disagree, you may be able to say it in a way that recognizes what or how another team member has communicated it, keeping the ambiance of good humor.

> Philip, a general manager managing a large leadership team employs an effective way of recognizing team members' participation. Every time someone makes a presentation, he critiques it and gives his view on its analysis and points made. His feedback is balanced, containing areas for improvement, and always includes a positive statement about the presenter or presentation. Philip is often prescriptive, stating what the person might consider next time. The mere fact that he is constantly commenting is recognition in and of itself.

Celebration can also be brought into the meeting environment. Sometimes, a round of applause for success achieved is a form of celebration. By finding ways to celebrate, the team increases its sense of self-esteem and identity. Some teams will celebrate a particular milestone at the end of a meeting with champagne or wine, making it a festive occasion.

If the team consistently incorporates celebration and recognition into meetings, it will positively transform the team, which will realize more and more success. Over time, the team will start to recognize itself as a successful and winning team with a High TQ!

8. Non-business activity—energizers, challenges, icebreakers, and movement

Part of the task of building a High Performance Team focuses on building deeper trust and relationships, yet these things typically get relegated to cocktail parties, dinners, and off-sites. Building in a little time for non-business activities adds spice, fun, and energy to the team. The non-business activity can be almost anything, but it's useful to include some type of physical movement that both energizes participants and preserves mental energy.

Meetings can be very stressful and engage all of our higher-level thinking. Participants need an opportunity to relax. Only about 10 minutes per meeting is required. A good time for this activity is after the break or at the beginning. One popular idea for incorporating icebreakers and short activities into meetings is to have everyone be responsible for a new activity at each meeting, thereby rotating responsibility and getting more engagement. You'll be surprised how much energy people put into something when it's '"their activity."

> The leader of one of my pharmaceutical clients does just this. She tasks each team member to come up with and lead a different icebreaker in each meeting. She commented that "this shifted the whole atmosphere and allowed us to keep positive momentum".

Some High Performance Teams choose to end every meeting with a social get-together, such as drinks before dinner. It's a good way to unwind and discuss issues informally.

Getting meetings right is a must for High Performance Teams. The leader needs to be willing to spend time on meeting effectiveness and get all team members involved.

MAKING BETTER TEAM DECISIONS

One of the key functions of the leader and team is decision making. Nothing impacts team success more than making the right decisions, yet leaders tend to spend very little time thinking about the decision-making process and methodology.

At my company, Focus One, we developed a team decision-making matrix to highlight different types of decisions and approaches for dealing with them. On the x-axis is the *complexity* of the issue, and on the y-axis lies the issue's *importance* to the team.

Team Desicion Making Matrix

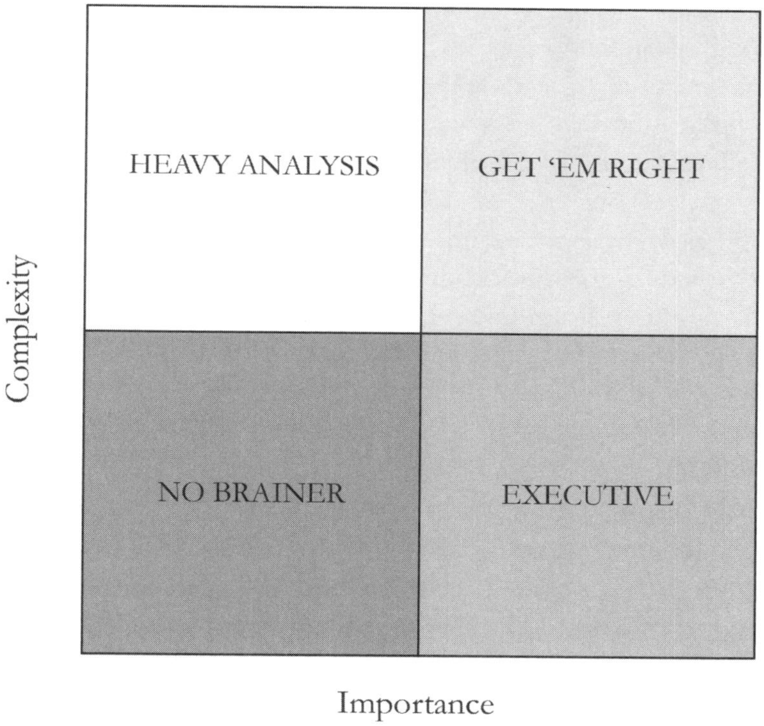

Figure 15.3

Complexity refers to how complicated the decision is. To make that decision, what degree of analysis is required? How much information is needed?

Importance also refers to the significance of the decision to concerned stakeholders. Deciding on an issue's importance may include considerations such as the ability to meet KPIs, number of people impacted, resources required, capital needed, markets

Nothing impacts team success more than making right decisions.

affected, supply chain requirements, business model modification, changes in strategy, rethinking of the vision, government involvement, number of customers, and others.

Get 'Em Right

High Complexity/High Importance decisions require significant analysis, potentially number crunching, and the time to conduct a thorough examination of the issues. Some decision-making tools, such as root-cause analysis or decision trees, may be useful. Implications may be significant to certain stakeholders; therefore the entire team as well as the key stakeholders typically need to be involved. These types of decisions are best debated in some detail and often require significant analysis based on reliable data. Examples include

- major employee programs and organizational changes
- significant strategy initiatives
- major capital expenditures
- new-product launches.

Executive

Low Complexity/High Importance decisions have significant impact on stakeholders though these decisions are relatively straightforward and don't require much data or analysis. Executive decisions can be made somewhat quickly, but stakeholders and the team need to be informed or involved in the decision, as the case may be. Examples include

- hiring/firing key executives
- key communication to staff and customers
- certain KPIs
- building customer relations.

Heavy Analysis

High Complexity/Low Importance decisions still require significant analysis and may need a lot of information. It may take some time to make these types of decisions, and they are usually not high on management's radar screen. The leader can make these decisions or delegate them to team members with particular expertise or interest. These decisions don't necessarily need to involve all team members. Examples include

- some IT programs
- certain supply chain or logistics decisions

- product launch planning
- some engineering projects.

No Brainers

Low Complexity/Low Importance decisions don't require much time or analysis. Leaders can make these decisions quickly or delegate them to team members. The entire team does not necessarily need to be involved. Examples include

- meeting attendees
- simple procurement
- staff hiring/firing
- overtime policy.

How does a High Performance Team handle these types of decisions?

DECISION TYPE	DECIDED BY	TEAM INVOLVEMENT
GET 'EM RIGHT	Team, with final say by leader	Extensive, with possible sub-groups for analysis
EXECUTIVE	Leader, with input from team	Endorsement with discussion, as necessary
HEAVY ANALYSIS	Key team members	Being informed prior to final decision
NO BRAINER	Key team members	Being informed

Figure 15.4

The guidelines in Figure 15.4 ensure that the team avoids 'rabbit holes' around decision making. How many times has the team gotten caught debating Heavy Analysis or No Brainer-decisions when it has not been necessary? The team needs to achieve clarity to the extent it gets involved with different kinds of decisions. Labeling decisions according to the matrix and keeping the decision making in perspective will save time and greatly improve effectiveness.

One leader who builds very effective teams is Penny Wan, from Amgen. I interviewed Penny and uncovered her secrets for leading effective teams.

CASE STUDY:
PENNY WAN
LEADING EFFECTIVE TEAMS AT AMGEN

Penny Wan is the vice president and regional general manager of Amgen's Japan and Asia Pacific (JAPAC) Region. She has led executive teams in the health and pharmaceutical field for more than 20 years. Amgen is one of the world's leading biopharmaceutical companies.

Penny believes that a key element of success is team composition, and her top priority upon joining the company in July 2014 was assembling her new regional team. Over the past three years, Penny and her team recognized that team dynamics is an evolving process and a journey.

She believes that the starting point for an organization that wants to realize its full potential is the management team. The seven principles below outline her philosophy and approach to building effective management teams.

1. Choose your team wisely, based strongly on members' own aspirations and values. The values of team members are key, and they need to be aligned with Amgen's fundamental mission of serving patients by delivering medicines to treat serious, unmet medical needs. In hiring team members, Penny expends a lot of energy looking beyond functional expertise. When she searches for candidates, she wants to know what each candidate is passionate about, and how he or she intends to make a difference. Ultimately, Penny built a team that was committed to making a positive impact in science for patients. Not surprisingly, team members score highly on compassion and willingness to help. They have a strong sense of ownership and jointly

> When searching for candidates, Penny wants to know what each candidate is passionate about, and how he or she intends to make a difference.

identify team goals and strategies that they are excited to pursue and achieve. They are a very competitive team and want to triumph across all fronts. In the end, Penny has carefully assembled an aligned team that is highly motivated to work together to deliver for patients in the JAPAC region.

2. Pick a diverse team that is willing to debate divergent views. For Penny, diversity goes beyond ethnicity and gender. It also includes diversity in styles, approaches, backgrounds, experience, age, and perspectives. The team shares profiles among its members to build awareness of other team members and an appreciation of their diversity. It is a deliberate process to invest in understanding where the members can truly work as a team and not just as a group. The diverse team, can by its nature, bring in different points of view and perspectives. While Penny acknowledges that it has been a process, she states, "The team has gotten to a place where it is fully comfortable taking on controversial topics, arguing, and coming to an agreement. It is not necessary to get consensus. If they agree too quickly, then someone will push in another direction to posit the opposite view. It's the definition of a great team."

3. Pay attention to meeting management and mix it up. Penny's core leadership team consists of nine members. They meet for two hours every week. The larger, cross-functional team consists of 18 members and meets monthly. Penny made an early decision to work through a smaller team that could drive a more agile and effective decision-making process focused on the key roles, while also keeping a broader committee structure to cascade important information and operationalize key decisions.

> It's clear within the leadership team that unless team members collaborate well, they cannot deliver.

4. Ensure open feedback to encourage engagement and trust. To encourage debate, the team needs the trust to speak openly while maintaining a level of comfort that "they are all in it together." When bringing in a new member, the team will initially focus on ensuring that the new person can engage with the rest of the team without fear. For those reticent individuals, it's about feedback and getting more engagement. Penny cites as an example, "You might get an expert, functional leader who is disciplined and good at his work, such as the supply chain, juxtaposed against a marketing team member who is more creative and flexible thinking. Initially, the supply chain person may feel stretched, and the marketing person may feel constrained. This is where open communication and feedback comes in. To understand, accept, and appreciate each other, team members must get used to constant feedback, building awareness about themselves and others." Thus, feedback is an invaluable tool that facilitates open sharing with the team and leads to functioning as a High Performance Team. At the end of the day, Penny's process fosters the ability to engage in direct and frank conversations within the team, which truly helps team effectiveness.

5. Showing up with the right behaviors and collaborating is essential. For Penny, aligning around what is important to the team and how it should operate and work together is fundamental. Implicit in that are the behaviors of the team members. While team members are distinct and need to be who they are, they should align on how they show up for each other and for the organization at large. They need to be clear about how they represent decisions to other stakeholders; team members want to carry the baton well. One fundamental behavior is collaboration. It's clear within the leadership team that unless team members collaborate well, they cannot deliver. They work in a matrix organization with a clear separation of duties, and it's only through effective collaboration that things get done. To facilitate collaboration, cross-functional teams are set up as a platform for people to work together.

6. Employing a decision-making model with clear roles is essential. Penny believes that decision making is a core function of the leadership team. The company deploys a standardized decision-making process that begins with clarifying roles and identifying each role's responsibilities for effective decision making. This is followed by making and communicating key decisions with clarity and discipline. Penny believes that it's important to have a clear decision owner; this may not always be the hierarchical business line. Very often, effective decision making is slowed or blocked as decisions get elevated to the highest-titled person in the room. It's the mark of a strong leader to let go of having to make the decision and empower teams to make their own decisions.

7. The leadership team needs to be accountable in both tangible and intangible ways to itself and the organization. Once decisions are made, accountability is fundamental. To the team, accountability is a mutual contract. Accountability is defined not just in terms of results but also around intangible areas, such as aspirations, attitudes, and competencies. Each team member needs not only to execute her responsibilities well but also be a trusted member of the team. Ultimately, it's not just the team members who need to be accountable to the team; it's the team, itself, that needs to be accountable to the organization.

Penny is a believer in the power of the leadership team. When team members can engage with trust and openness, they can find solutions to any challenges. When other leaders start to believe in the team, too, magic happens.

PENNY'S FORMULA
Creating an Effective Leadership Team[54]

1. Choose your team wisely, based strongly on members' own aspirations and values.
2. Pick a diverse team that is willing to debate divergent views.
3. Pay attention to meeting management and mix it up.
4. Ensure open feedback to encourage engagement and trust.
5. Show up with the right behaviors and be ready to collaborate.
6. Employ a decision-making model with clear roles.
7. Task the leadership team with accountability, in both tangible and intangible ways, to both itself and the organization.

Figure 15.5

16

ELEMENT #6
FUN

I LOVE THIS TEAM!

Lessons from a Swiss Client

A Swiss client's team and I were heavily into some feedback exercises during a TQ-team off-site when I sensed it was time for a break. I suggested to the team that it was time for some fun. Most readily agreed, however Heinz, one of the leaders, raised his hand and promptly admonished, "Fun? How can we have fun? This is business!" It was inconceivable to him that a leadership team could have fun together.

> Fun brings positive energy to the team, allowing a shift to happen.

The Team's TQ was relatively low, and the lack of fun, energy, and emotion was a key reason. Fortunately most of the team members understood this and convinced Heinz that indeed "We need to build some 'fun time' into our team activities and rituals."

Yes, there are those who believe that serious business means that there is no room for fun. On the other hand, others understand that the element of fun provides the impetus to make the impossible possible. Most of us may not even have thought about it, but the roots of *motion* and *emotion* are virtually identical. *Movere*, from the Latin, means 'to move.' *Exmovere* or *emovere* means 'to move out, hence to excite.' So taking action stirs something up, moves something inside of us."[55] Fun indeed brings positive energy to the picture and to any situation. It also can create a shift, allowing our brains to view issues from a different perspective.

Why Fun?

First of all, *fun relaxes us*; it de-stresses. In the "serious business" environment that we all face, we are overloaded with stress. Our psyches need an outlet and release, and experiencing fun does just that. When people are relaxed, they perform better.

Second, *fun motivates*. We are motivated to do what we enjoy, and motivated to do more of it. We will get good at the task, and it might even develop into a core skill. Fun is a strong motivating factor. The more fun a team has while pursuing its goal, the more members want to be with the team, and show up and perform for the team.

Third, fun creates *camaraderie*. When you go beyond serious work and start to enjoy each other's company, whether at work or play, you develop solidarity with the team. This engenders strong trust and relationships.

Finally, fun creates *energy*—the driving force that will achieve the vision. Fun unleashes the energy so that more of it is available to draw upon through the tough times.

WORK HARD; PLAY HARD

Most High Performance Teams work hard and play hard. Team members are highly committed to the team as well as to their goals.

At PepsiCo, the regional president understood the value of fun. He took the leadership team on annual trips to celebrate being together. These trips took us to exotic places like Thailand, Egypt, Australia, and New Zealand. We took our playing and fun seriously in between business meetings. The trips represented an investment of time, money, and energy in the team's welfare and well-being in an environment where we could relax, have fun, and develop camaraderie. Team members took away the message that "If the company is willing to invest in the team and in me, then I need to show up as an effective team member." Out of this came a deepening of relationships. Looking back, we created great memories during these outings and bonded with each other, which had long-term benefits.

An added benefit to relaxing and playing together is that you get to know the people you work with on a new level. We all desire to know more about our fellow team members with whom we spend so many working hours. Ordinary workplace relationships can be rather one dimensional. Yet when we add the element of play to it, we learn all sorts of things we didn't know. Play deepens and enhances our perspective on our fellow team members and usually results in an added level of respect.

There are many ways to deepen relationships through fun and play. Whenever possible, conduct business off-site and add some fun activities into the mix. When I conduct off-sites, I always include plenty of icebreakers and brief team activities among the business meetings. This keeps the energy going and deepens the sense of team and bonding. Wherever possible, I'll debrief the team after an activity to ensure that there was some additional team learning that resulted.

For example, in a two-day, *business-focused* off-site meeting, which was *not purely devoted to building the team*, I would schedule a program to look something like this:

BUSINESS OFF-SITE
Day One
Morning start: deepening-relationships icebreaker
Business
Break and icebreaker
Business
Lunch and short team activity
Business
Break and icebreaker
Business
Closing activity
Day Two
Morning start: deepening-relationships icebreaker
Business
Break and icebreaker
Business
Lunch
Team activity for the entire afternoon
Dinner and closing activity

Figure 16.1

There are many variations on the above type of schedule. The important thing is to customize each off-site according to the needs of the group.

On Day One (above), I built in four business sessions of 1½ hours each, and four icebreaker/team activities lasting between 10 and 30 minutes each. On Day Two, the whole afternoon is devoted to a fun and usually challenging activity. Team members love these types of events, and they result in accolades with glowing testimonials about the team and the activities.

It makes for a high-octane two days. The added benefit is that team members are more refreshed and able to function in the business context more effectively. The combination of activity, fun, emotion, and movement stimulates their brains and ramps up energy. Their off-sites and meetings are a pleasure, and everyone looks forward to them. Within a short period of time, it can change the whole dynamic in a team. Furthermore, it utilizes both left and right sides of the brain, and stimulates body, emotion, and mental activity. That's a far cry from the typical business meetings that are essentially cerebral.

CAMARADERIE

In the chapter on alignment, we discussed peer pressure. This touches on the power of camaraderie. In essence, camaraderie is about people who spend a lot of time together creating mutual friendship and forging trust. This means that team members truly enjoy being together and in each other's company. It reflects the power of being together as a unit and working on something bigger than any individual.

Much has been written about the incredible solidarity shared by troops, as evidenced in this article by Geoff Ziezulewicz from *Stars and Stripes*:

> *Lessons from the Brotherhood of Combat*
> Call it what you want. Band of Brothers. The Brotherhood of Combat. It's a familiar concept these days as America's sons and daughters fight on two fronts. Even for people who don't fight the wars.
>
> It's an unbreakable trust and kinship forged as men push their brains and bodies to the limits each day, together, in an environment that won't forgive them should one man mess up. One guy keeps the next guy going, to keep all the brothers from falling.
>
> That bond is found in shared sweat, blood and Gatorade, and in a can of chew passed around before a patrol, be it

on an unfathomably smelly Baghdad street or high in the Afghan mountains.

"When I'm with one of these guys, I feel safe," said Brackett, 24. "Just one of them. When I'm with them all, I'm invincible; you know what I'm saying? That's how cool it is.

". . . They'll never understand unless they're in it," he said. "Never. I have an identical twin brother; we've been close our whole life. He wouldn't understand. He's not been in.

" . . . It's beyond friendship," Brackett said. "You may not like the person," he said, but you'll work with this person and give your life for this man, every time. It doesn't matter if you hang out on the weekends. . . . You have to pass on that friendship, that trust, so that this kind of connection here never fades," he said. "It's our job to make sure that trust and that connection travel on. . . . I never understood it until now."[56]

The camaraderie that is felt by troops can also be felt by a team with High TQ. It's a phenomenon in which team members who might not normally be friends can feel a close kinship and connection by virtue of being on the same High Performance Team. It's the same camaraderie felt within winning sports teams.

The amazing thing about camaraderie is the trust and friendship it engenders. Members of High Performance Teams experience this when others do things for them that are, perhaps, uncalled for. There is a sense that "We are all in it together, and we need to show up and help each other succeed."

So how do you create that sense of camaraderie? The first step is showing up for each other. Then the team needs to have a purpose, vision, and values that are clearly articulated. That way, everyone is marching toward the same goal and knows what's important to the team. As clichéd as that sounds, alignment is a prerequisite to building camaraderie quickly. Finally, it means doing more than just working together. To truly build camaraderie, heartfelt recognition and celebration must become a part of the team DNA. Knowing each other better helps to invoke a feeling of kinship. Many of the teams I work with reach the point at which their team begins to feel like family. There is closeness and trust, which engenders this type of feeling.

FUN MOTIVATES

In the vast majority of teams, members are doing their jobs—simply going through the motions to live up to expectations, to hit and hopefully exceed goals. People are motivated by many things. Obviously money is a fundamental reason that people work—to make a living. For many, having a job with some security is enough.

That's a base level of motivation. The chance of a promotion, whether it's to a better job or salary, is another level of motivation. It can propel staff to the next level of performance yet it's only a temporary fix.

Beyond the basic levels of motivation, the most powerful team motivation comes from having compelling goals and vision, and working together to achieve them. It's called the "winning mentality" in that team members equate achieving and exceeding goals with winning.

> The most powerful team motivation comes from having compelling goals and vision, and working together to achieve them.

Then there is the all-important area of doing what you love and enjoying your work. Harrison Assessments is an excellent tool and operates from the concept of "Enjoyment Performance Methodology,"[57] as illustrated in figure 16.2.

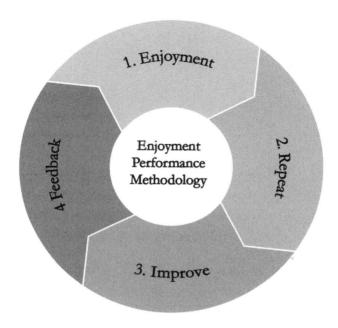

Figure 16.2

According to a Harrison Assessment report, "Enjoyment and performance are linked because the level of enjoyment that an employee has while performing a particular activity is directly related to the level of their performance relative to that activity.

"When people enjoy a task, they tend to do it more and get better at it. Like a self-fulfilling prophecy, good performance creates acknowledgment and/or positive self-regard, which then causes people to enjoy the task even more."[58]

The implication, of course, is that when team members are doing work, they enjoy, their motivation increases, and performance improves. It is, therefore, the team leader's task to ensure that all team members are engaged in a high percentage of work that they love to do.

> When team members are doing work they enjoy, their motivation increases and performance will improve.

273

GETTING MORE PASSION OUT OF YOUR DAY

One of the tools I use with clients is called "Getting More Passion out of Your Day." The concept is to classify work into three areas:

1. *Yahoos:* Doing what you love
2. *Ho-hums:* Doing what you are ambivalent toward
3. *Boohoos:* Doing what you dislike

The Yahoos need to compose at least 30 percent of an employee's total work time in order to create strong engagement and motivation. If it's not as high as 30 percent, employees might consider shifting the mix of their responsibilities through offloading—delegating some of the Ho-hums or Boohoos.

They key is to focus and spend more of employees' time on the activities they love doing. It is up to the team leader to open the door for this type of discussion and be willing to shift work around, if necessary. The good "troopers" will do the work eagerly, but they may not stay around too long if they are stuck with what they dislike.

One client, the chief financial officer (CFO) of a multinational corporation, had a particularly apt philosophy: "I hire people who love doing what I hate doing, and therefore I'm able to spend 80 percent of my time on what I enjoy!"

A more advanced level of High Performance Team motivation comes about when team members simply enjoy being together. It becomes a pleasure to do work with and for the team. There is a sense of satisfaction knowing that team members have had the chance to help each other succeed and that the team can succeed as a whole. Team members become motivated to show up and deliver for the sake of the team, which almost becomes second nature.

GETTING MORE PASSION OUT OF YOUR DAY		
Yahoos (Love doing)	*Ho-Hums* (Just okay)	*Boohoos* (Hate doing)
• • • • •	• • • • •	• • • • •
% of time:	% of time:	% of time:
Where are you now?		
Where do you want to be?		

Figure 16.3

E-MOTION = ENERGY IN MOTION

High Performance Teams possess the drive to move forward. The drive comes from emotion, which is a kind of "energy in motion" to make things happen. In other words, High Performance Teams are also "high-energy teams." There is a bias toward making decisions, executing responsibilities, and creating winning results.

High TQ teams create momentum. They celebrate and recognize after initial successes; a few small successes increase confidence. When the team fails, its members pick themselves up quickly and move forward. Their commitment is to their goals and to each other.

Despite their similarities to sports teams, business or corporate teams

> "I hire people who love doing what I hate doing, and therefore I'm able to spend 80 percent of my time on what I enjoy!"

275

are also distinct. The emotion encountered with High Performance Teams is distinct from the rapid peaks and troughs found in any given sports match. It is less about short-term successes and highs, and more about longer-term successes and mutual commitment to goals and to each other.

TEAM SPIRIT IS THE RESULT

Through engaging in the 2-Step HPT process, team spirit naturally arises. You can't achieve it just by wishing for it. It results from the interaction around purposeful activity. For example, when a team is marching toward a goal with intensity, team spirit will naturally arise. When a team is working together with high openness, feedback, trust, alignment, and collaboration, the result will be team spirit.

There is a sense that when a team feels it is "winning" or on the path to winning, strong team spirit develops. This is true for sports teams and is equally true in corporate teams. Winning sets up positive emotions. At this point, it is important to recognize the winning and celebrate it to strengthen the team's spirit. Celebration maximizes the opportunity to build a stronger spirit.

Another key shift in engendering team spirit is the point at which the individual puts the team first.

In practical terms, this means looking out for, supporting, collaborating, and helping each other. When all team members arrive at this point, something magical takes place. There is a shift in the team's energy, and a quantum leap in team spirit occurs. In other words, a conscious effort by all team members brings a significant uptick in individual TQ, which results in a soaring Collective TQ.

RECOGNIZE, CELEBRATE, AND REWARD RESULTS

In previous chapters, we spoke about the power of recognition and celebration. These become especially relevant when the team meets goals and achieves milestones. Yet it is not just about the big goals: it can be about small things that create the desired team culture. These small things might be team members or staff living a value, finding success in integrating the vision, displaying passion around a certain initiative, or practicing a level of collaboration or cooperation.

Celebration: Some teams celebrate only once a year, if at all. Unfortunately, they miss out on its power. Celebration lends a positive self-image to the team. The psychology of it is simple. Every person or every team wants to feel good about something they have done. The better you feel about yourself, the more effort you apply toward continuing to do good things. Therefore, celebration breeds success. It also strengthens one's identity as a winning team. Teams don't do enough celebrating. High Performance Teams know this and celebrate whenever they get a chance..

I always encourage teams to celebrate in ways big and small. A small celebration might be just an expression of emotion or recognition. It might include wine or champagne. It could graduate into dinner, drinks, or a night out on the town. Or it could be as big as a team trip. The celebrations make all the toil and hard work worthwhile. They reinforce the things that are working. They recognize the team and the individual in connection to the team.

Recognition can be more frequent and subtler than celebration. I worked with the Hospital Authority of Hong Kong, which was facing a challenge in finding authentic ways to recognize the staff. This client decided to brainstorm ways to recognize his team, and he came up with the following list (see figure 14.3).

> Recognition, celebration, and reward are powerful tools for sustaining outstanding team results.

As the list illustrates, with a bit of creativity, you can think of many ways to recognize someone. Pay attention, use empathy, and be willing to share your thoughts.

Reward is a stronger and more tangible form of recognition that demonstrates the fruits of success. Rewards can be doled out on several levels; the first of these is the individual level, which we witness more often in terms of promotions, financial incentives, perks, and so on. And the second level addresses reward from a team perspective: It's important that the team reward itself when it achieves success, and. there are many ideas for this, including trips, parties, bonuses, and team perks. The team rewards reinforce the identity and meaning of being part of the team. It makes the team experience even more tangible.

When handled intelligently and genuinely, recognition, celebration, and reward are powerful tools to perpetuate outstanding results and the continued success of the team.

WAYS TO RECOGNIZE	
Plaque	Drinks
Certificate	Telephone recognition
Medal	Appreciative responses: e.g., emails, letters
Star of the Week	
Share success story	Praise
Newsletter	Promotion
Chocolate	Money
Bonus	Outstanding staff/team award
Deputize	Verbal appreciation
Dinner for two	Wink
More resources	Support
Succession planning	Lunch
Appreciation cards	Afternoon tea
Positive body language	Sponsor initiatives

Figure 14.3

If *effectiveness* represents the mechanics of a High Performance Team, then *fun* represents the energy and drive. Implicit in fun is motivation, positivity, and camaraderie. Investing in your teams to enjoy the experience together will reap benefits beyond expectations.

17

ELEMENT #7
ALIGNMENT

OUR WAY OR THE HIGHWAY

In our TQ HealthCheck, the first question is, "Is our team aligned around a compelling vision (mission/purpose) or common goals?" Alignment is a critical component of team quotient. Many of us have experienced the perils of not getting others on board.

Lessons from PepsiCo's Distribution System
During my days in PepsiCo, I learned the lesson of alignment the hard way. The implementation of a new third-party distribution system in China was on my agenda. Carbonated soft-drink manufacturers pride themselves on their logistics. They love to expand through advanced "direct delivery" systems with high efficiency, which implies a significant direct investment in trucks, warehouses, and drivers. However China presented a unique set of challenges given its size and the consequent need to invest heavily in infrastructure. We found another way. The idea was that by using distributors and wholesalers to expand our footprint, we could achieve higher levels of store and city penetration

much faster. Moreover, using third parties was more cost effective than investing in trucks and warehouses. The key was executing the requisite control mechanisms to ensure the quality of execution while managing accounts receivables. After detailed planning and considering several models, we decided to pilot a plan in South China.

After the successful test, I managed to convince most of our bottler general managers that this was the way to go. At least I thought everyone was on board. Right around that time, Proctor and Gamble (P&G) had experienced some nasty issues around accounts receivables in China and barely averted a collapse of its wholesale system. One of my peers, "Tony," was a vice president with expertise in direct delivery; I hadn't aligned him with the program. When he caught word of the P&G case, he blew a fuse, fearing that the same could happen to us. Tony, a big, burly man who rode a Harley and loved trucks and logistics, was a proponent of "direct delivery." Tony weighed in with his concerns and raised them with the president of the China Region. This was a setback I hadn't foreseen, and it caused a schism in my team. As a result, we had to rework our models to ensure that they were robust enough to meet the required standards of control. Ultimately, we were successful in launching the third-party system, but I lost three months of valuable time and strained my relationship with Tony.

The fact was that I had never really aligned all my team members, including Tony, nor had I done the contingency planning necessary to address the potential downsides of that approach. This resulted in two "camps" on the subject within the leadership team, which was unhealthy from an execution perspective. The mistake I made, knowing that the proponent of direct delivery held strong opinions, was not doing the hard work of truly aligning the team and addressing everyone's concerns. Instead, I relied on the regional president to make an executive decision, which further alienated some team members. At PepsiCo, alignment was a necessary part of the unspoken culture. If you wanted to get something done, you had better get your entire team on your side.

ALIGNMENT VS. CONSENSUS

Consensus implies that most team members are in agreement. It can be a powerful and useful tool to gain agreement in a team environment, however consensus can often be forced or faked. This can lead to "group think," in which the group superficially agrees because they want to please the boss or preserve harmony in the team, yet they may or may not be aligned. Team leaders often mistakenly believe they have alignment just because there is consensus.

> Team leaders often mistakenly believe they have alignment just because there is consensus.

One of the definitions of *alignment* is 'support and alliance.' Consensus, on the other hand, implies 'broad unanimity.' Alignment is such an apt concept for High Performance Teams because it implies that *support* is required among all team members. It doesn't always imply agreement because you can disagree and still support an initiative—something that happens in all teams. The word *alliance* is also a good descriptive given its deeper meaning of supporting the "cause" or "values" of the group.

THE "VIVRE FAT" CONTEXT OF ALIGNMENT

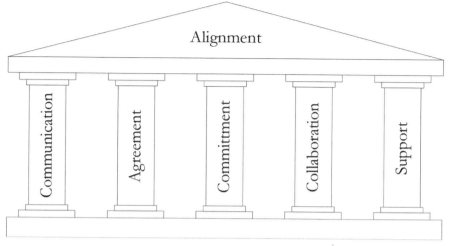

Figure 17.1

In our High Performance Team model VIVRE FAT, the *A* stands for "alignment." It deserves its place as one of the critical elements of the model. Essentially, there are five pillars that support alignment in the team context: communication, agreement, commitment, collaboration, and support Put another way, the team *communicates* the situation and issues, seeks *agreement* on a path forward, *commits* to a course of action, and finally *collaborates* in the plan's execution, with mutual *support* throughout the entire alignment process.

Communicating to Create Alignment

In any given process, Communication will be one of the major elements of success. Getting the communication right is a priority for the team leader. That's certainly true with High Performance Teams. Communication to align team members is a prerequisite for any team activity or scope, whether it's related to vision, direction, purpose, values, feedback, trust, or projects. These all need to be clearly articulated in order to achieve the requisite clarity.

The challenge in a team environment is that what needs to be said often doesn't get said. We all go about our business with thoughts and holdbacks that may be preventing us from moving the team to the next level. Some teams I have worked with do the RearView Feedback exercise (as outlined in the next chapter on "Trust") every six months to ensure that everyone is on the same track and communicates what needs to be said. It also exposes holdbacks that need to be expressed.

There are also certain things that need to be communicated among the wider team or organization. Naturally, these include the vision, goals, values, and commensurate expectations on behavior. The team leader and all team members need to ensure that all relevant members of their own teams have clarity around these issues. Otherwise, the team leader is relying on assumptions that things will get done. Misunderstandings and the problems that result from them can be traced back to a lack of communication, leading to the need to over-communicate. A few questions should be posed to ensure messages are getting through to the wider team or organization.

Ask: Do these people or parties:
- have the information they need to get it done?
- know the five W's and 1 H: *What, Who, Where, Why, When,* and *How?*
- have any major unanswered questions?
- have the resources required to get it done?
- have the chance to challenge assumptions, if necessary?

Are We in Agreement?

Once the communication has taken place and the issues have been discussed and debated, the team needs to agree to a curse of action. That agreement can take a variety of forms, including "Getting to yes," "Agree to disagree," "Agree in principle," "It's my way or the highway," or "Great point but . . ." Many of us have used these phrases to describe something less than complete agreement. In fact, we all try desperately to get people to agree with us, and most of us don't like to directly disagree. In a team environment, it's often not easy to get true unanimous agreement.

Whether team members agree or disagree on various topics, there are a few things they all need to agree on:

- vision or direction
  - key strategies
  - values, and how we conduct ourselves

It may sound like a broken record, but these things not only must be communicated, they need agreement. In this sense, agreement is more about embracing the process.

When it comes to vision/strategies/values, all must be carefully analyzed to ensure that everyone understands and embraces them. Otherwise, there will be schisms down the road, and execution will suffer. I recommend that teams look at these three items from every angle to ensure the key aspects are being covered and that no stone lies unturned. Playing devil's advocate helps uncover inconsistencies or potential roadblocks.

Now that we have established that true agreement is essential on vision/strategies/values, what about other areas? I have found that the best way is to identify a champion or strong proponent for any particular area. The champion's job is to make a case for the particular issue with all the data and arguments at hand. It's then a question of engaging in a spirited discussion around the issues. This means being open to exploring, challenging, and, of course, disagreeing.

Impersonal conflict around the issues is healthy; personal conflict is toxic. Therefore impersonal conflict and disagreement around issues should be encouraged while entertaining diverse views. It need not be a raging debate. The facilitator of the meeting or the team leader needs to live with a certain level of impersonal conflict and seek out relevant team members' views rather than be content to have a few heavy hitters on board who are pushing hard for one perspective or another.

Ready to Commit?

Once there is agreement, members need to make a commitment. This is all too often where execution falls down. I often hear some variation of this thought: "We agreed to take this action, but a month later during our meeting review, we discovered that nothing had been done!" This often implies a lack of clear commitment.

Commitment can come in many forms. Sometimes it's a simple as action planning and identifying those who will be responsible.

Whenever I conduct a High Performance Team Program, I always conclude by asking for individual commitments to the team. This is because of the power that commitment holds in achieving results. When team members commit in front of others, they feel an obligation to deliver.

Verbally agreeing at the end of a program is just one form of commitment. In fact, whether we realize it or not, we have made many commitments spoken and unspoken, conscious and unconscious, to teammates. This is another reason why the identity of the team is so critical. The stronger the team identity, the more seriously its members will embrace their commitments. The opposite also holds true. Some team members don't want to get too close to the team out of fear of the commitments and accountability it entails. For those interested in leading a relaxed, happy existence, participating in a High Performance Team may seem like a potential threat to their comfort level. The answer, therefore, is to ensure that the payoff for being part of a High Performance Team is significant for each participant.

Team commitments work due to unspoken peer pressure. Peer pressure is powerful, and it's hard to know which is more significant—the fear of letting others down or desire for the glory of being recognized. Certainly, fear is a key motivator to do what's necessary to, at least, *hit the target.* Then the recognition will propel the individual to *exceed the target.* In any given team, there will be those who stand out; perhaps we can call them the "stars." Stars tend to succeed, and they thrive on recognition. This has the risk of leading to jealousy and a perception of favoritism. Therefore, team leaders need to heap recognition upon those who may not be stars but are still delivering results. This encourages them to ramp up their performance.

One way to identify traits that deserve recognition is by seeing who volunteers for projects or initiatives. Volunteering not only indicates that one is willing to stick his neck out and contribute to the team but also makes it more difficult to back down. Smart team

leaders know how to reward these commitments with visibility and recognition.
If team members aren't volunteering to
tackle certain projects, the team leader
must nominate individuals or groups to
handle those projects. The caveat around
nominations is that they need to be perceived as fair and not overly burdensome
to the individual. To nominate someone,
the leader needs to know the individual
and the resources she has at her disposal.

> Smart team
> leaders know
> how to reward
> commitments
> with visibility
> and recognition.

Collaboration: It's More Than Cooperation

Collaboration is essentially the act of working with or alongside
someone, usually on a project or initiative. Once a team member
commits to any strategy, action, initiative, or program, the leader
must ensure collaboration within the team in order to ensure the
project's realization. Often, there is an element of sharing ownership. Cooperation, however, is broader than collaboration, and
refers to providing help or support when it is needed.

A few years ago, I conducted a team program in China as
part of a joint venture between a European pharmaceutical company and the local Chinese partner. The general manager at the
time was having issues with team collaboration, and we decided
to focus the team workshop on this theme. Oddly, there is no
direct translation for the word *collaboration* in Chinese. It often
gets translated as *hézuò* (合作), which means "to cooperate." The
difference between the two words became very tangible in our
workshop because the team was having a hard time capturing the
true spirit of collaboration. They didn't realize that collaboration
was more than just getting along and being helpful or supportive.

High Performance Teams want to be cooperative, yet they
also aspire to go beyond cooperation to collaboration. For important team initiatives and projects, collaboration is essential, going
beyond departmental silos that just deliver results. If we are all
operating from a silo mentality, we don't have much of a team.

Lessons from an Executive Search Client

While helping my executive-search client with team projects, I found that many of the partners were supportive of the need for a team. There were, however, a few outliers who were happy to deliver strong results in their own practice areas without concern for the team's focus. In the back of their minds was the thought that, "As long as I deliver, do I really have to spend time on the team?" It became apparent that they could go solo with many of their executive searches, yet for some clients, collaboration was essential, particularly in the larger and more complex cases, and with servicing clients, recruiting consultants, and building culture. Fundamentally, a team of silos does not engender a positive working atmosphere. By default, everyone ends up being in it for their own skin. This atmosphere occasionally becomes toxic. We identified where the team *needed to collaborate*, including client initiatives and other identified projects. These provided the impetus to build a strong and collaborative team.

To collaborate effectively, the team needs to identify which projects require what form of collaboration and then identify the roles that each team member must play. But there needs to be a willingness to collaborate. I have worked with countless companies at which team members paid lip service to supporting projects yet didn't really intend to spend much effort on it. The team leader must make the collaboration visible within the team and then review and recognize individual participants along the way.

> To collaborate effectively, the team defines which projects need what collaboration, with clear role identification.

It is also crucial to create the right level of visibility for a project requiring collaboration. Unilaterally announcing a project without discussing it in team meetings first almost ensures that the project will die.

Finally, collaboration often extends beyond the immediate team to other levels of the company or stakeholders. The beauty of a High Performance Team that has firmly established a collaborative environment is that other stakeholders will feel that sense of working as part of a team. It becomes infectious, and the team becomes known for its collaborative nature.

Support: Do My Teammates Have My Back?

Underpinning the entire alignment process is support. When I poll teams on the desired characteristics of High Performance Teams, most people include the description, supportive. Most people want supportive environments in which they feel that team members have their backs. They also want to be able to take a few risks without being shot down.

Support begins with an attitude, which translates into action. The question is, are the team members there to support their fellow members or to promote their own agendas? Real support comes with the attitude, "How can I support my fellow team members so that we all succeed?" Of course, supports starts with the leader who sets the tone by demonstrating support for team members, as described below. Some team leaders believe it's their role to challenge team members, and that's fine as long as the *intention* is to support the team.

A Primary Form of Support Is Feedback

Providing feedback, whether it's constructive criticism or recognition, is essential to bring fellow team members to the next level. It's part of creating a feedback culture that High Performance Teams relish and promote. Feedback is the most powerful way to support team members to correct their actions and improve their performance.

At a deep level, we all want to be surrounded by supportive team members. We know there are many areas where we can improve, and need the support of others to show us how. Yet because most of us have strong, built-in defense mechanisms, we don't always appear open to support and feedback. This is the paradox that members face in a team environment.

How, Then, to Engender a Strong, Supportive Culture?

It starts with the team leader and their skills. The first thing the leader must do is live by example. The commitment is reflected in the attitude, "I am here to support you to do better and will continuously provide feedback wherever I can to help you."

To set the tone, the team leader needs mutual team member support. This should be part of the values discussion. Being supportive can be a value or may be a subset of a value, but it must be treated as an expectation.

Support does not come only through words and intentions. The strongest support can be demonstrated through giving one's time to others to support them in whatever they need. In my PepsiCo example at the beginning of this chapter, I referred to the third-party distribution system that we implemented. To accomplish this, I needed an enormous amount of support from others. One of my colleagues supported me by providing concrete examples from his work in India on third-party distribution systems, and he was willing to create a pilot system in South China. This level of support was essential to codifying and proving the utility of the system. The distribution system also needed support from all the bottlers, sales, distribution staff, and back-end staff who were there to give the initiative a chance to fly.

The other form of support is through providing *resources.* Initiatives succeed and fail in large measure based on the resources devoted to them. A good team leader can recognize the need for certain resources, even when team members may not. The leader also plays the key role of challenging team members in ensuring that they have all the resources they need to execute their tasks The biggest form of support involves fighting for the needed resources.

AN ALIGNED TEAM IS AN INTELLIGENT TEAM

Alignment in a team is tantamount to a car firing on all cylinders, which is why it is a key element of TQ. Reaching alignment utilizing communication, agreement commitment, collaboration, and support pulls the team together; this is when breakthroughs occur. It's the alignment that allows the team to move beyond individual intelligence to team intelligence.

Without alignment, the team members (by default) will operate in silos. A lot of smart people will look after themselves and their departments in the absence of a real team.

Alignment makes the job of the team leader easier. The leader can step back a bit, knowing that all team members are working together intelligently. She doesn't have to direct the team or do all the thinking for them.

18

ELEMENT #8
TRUST

THE ELUSIVE YET ESSENTIAL INGREDIENT

Lessons from a European Executive Search Client
While working with a European executive-search firm on their TQ, I noticed that two of the consultants (Mark and Carrie) were not on speaking terms. They often blamed and criticized each other for some client complaints. In essence, their sense of trust was practically nonexistent. I realized that for this team, trust was the number-one priority. We devoted a whole afternoon to trust building, utilizing our RearView Feedback exercise. The results were beyond expectations. At the end of the session, Mark and Carrie were beaming and hugging. It completely transformed their relationship.

> Clients say trust is the most essential ingredient, yet it is the hardest to build.

When I ask clients what is the most essential ingredient for building a High Performance Team, nine times out of ten they respond, "Trust." Yet trust is also the most difficult element to create. Many people cite how many years it takes to establish and how easy it is to break. I am going to show you how *to build trust quickly, effectively, and sustainably.*

WHY SHOULD I TRUST YOU?

Yes, why should teammates trust each other? It's a good question.

In answer, here are some of the thoughts echoed by many team members I have interviewed over the years;

- "After all, you may not know what I really think of you."
- "I have seen how you do things, and I have no confidence that you are really a friend of mine or that you have my back."
- "You have done nothing thus far to earn my trust. Conversely, you have done things to make me doubt you. After all, we are all in it for ourselves, right?"

Our instinct is not to trust others immediately; we should, at least, begin with a healthy dose of wariness. Trust is a mutual affair; if I trust you, but you don't trust me, it's not trust. Trust is the most fragile factor in a relationship: hard to gain; easy to lose. It's much safer and easier not to trust. No one wants to be played, used, or fooled. The real answer is this: We won't trust until that trust is earned.

The root cause of lack of trust is our natural, self-serving intentions that put our own needs above others. What does that mean? During childhood, the focus was on meeting our own personal needs. As babies, we cried when we were hungry. As toddlers, we threw tantrums when we wanted something. As children, we constantly sought attention and ways of having our own needs met.

As adults who have learned how to interact with society, many of us have repressed our self-serving intentions. Yet the inner child is alive and well. Moreover, isn't the desire for fame, wealth, accolades, recognition, and achievement a reflection of the need to satisfy the self? At our core, most of us are still self-serving (even if we mask it), putting our own needs above others.' Being conscious of that fact means that *not* trusting others is a necessary yet unconscious mechanism of self-preservation.

By the way, this self-preservation mechanism is the reason that most teams are not true teams but, rather, function as a group of individuals. The key to begin trusting, then, is finding a reason to trust. The reason lies in reason, itself.

Follow the logic: Relationships are essential for success in any collective endeavor and particularly in teams. Forming and building relationships may make the difference between success and failure. A key component of a relationship is building a *degree* of trust, not necessarily finding absolute trust. A successful relationship will invariably have more trust than an unsuccessful one; the more you trust another person, the greater the chance of building a strong relationship. When you give trust, you likely receive some in return, and your relationship strengthens. If it's not mutual, it's not much of a relationship. Therefore, if you believe that developing trust is key to successful relationships, and that relationships are key to success in any collective endeavor, you would do well to build trust.

How does this apply to teams? As opposed to binary relationships, we are talking about multiple relationships in a collective environment where there is a common purpose. These relationships are commonly referred to as a team. Forming strong relationships within the team is critical to its success, so you must start doling out some trust. This does not mean trusting blindly; it does mean trusting with some measure and building it over time.

OBSTACLES TO TRUST

We have examined some of the causes for a lack of trust. Yet we all witness more tangible trust issues between team members from time to time.

1. Different points of view. If you and I disagree, that in and of itself is no reason not to trust each other. Yet if our perspectives put us in different camps, that may impact our trust. You are from a different camp with different motivations from mine, and on this issue you are my adversary. Therefore, I might not trust you. In fact, in a team environment, most people gravitate toward like camps that hold similar viewpoints on many issues. Different camps with different perspectives can be adversarial.

2. Conflicts. Different points of view grow into conflicts when they remain polarized with no resolution. These conflicts can become personal. Adversaries can even become enemies. Conflicts are exacerbated due to *assumptions* about the other person's actions and intentions.

3. Untrustworthy behavior. When someone's actions or words have negatively impacted another person, trust is immediately broken or damaged. In this case, the situation is exacerbated when the party taking action denies, defends, or justifies its actions or words. The key, in this instance is to admit to the action, state why the action was taken or words spoken, and apologize. This is not easy to do in a corporate or team environment, but without coming to terms with the issue, there is little chance of rapprochement.

4. Hearsay is very common in the form of rumor, gossip, and even facts. It can be damaging. Hearsay may raise doubt that the target of the hearsay is unable to address. Indeed, it takes some consciousness for the person listening to hearsay to verify whether it's true and not to jump to conclusions. My experience is that a person who participates in something that appears untrustworthy will always have a reason and justification for such action. Issues are complex, and rather than rushing to conclusions, it's better to keep an open mind and attempt to understand the possible context of the action taken.

Lessons from Kodak

In my early corporate days with Kodak, my first overseas position was in Mexico. At the time, there were challenges with some of the local managers, who seemed to be getting too close to certain customers. Kodak brought in a new general manager, Dick, to clean up the situation. He ended up firing several managers. The word on the street was that you couldn't trust Dick. He earned a reputation for "firing with a smile." People would spend hours in his office and walk out smiling—even if they had just been fired! Dick had a talent for making managers feel good about themselves even when they lost their jobs. As I got to know Dick, I realized that he had a task to do. In fact, Dick was a pretty straightforward guy when you got to know him. I had to understand the context of his actions and not infer that he was, de facto, untrustworthy.

5. Chemistry. A major source of lack of trust is plain chemistry. Chemistry may stem from the idea that this person "isn't like me" or represents a "different management style." Sometimes, another team member may just "turn me off." This could be related to a clash of values or to certain behaviors or characteristics relating to your pet peeves. Often what you see in the person is simply a reflection of those hidden things you don't see or accept in yourself. This is why I often use assessment tools to expose the differing personalities and leadership styles on the team. This awareness is useful in helping people open their minds and begin to accept others so that trust ultimately can take seed.

6. Competence. The question is: Do I believe you are competent at your job? Can you handle the issue at hand, and can you deliver a result? If not, whatever you say may be colored by my lack of confidence in you.

Lessons from PepsiCo Sales Management
While I was the vice president of sales at PepsiCo, our team had to satisfy many stakeholders. One key stakeholder oversaw operations. He had a basic issue with one of my sales directors, believing him to be deficient in several areas. Whenever these two met, the head of operations discounted whatever my sales director had said, leading to a lack of confidence in his competence. My opinion was quite different. I saw the issue to be one of chemistry and differing styles. The head of operations was quite direct,

specific, and detailed. Much like many sales people, my sales director was somewhat elusive with facts and promised big results with generalities. The fact was that he always delivered results, yet his style and issues got in the way of having a trusting relationship with the head of operations.

WHAT DOES TRUST REALLY MEAN?

Trust is one of those words, like integrity,' that has several meanings and connotations. So when we talk about trust, we need to be clear about what type of trust we are referring to. Used in the wrong context, it can be misleading.

1. To do your job. This is simply about doing your job and delivering for the team. It is trust that says, "I have confidence that you can and will do your job." This is related to the issue of competence, above. The fact is that this type of trust is often colored by chemistry or style issues, which need to be recognized. How

> There are often trust issues around the ability of the leader to lead or the follower to follow.

many times have we heard, "Nice guy, but he's not up to the job"? There are often trust issues around the ability of the leader to lea, or the ability of a follower to follow.

2. Do what you say you'll do. This is about "walking your talk." Do I have confidence that when you say you will do something it will get done? Or do I believe that much of what you say is "B.S." and won't get done as you say it will. The "actions speak louder than words" axiom applies here. It's about credibility.

3. Are you truthful? At a basic level of trust, do we experience that what you say as true? Or do we experience you lying or stretching the truth? This is a tough one, since once you are branded as a liar it's hard to recover.

4. Show a backbone. To what extent does the person stand up for what he believes in rather than being swayed or influenced by others? This is the sense of backbone or spine—standing up for one's convictions.

5. Stand up for each other. An important and fundamental level of trust has to do with the extent to which we stand up for each other. Do you talk behind my back and throw me under the bus, or do you defend me? Are you objective in your comments about me or do you denigrate me for personal gain? This involves self-preservation; therefore, this form of trust may be felt at a visceral level. At the team level, it relates to the degree to which a team member will stand up and fight for the team—their commitment to other team members.

> Trust means being credible with the right intentions.

When we define trust, the five forms of trust above can be described as having to do with credibility and having the right intentions.

Does someone's word have credibility, and do people believe in her actions and abilities to do her job? Does the team member have the right intentions such that people believe he will do the right thing by the team?

It is important not to overgeneralize the issue of trust. It's also essential to know what type of trust to which we are referring. When you say, "I don't trust him," you may be referring to someone's credibility whereas the listener may think you are talking about their intentions.

Now that we understand what trust is and why someone may not have it, we need to understand how to build it within our team quickly and expediently.

TEAM FEEDBACK:
THE SILVER BULLET FOR BUILDING TRUST

Earlier in the book, I mentioned that there is a quick and effective way to build trust. It is feedback; not just any feedback, but structured feedback at the team level.

When we think about feedback, we typically think of what is given one-on-one, often in private. We recognize certain guidelines for providing feedback to another person at work, such as getting permission to provide feedback; being specific and factual, using "I" rather than "you"; and employing the "sandwich technique." Indeed, the best-managed organizations are proficient at incorporating feedback into their management routine.

Lessons from Apple

Apple has a feedback culture and uses it adeptly to inspire everyone to continue improving. Jerry, for example, came from a traditional company background and joined Apple mid-career. Jerry receives frequent feedback and is expected to consider it seriously and modify his approach accordingly. The process is ongoing—not something that ends when you reach a certain level. If you are to be a happy and productive team member at Apple, you need to embrace this self-change process. Feedback allows people to slice through the company hierarchy. The CEO can walk into an Apple store and store members can give him direct feedback.

Feedback works well at the individual level. A problem with using individual feedback techniques at the team level, however, is that it can be counterproductive. When confronted with personal feedback in a team context, it's human nature to clarify, dispute, and defend oneself. The situation can become confrontational and stressful, and it rarely works well. However there is another "brand" of feedback that I have developed specifically for use in teams that is very effective and powerful. Below is a client example of what kind of feedback works and what doesn't.

Lessons from Cathay Pacific Airways

During a team program at Cathay Pacific Airways, I suggested that the team leader adopt a team-feedback process to build trust. He said, "No way. I tried using feedback last year, and it turned out to be disastrous. People were defending themselves, and it led nowhere." I backed off, returned a week later, and again suggested that he engage in this special brand of team feedback for building trust. He replied, "We should find another way. That's too risky." Two weeks later, I returned for the third time. This time I told him I "guaranteed" that the team-feedback process would work and be instrumental in building trust while bringing the team closer together. At that point, he said, "If you guarantee it, we will try it." The process worked like a charm and was a turning point in building trust and a stronger team culture.

So what is this "brand" of feedback? *It is safe, structured feedback at the team level.* The key is not to bring personal performance, strengths, or weaknesses into the picture but rather to focus on the team members' *contribution to the team.* The principle is that we are most interested in how team members show up for the team, for the team's benefit and its health.

Here we need to mention the when and where of providing feedback. I find it most useful to provide feedback in the middle or towards the end of any offsite meeting. If possible, don't do this at the office. People need to warm up to feel comfortable and open to new information. They also need quality time with the team after receiving the feedback. You will discover that, after you conduct the feedback exercises, the team's closeness, trust, and effectiveness improves. The team begins to relax and have fun together.

"RearView Feedback"—Going Deeper with the Team

Following is the most expedient and effective way to build trust quickly in a team environment. It's a technique that I've used successfully in hundreds of teams. The point is to follow the structure and process carefully. Control is essential.

I call this RearView Feedback because this is the feedback *in relation to the team,* on areas that team members may not see about themselves. It works best with 5 to 12 participants. (For a greater number of participants, see the exercise called "Feedback Mingle.")

RearView Feedback: Form chairs in a circle. At the head of the circle will be what is known as the "Love Seat." Whoever wants to go first sits in the Love Seat. Each team member gives structured feedback, one by one, to the person on the Love Seat. After all members have given feedback, the next person rotates into the Love Seat and receives feedback. Continue rotating them until all have received feedback.

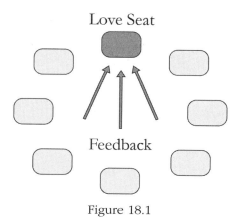

Figure 18.1

Structured Feedback: The team leader should put the following on a flip chart or a screen behind the person in the Love Seat:

"[Name], what I appreciate about your contribution to the team is . . ."
"[Name], where you might contribute more to the team is . . ."

Whoever is giving feedback reads each sentence above and finishes it with their own structured feedback to the person in the Love Seat. At the end of the session, all team members should thank each other and have a bit of time for mingling. *Always* take a break after RearView Feedback.

Feedback must be concise and focused and last about 60 to 90 seconds for each person giving the feedback. If it drags on, the facilitator should cut off the speaker. This is important for two reasons. First, people can remember only a few things. Having ten people provide feedback is already substantial, so it needs to be

THE LEADER'S OPERATING MANUAL

clear and to the point. Second, time management is essential. Ten people providing feedback for 60 to 90 seconds each makes this exercise last between 90 and 135 minutes. (Two-and-a-half hours is really the max; otherwise people lose focus and get tired.) This is a very intense exercise. If you really feel you need to run longer, take a break.

I tee up this exercise as follows:

> "We are going to do a powerful exercise to build trust, to get closer as a team, and learn how we can all be more effective team members. You will be giving and receiving one of the most valuable gifts in your career to and from your team members. What we are talking about is team feedback. This feedback is not about your personal performance; rather it's about your "contribution to the team." It requires complete honesty and focus on the person to whom you are providing feedback. Don't use the third person "he" or "she"; use the name of the person. You may not elaborate, tell stories, or make judgments. Your task is simply to provide quick feedback on the person's contribution to the team. If you don't know the person well, just use your intuition to provide feedback on whatever comes to mind. Trust yourself to give the right feedback. Remember, the more honest and valuable feedback you give, the more honest and valuable feedback you will receive.

> The person receiving the feedback is *not* to take notes. You are to absorb the comments as much as possible, and if you are comfortable, make eye contact with the person providing feedback. You are allowed to say only two words: "Thank you." If you wish clarification, you can ask for it offline. Please take a break now as there will be no breaks during the exercise."

During RearView Feedback, the individual in the Love Seat is not allowed to take notes because you want him to be totally focused. However, the facilitator or a scribe should take notes and send them to each team member separately after the program. This will be highly appreciated by team members. Some treasure the feedback for years.

This exercise can completely transform the energy of the team, and members will feel the kind of closeness, as if they have known each other for years. I have witnessed situations with palpable team conflicts that dissolved through this exercise (as with the executive-search client mentioned at the beginning of the chapter).

This activity provides some important benchmarks for people to conduct high-quality work on themselves.

At the end of the off-site, I ask for *personal commitments* based on the feedback received. The lessons gleaned from RearView Feedback always provide good information to build upon.

If you have more than 12 people in the team and you want to do a feedback exercise, you have three options.

1. You can do the RearView Feedback but limit the number of people giving feedback to the person in the Love Seat to between 6 and 8. The only downside of this is that some people may have an opportunity to "opt out of giving feedback." In this variation, you will need to monitor and count to ensure that you don't overrun.

2. You can conduct RearView Feedback while splitting into two groups. In this case, you will need two facilitators. Organize those team members who work frequently with each other and those who may have conflicts with each other in the same group. Two groups work just as well as one; the only downside is that not all will be able to hear everyone else's feedback.

3. You can also conduct a Feedback Mingle, which is described below.

Feedback Mingle: "Trust Lite"

In this exercise, the idea is to mingle and give feedback to as many people as possible. This follows the same concept as RearView Feedback in that the feedback words are the same, but instead of giving and receiving feedback in a group, you offer it one-on-one while mingling within the group, as follows. Instructions are as follows:

> The principles of Feedback Mingle are to provide honest, direct feedback about one's contribution to the team. Please write the following two sentences in your notebook:
>
> *"[Name], what I appreciate about your contribution to the team is . . ."*
>
> *"[Name], where you might contribute more to the team is . . .*
> Now proceed to give and receive feedback with each person on the team, one by one. Each give and take should last no more than two minutes. Once you finish the feedback with one person, find another free person and give and receive feedback until you have completed the exercise with everybody. Take notes on what the person providing feedback to you has said (unlike in RearView Feedback, individual notes are important to be able to review later as the facilitator has no opportunity to take notes for everyone). After everyone has finished, review your notes and circle the feedback you find most useful.

WHAT DO I DO WITH MY FEEDBACK?

Having run the exercise(s), you will discover some powerful information. It's important to encourage team members to review and absorb what they have heard and make note of what resonates with them and what they would like to work on. Ask each participant to commit to working on these areas for improvement.

When the team returns to the workplace, team members are encouraged to continue providing feedback, both as recognition when they are performing well or being "on," and as encouragement when they are "off."

In summary, the feedback exercises are a safe, structured, and powerful way to build trust and bring the team closer together. It is truly the silver bullet of trust. Make sure you plan and think through the exercise thoroughly. Stick to the principles and pay attention to structure and timing.

Finally, many teams do the trust exercises multiple times, say every six months. It's a great way to keep bringing the team closer together over time.

Given the elusive nature of sustained trust in an organization, it takes a bit of effort to find it. However, one such company is Global Sources, which puts trust in the forefront of its team values. In interviewing the executive chairman, Merle Hinrich, I found trust to be a core value of his executive team, as illustrated in the case study below:

CASE STUDY:
MERLE HINRICH AT GLOBAL SOURCES
CREATING A SUSTAINABLE MANAGEMENT TEAM
THROUGH TRUST AND TRANSPARENCY

Global Sources, publicly listed on NASDAQ since 2000, is a leading business-to-business media company and a primary facilitator of trade with Greater China. "The core business facilitates trade between Asia and the world using English-language media, such as online marketplaces, trade shows, magazines, and apps. More than one million international buyers, including 95 of the world's top 100 retailers, use these services to obtain product and company information to help them source more profitably from overseas supply markets."[59]

Merle Hinrich, executive chairman, co-founded Asian Sources in 1970, which later morphed into Global Sources. Under Merle's leadership, the company was the pioneer in the use of the Internet for international trade, launching Asia's first B2B online marketplace in 1996. *The Economist* magazine recognized Hinrich as "Asia's e-commerce king," while *Forbes Global* magazine has repeatedly voted Global Sources as "Best of the Web."[60] The company has 2,500 employees, with more than 30 offices worldwide. Each has a manager who reports to regional managers. The senior management team consists of four product- and business-unit heads, the HR head, CFO, CIO, COO, and CEO.

In early 2016, I interviewed Merle Hinrich about his success in building the senior management team of Global Sources and his other venture, Hinrich Foundation, whose mission is promoting sustainable global trade. It became clear that one of the underpinnings of success is the quality and continuity of the firm's people. According to Global Sources' HR head, Philip Chatting, the top 25 people have been with the company for an average of 25 years. Therefore, one of Merle's core strengths and success factors is the ability to instill *loyalty* in his people and team. A case in point is the outgoing CEO, Spenser Au, who came up through ranks. Starting as an account executive in 1978, Au spent 39 years with Global Sources and was recognized all the way up to the top.

What accounts for this loyalty? There is a comfort level in working at Global Sources, and people trust they will be treated fairly over the long term. They know what to expect and realize that loyalty and performance will be rewarded. As Au's career trajectory demonstrates, there is nothing stopping a person from reaching the top. People absorb the culture of Global Sources and continue to sustain it over time.

Merle's own management philosophy can be summed up in the triangle below. At the top is the individual, in the middle is the team, and at the bottom, supporting it all, is communication.

Merle believes that to be a successful team, individuals need to work on their own personal development. It all starts with the individual. He employed the services of consultant John DeFoore to work with his senior management team. According to Merle, DeFoore works with executives at an individual level *specific to the person*. He delves into the personal aspects of the individual's life; himself, his spouse, mother, father, etc., to the point that the executive truly knows himself. DeFoore works with individuals to determine if they are happy in their

> Trust only comes when you know who you are and can be transparent.

private worlds. If they are happy in their personal lives, they have a good chance of being happy with others. Because the information is personal, the discussions are also private. It's public only to the extent the individual wants it to be. The goal is to know one-self and get comfortable with who one is as a person. Through this work, executives have experienced personal breakthroughs that have made them better people, allowing them to open up and be more transparent in a multicultural environment.

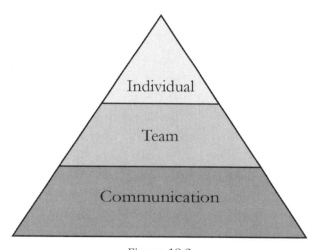

Figure 18.2

It is with this level of *transparency* that the individual can operate in a team environment at a deeper level. This engenders a greater sense of trust with each other, which is a key value of the senior management team. Merle believes that trust only comes from knowing who you are and being transparent.

DeFoore also worked on the team level with roundtable debates. It was agreed that anything could be said without criticism. The idea was to say it straight out, not behind someone's back.

To nurture trust, vulnerability is essential. Vulnerability relates to anything that might be shared with an individual or team—emotions, facts, results, issues, challenges, and so on. In a small executive team, there is no situation that doesn't carry some substantial pros and cons and potential risks. The key is getting the team to feel comfortable to open up about the challenges and risks of any given issue and to trust that the team will be there to support, not criticize.

Merle posits that the ability to lead is the extent to which one can be honest and open with the team, organization, and customer. This attitude flows throughout the entire organization.

Merle considers that *communication is all about alignment* across a variety of ethnicities, languages, and genders. Team alignment is the desired outcome of communication, whether it's about vision, goals, direction, strategies, or decisions. Global Sources senior management team is also aligned around a certain team language, using specific words and expressions such as "the little girl or boy in me,"(the child within) and "outside of the eight dots" (thinking outside the box). Amazingly, the Global Sources senior management team is able to open up about their thoughts and fears, knowing that they won't be judged, because the entire senior level of management has been through the same program. This has resulted in alignment and unity within the management team.

> Team alignment is the desired outcome of communication.

Another key value of the team is respect. Respect is closely associated with trust, vulnerability, and openness. The management team at Global Sources displays a high degree of respect, not only for mutual business skills and acumen, but just as importantly for the personal journey all have gone through and the willingness to share and be vulnerable. There is also the respect for each other's time. At Global Sources, *time management* is critical to working effectively as a team. Everyone needs to have a common understanding of the importance of time. If a team member is late, that can be interpreted as lack of respect. If work is delivered late, it's a letdown to the team. Ultimately, if time cannot

> Feedback is given with the best of intentions to mutually support one another's growth.

be respected, the individual will have a challenge continuing as a team member.

Feedback becomes a crucial tool for a team to work effectively. At Global Sources, feedback starts at the one-on-one level, going to the core of an individual while understanding the source of the strengths and areas for improvement. Only when this is done can feedback be engaged on a team level. Giving feedback can be tedious and tiring and is a massive job, yet it's essential to support people's growth. It can only be engaged at a deep level when one has done the personal work and trust is present. Feedback is given with the best of intentions to mutually support one another's growth.

Merle recognizes that effective *conflict management* is the mark of a strong senior management team. One needs to be clear about one's own style and whether it is hierarchical or consensus based. In Asia, he finds it is critical to listen, listen, listen, and arrive at the nuances of the subject. It's never black or white; rather there are many shades of gray. In Asia, 50 percent is gray. Regardless of which end of the spectrum you are at, you better learn to listen, question, and conduct the discussion to get clear answers.

From a management perspective it's important to listen thoroughly first to gain trust and get all the issues out on the table. If consensus doesn't work, it is necessary to make an executive decision. The CEO needs to be prepared to make this call. Asians expect leadership and a strong hand, with the backdrop of the parental relationship and family. Merle strives to create a family environment with deep relationships. He cites Japan's traditional policy of retirement at 55 years old; the company has the ability to hire retirees back on a consulting basis, allowing firms to move people out in a friendly, emotionally attached way.

One of the practical parts of the triangle that cuts across individual, team, and communication is Global Sources' method of identifying and tracking commitments. This is done

> Merle recognizes that effective conflict management is the mark of a strong senior management team.

in the form of a Job Objectives Analysis (JOA), a rolling, six-month plan of specific commitments with dates, which is reviewed every three months, two levels up (with the manager). The JOA forms the basis of a structured dialogue. The performance component and financial incentives attached to the plan are its "teeth." The JOA became an important tool to manage the complexity of having 30 offices and a highly time-dependent business. Deliverables need to be clearly delineated and communicated so that everyone has clarity about expectations. The JOA goes beyond the executive team, cutting through the entire spectrum of the company, and is the structural glue that holds the company together.

Global Sources is a unique organization with remarkable employee loyalty. Merle's leadership philosophy and approach to forming an effective management team is notable, centered on shared values and a willingness to do the personal work necessary to improve. It's a formula that has withstood the test of time and produced a resilient company culture.

SUCCESS OF MERLE HINRICH'S TEAM APPROACH[61]
(Takeaways)

1. The personal work is done first at an individual level.
2. The dynamic triangle of individual, team, and communication must be considered.
3. Aligned values form the glue of a durable team and company culture.
4. Trust and transparency are cornerstones to successful communication.
5. Vulnerability allows for an open examination of the risks and issues.
6. Respect needs to be built in to achieve effective team relationships.
7. Feedback is a key team enabler that encourages individual and team growth.
8. The team needs to become adept at conflict management.
9. The JOA commits and aligns the entire organization.

Figure 18.3

19

PUTTING IT ALL TOGETHER

YOUR TEAM CHARTER

Lessons from a Global Industrial Goods Company
Jennifer leads a team at a global industrial goods company. We had just completed a two-day TQ program with her team. The team said that they could feel the transformation happening and were excited to get back to work and operate as a High Performance Team. Jennifer wisely commented, "We have done great work, but what do we have to show for it?" She was right. You need more than good experiences, plans, rituals, and initiatives to take away a team program. You need to be able to sum it up with a one-page team charter. At the end of the off-site, the team members worked on their team charter. It became not only a document that they would refer back to, but it also became a key document to share with the rest of the organization. Essentially, the team charter became a work of pride.

Many leadership teams do great work in their off-sites to build their Team Quotient. They invest in captivating team activities with a proportionate improvement of understanding. Some teams spend lavishly on their executives to make them feel special, but after all the "great experiences" and after going back to the daily grind and pressures, how much has the team truly transformed? How many of the agreements are actually put in place? To what extent are the team understanding and agreements integrated into the larger team or organization?

The team charter compels the team to define and take a stand for what is important.

Ensuring Your Team Gets Traction

Throughout the years, I have learned the most effective way to ensure that the team gains traction is by recording the knowledge gains and plans and making them visible in a way that holds everyone accountable and keeps them focused. One of the best tools for accomplishing this is the team charter. Essentially, the team charter is a condensed form of the agreements to which the leadership team has committed and for which it holds itself accountable. It compels the team to define and take a stand for what is important. Ideally, it's one or two pages long.

The team charter is the contract to which *all team members agree*. It is not something just put up on the wall; rather it is a living document. It describes the intent of the team that all share. The team charter also provides the scope and boundaries under which the team will operate and conduct itself.

Who Creates the Team Charter?

The team charter is an outcome of the collective work of the entire team. Much of the input for the team charter is created at off-site events at which each of the team-charter elements are focused on and ferreted out. It is essential that the team charter be seen as the work of the leadership team as opposed to being that of the leader or just a few people. This will create the necessary ownership to ensure that the team charter is taken seriously and gives everyone the feeling that "this is our baby."

Ultimately, once all the key elements of the team charter have been created and have been agreed upon within the team, several team members may take up the torch of producing the actual charter document.

TEAM CHARTER ELEMENTS

Essentially, the team charter is a culmination of all the work the team has done in Steps 1 and 2 of its High Performance Team journey. It embodies the key aspects of VIVRE FAT: vision/identity/ values/results/effectiveness/fun/ alignment/trust.

Vision/purpose: In your team charter, the vision usually refers to the team vision as opposed to the company vision. Ideally, the team vision embodies a multiyear perspective so it won't have to be changed every year. As mentioned in the chapter on vision, it's up to you to decide how to scope it out, and decide if you want a purpose or mission statement separate from your vision.

Values: Values compose an essential part of the team charter. They may include a statement of your team values (as opposed to corporate values) and possibly definitions for each. Some teams may also attach behaviors as a part of values. For example, say one of the values is passion. The corresponding behavior might be showing up with "energy, focus, and drive." It all depends on how prescriptive you want to become in the team charter.

Meetings: Given that meetings are the venue in which most team interaction takes place, it may be useful to prescribe how we conduct them and how to be most effective. For example, formal leadership-team meetings might contain guidelines such as:

- type/frequency
- preparation (pre-reads/work)
- roles: scribe, rabbit-hole watcher, timekeeper, facilitator, observer
- content: 20 percent follow-up/update, 40 percent important issues, 30 percent decision making, and 10 percent reflection/fun.

The idea is to decide on the focus of the meetings and provide a guideline for such.

Rituals: Rituals are a key to ensuring that the team continues its momentum and stays on track, avoiding the risk of falling into old and undesirable behaviors. Listing out the key rituals—or things the team will do consistently to ensure its success—places importance on those elements.

Success definition and measurements: When a team defines what success looks like, it is well on its way to achieving success. Essentially, the *success* definition describes not only success but also how the team measures itself.

Mantra/slogan: A powerful way to capture what the team is about is through a mantra or internal slogan, which can be a fun and catchy way to bring the positive influence of the leadership team to the larger team or organization. It also creates a stronger sense of leadership–team identity.

Photo/signature: To personalize the team charter, it's best to have a photo of all members with their signatures. There is something powerful about having leadership members sign the charter. Putting one's name to it adds more weight and implies greater commitment. Given that team members come and go, this may be a separate page, which is easily updated.

Updating the Team Charter

Things change from year to year, and therefore the team charter needs an annual review. This is best done during an annual off-site. I suggest allocating each element for review by a few individuals, and then coming together, discussing, and agreeing to the revised charter. The elements that need most tweaking and updating tend to be the vision, rituals, success definition, and, oddly, the photo and signatures.

The team charter inspires other team managers to take the cue and move their own teams to high performance.

The Team Charter Is a Visible Document

Remember that the leadership-team charter is something that should be publicly displayed within each team member's department. By making it visible, team members will take the charter more seriously and make it a reality. Furthermore, it will serve as an aspirational element to managers and staff who will be impressed that the leadership team takes its role seriously. It also allows people to read what is important to the leadership while "personalizing" the leadership team.

Below is a sample team charter from a pharmaceutical company's leadership team. Note that each charter is distinct, representing the unique qualities of the team.

LEADERSHIP-TEAM CHARTER
(Example)

Our Mantra Is: Care with Compassion

We are the Pharma Leadership Team (PLT) (with photo)
John Hunt, Mary Chen, Koji Watanabe, Klaus Engelhard,
Petra Bauer, George Mason, Alisha Agarwal, Bruno
Francois, Sandy Jarvis, Anita Lopez, Frank Ksoh.

VISION
Through our PLT commitment to a High TQ, we will drive our
business growth 2x above the industry average, achieving strong
satisfaction among the medical community and patients, and thereby
enhancing our company image as innovative and caring.

PURPOSE
Our purpose is to demonstrate care with compassion
to our patients, people, and stakeholders.

VALUES
We are committed to the values embodied by C.A.R.E.:
Commitment to what is promised, to each other, and to our stakeholders.
Acumen in our business, our decisions, and doing the right thing.
Respect for each other, our styles and preferences, and mutual contributions.
Excellence in our interactions, our work, and results.

MEETINGS
We meet monthly as a leadership team, on time, with full attendance.
We prepare in advance with an agenda, pre-reads, and pre-work.

We achieve meeting excellence through our rotating roles as:
- Observer: To provide feedback and teach
- Timekeeper: To stay on track
- Rabbit-hole watcher: To keep us focused
- Facilitator: To maintain the flow
- Scribe: To document and ensure follow up

We stay focused on what really matters by following the agenda principles:
- Start: Reflection/sharing of key understanding by each member – 5%
- Follow-up and reporting of business results and initiatives: 20%
- Discuss key issues critical to our success: 40%
- Engage icebreakers to be led by team members in turn: 5%
- Consider key decisions that affect all of us: 30%
- End each meeting on a high note with celebration

RITUALS

We commit to the following to keep our momentum:
- Monthly get together outside of the office for fun
- One-on-one rotating coffee break chats with each PLT—15 to 30 minutes outside of the office
- Weekly contribute to success blog
- Friday afternoon: 20 minutes for drinks end of week
- Quarterly review of key team initiatives
- Frequent on-the-spot recognition and feedback to each other

SUCCESS MEANS AND IS MEASURED BY . . .

1. Leading a highly motivated workforce: Accessed through engagement survey or comments on employee blog
2. Living our values: Getting feedback from our stakeholders
3. Reaching our goals: Pursue key KPI achievements
4. Achieving critical initiatives: Measured by milestone accomplishments
5. Being a High Performance Team: Conduct TQ HealthCheck
6. Targeted recognition on achievements: Recognition provided by key stakeholders

Figure 19.1

The focus on creating a charter when a strong mission exists cannot be underestimated. I interviewed Dan Booher, former development head of Kohl's, and he recounted his story about developing his team for a high-stakes mission.

CASE STUDY:
DAN BOOHER
BUILDING A HIGH PERFORMANCE TEAM
AT KOHL'S

Kohl's Corporation is an American department store retail chain and the second largest department store by retail sales in the United States after Macy's.[62] In 2002, Kohl's brought Dan Booher on board with the mission of ramping up the store development program. At the time, Kohl's was opening (with considerable difficulty) about 50 stores per year, and the company wanted to at least double this to 100 stores annually. Dan believed that this couldn't be done properly with Kohl's existing structure and resources. At that time, very few companies were opening 100 stores per year. In 2002, Larry Montgomery, the CEO with a deep, gravelly voice and type-A personality, said to Dan: "One-hundred stores a year: Can you do that"? Dan took up the challenge under the proviso of being able to revamp the store development organization. This would entail making changes to people, processes, and systems.

It was Game On. In the beginning, the board directive was to "Make it happen," and that was it. There were no concrete plans, so Dan and team had to start the process from scratch. Dan didn't realize the gargantuan task ahead of him.

Fundamentally, the existing systems were antiquated and the organization had no clear financial picture. Dan asked the woman who processed the construction invoices what percentage of invoices were processed and paid the first time.; it was only 2 percent! From a functional standpoint, the company was spending a lot on staff whose main task was to rectify vendor invoices. The goal was the inverse: 98 percent of invoices needed to go through the first time.

Reaching that goal required a special electronic modeling process, so Dan's team decided to invest in a software company called Expesite, which also worked with Home Depot, Wendy's, and Tim Horton's. This would allow Kohl's to monitor progress as well as track accountability. Every piece of data was assigned to an identified individual. To make this happen, Dan had to get involvement from the CEO, CFO, and general counsel as this required a major change in the way Kohl's processed, monitored, and reported on vendors.

It took a massive effort to revamp the operation, not to mention getting the right people in place. Their new target was to open 127 stores in the coming year, with 100-plus stores to open in subsequent years. Dan's team realized it couldn't just be an internal effort and that all key stakeholders needed to be engaged. When they were ready to push the button, Dan got all the vendors, contractors, designers, and equipment suppliers together in a rented ballroom at a nearby hotel and conducted a three-day event to get everyone aligned. They brought everyone up to speed and on the same page while establishing clear imperatives for execution. They also introduced a very clear expectation and measurement process. The higher you scored, the more business you could expect to receive.

Through intense efforts, real estate contracts started rolling in, and 127 stores were envisioned to open in 2006, with *80 of them opening on one day in October.* No one had ever opened 80 large-format stores in one day!

At a meeting some years later, the CEO of Walgreens, Dave Bernauer, told Dan, "I asked my guys at Walgreens, 'How come you guys can't do that?'"

Opening 127 stores in one year required a cohesive team approach. Dan determined that he didn't have the right people in place. In the past, all decisions went through one person, which was highly ineffective; there was no bench strength. The design side of store creation was lacking so Dan brought in the director of design from Target. Dan's imperative was to select the right people and then build a team under them. Searching for skill was a given, yet attitude was paramount. *Dan wanted people with the right mind-set to do what had never been done.* Everyone had to work toward the ultimate goal without distraction.

Sometimes building the team is a long-term goal. Dan came on board in December 2002, built his team over a five-year period, and in 2006 they were ready for kickoff. They needed to develop out a "different engine" and figure out how to build it. Dan's analogy was, "You've got this big tractor-trailer rig that used to be driven by a Ford 150 pickup, and we have to retool it into a powerful Peterbilt engine to pull this thing."

Dan started with a core leadership team of six people in functional areas such as design and engineering. Initially, the team met weekly. They were all smart and capable people; they understood the purpose and direction of the team; and they comprehended what needed to be done and why, but the team's vision, strategy, and functionality to meet the challenge required a complete makeover. Over numerous weekly meetings, Dan built his High Performance Team. Throughout the process, they began to realize that they needed a strategy that was easy to understand and articulate. The core team then created a one-page document—effectively a *charter for the team and organization.* It needed to be carefully documented in order to integrate it throughout the broader development team.

After a number of meetings with his core team, Dan realized that he needed to get his whole organization of 150 staff on board, so he assembled them in the conference room and went through the detailed strategy and update. People said, "This is the first time we've had everyone together in the same room." Once the core team shared the charter and aligned everyone on the strategy, the process became natural and relatively straightforward.

Recognition was the key factor in keeping the team highly motivated.

After opening 127 stores, Kohl's had the ability to open 100-plus annually. To maintain the momentum, the company needed to maintain standards for continued long-term implementation. Ongoing efforts were made to explain and align the bigger picture within the organization. The team did lots of recognition, and people lapped up the acknowledgment by their peers. Despite all the intensity, *recognition was the key factor in keeping the team highly motivated.*

**DAN BOOHER'S LESSONS FROM
KOHL'S DEVELOPMENT STRATEGY[63]**

Every business challenge requires a tailored approach. For a ground-breaking strategy, a reengineered long-term approach was required:

1. Spend the time to build the right team and strategy, and start from ground zero if necessary.
2. Get it right with your core team first.
3. Make sure you have your team charter and strategy set and well documented.
4. Involve and align the entire organization (internal and external) and integrate the strategy.
5. Bring in key external stakeholders to communicate and align the strategy.
6. To keep quality momentum, invest in the standards.
7. Recognize, recognize, recognize.

Figure 19.2

———

The team charter helps a team pull it all together. It summarizes the experiences and agreements on paper, which can be reviewed and shared. The team charter is simple, yet powerful. It reinforces the team identity and serves as a reminder to all team members about what is important.

It might take some time and several off-sites to create the team charter. It's not something that should be rushed; rather, it should only be finalized when the team feels that the key aspects have been aligned.

20

YOUR NEXT STEPS

MAKING IT EASY

By now you should have a comprehensive view of how to build your High Performance Team. The steps to move to High TQ have been discussed in some detail based on proven cases. Given that every team is unique and that includes *your team*, where do you start? After all, your team currently may be anywhere along the spectrum from dysfunctional to high performance.

In this book, we have detailed how to achieve High TQ, yet keeping it simple is your best policy for reaching your goal of a High Performance Team. The first task is clearly understanding where the team is now. You can follow the 2-Step HPT process as outlined in Chapter 4. It begins with the following steps.

Assessing the Team

Begin by assessing where your team is now. If you want just a snapshot, you can conduct the One-Word exercise from Chapter 7—Assess; it will take only 10 minutes of your team's time. You will want to follow this with an assessment of both your personal and Collective TQ; this can be accomplished by taking the TQ HealthCheck at www.douglasgerber.com, or as outlined in Chapter 7. These steps are simple and easy, and will quickly provide a very good feeling of where your team is on the TQ continuum. The diagnosis of your team's strengths and challenges will reveal a clear focus. Once you have completed these steps, it would be appropriate to create *alignment* within the team to decide on the next steps.

If you decide to move to the next level, consider conducting individual interviews with team members to dig deeper into the real issues and challenges, as well as gathering everyone's views. This is best conducted by someone outside the immediate team who may be internal or external to the company. The more distant the interviewer is from the team's operations, the more openness and honesty you are likely to get.

Transform

Once you have conducted the interviews and the TQ HealthCheck, you will have a very good idea of the state of your team along with its challenges and directions. This is the time to decide on the focus and priorities for building the Team Quotient. *The beauty of the process is that you don't have to tackle everything at once.* You may decide to focus initially on the low-hanging fruit. For example, I have clients who decide to spend a half- or full day on just the mission or vision. That is always a good place to start. They may supplement that by handling key challenges or addressing the team's "elephant in the room." Other teams may decide they want to concentrate on the relationship side of the equation, focusing on building trust and providing safe, structured feedback, along with activities that combine fun and building camaraderie. Still others—and I would say at least half the teams I work with choose this option—decide to conduct a two- to three-day comprehensive off-site to work on all the aspects in the team charter, such as vision, success definition, values and behaviors, meetings best practices, trust and feedback, and rituals.

> The beauty of the process is that you don't have to tackle everything at once.

From Transform to Integrate

Once you have considerable traction with the Transform phase, you need to move to Integrating. *The biggest mistake teams make is not putting enough time, energy, and focus into integration.* Building a team can be fun and exhilarating. The progress will feel palpable, and you may experience transformational shifts. Yet those shifts are only as good as how well you integrate them into your day-to-day interaction. That, by its very nature, is the definition of transformation. Here are a few pointers to consider for integration:

> The biggest mistake on the team journey is not putting enough time, energy, and focus on integration.

- *Action planning* may be mundane, yet it is essential for bridging the gap between experiencing the shift in an off-site environment and actually integrating it into work. Therefore, at the end of any off-site, we dedicate ample time for action planning and creating commitments. Remember that the aim is to create new behaviors and ways of interaction; these need to be clearly defined. Many of the actions come in the form of larger initiatives that need a champion. The role of the champion is to lead the initiative to success.
- Coming up with *rituals* that the team will conduct regularly is an essential tenet of the integration phase. The rituals connect us back to the original intentions and help ground and center the team with the required energy and mindset.

Keep Up the Momentum—Renew and Enhance

After 6 to 12 months, the team may decide it needs to renew and enhance its commitment to the original goals. No doubt the team will have learned much about itself over that time, and it's appropriate to reflect on a few questions. To what extent have the initiatives been actualized? Is the team exhibiting the values and behaviors it set for itself? Is it charging forward with momentum or falling back into old habits? Have old conflicts resurfaced? Is the team getting bogged down in new issues? Are there new team members who require onboarding? To what extent is the core or extended team progressing with what was intended? How is the trust level? In essence, what's working and what isn't? The team must expect to have ups and downs and may progress at rate of "two steps forward, one step back." Therefore, reconnecting is essential for keeping up the momentum and moving to the next level.

The *Renew* phase is best conducted again through an off-site program, where possible. If this isn't possible, it can be accomplished in an environment in which there are no interruptions, allowing for complete focus. Many teams I work with will revisit the One-Word exercise as well as retake the TQ HealthCheck. One of the main purposes of the TQ HealthCheck is to revisit the state of the team over time, track progress, and diagnose areas requiring further attention. The Renew process essentially allows for a focused approach for concentrating on those areas that need more work. For example, teams will often decide they want to deepen trust, reconnecting again through the RearView Feedback exercise. The Renew process also allows for a re-examination of issues and challenges that may have cropped up over time.

Usually, teams will take advantage of the Renew time to *Enhance*. There may be a new focus area that deserves attention, such as collaboration. Or possibly the team will want to focus on enhancing communication, or revisiting rituals.

Finally, many teams decide they want to go through the *Certification* process. Becoming certified as a High Performance Team is an act of pride. It allows the team to coalesce around an aspirational goal that encourages a collective will to succeed.

KEEP IT SIMPLE OR GO COMPREHENSIVE

Essentially you, as a team leader or as a team, need to decide how fast or slowly, focused or comprehensively you want to engage the team. Many teams decide to engage in the 2-Step Build–Integrate cycle several times. Or you may decide to take a rapid, supercharged approach, aiming for high performance within six months. Alternatively, you may wish to take your time and spend a couple of years getting there or take an incremental approach: take one step, assess, and determine where to go next. This is the elegance of the model: You can take it at your own pace. It allows flexibility as long as you know where you are going and are consciously working toward your team goals in an aligned fashion.

Respecting that each team is unique and in a different place when you begin this process, it will be up to you and your team to select the appropriate approach. No matter which approach you take, if you follow the prescriptions diligently over time, your TQ will increase until you reach the state of high performance.

Throughout these pages we have ventured on a comprehensive journey together. My final advice is to GET STARTED NOW! Make a decision, align the team, and begin. Committing to increasing your TQ and becoming a High Performance Team will reap unimagined benefits, including realizing positive results, enjoying competitive advantage, and creating a more effective team environment with stimulating meetings and interactions.

The sense of pride and identity produced by being part of a High Performance Team is unparalleled, leading to a rewarding and deeply satisfying team and personal experience.

In this book we have illustrated many examples of successful High Performance Teams, ranging from the sporting achievements of Die Mannschaft and Leicester City, to the successful turnaround at Ford Motor Company and GSK, to the unique team-leadership qualities at Amgen, BSD, Cathay Pacific, Global Sources, Kohl's, Integra Telecom, Kimberly-Clark, MTR Corp., and other companies.

But perhaps the greatest example of a team achieving the ultimate in success is the remarkable story of the recovery of Apollo 13 from near disaster. To quote the then-Apollo Mission Controller Gene Krantz in the recently released documentary on the Apollo story, *Mission Control: The Unsung Heroes of Apollo.*

> "We came into this room as a team, and we will leave as a team. . . . Somehow or other, when we came together, we became capable of doing the impossible."[64]

An epic quote from a great leader.

BIBLIOGRAPHY

Bach, David, "Is Germany's World Cup Triumph a Triumph of Management?" *Yale Insights*, last modified July 15, 2014, http://insights.som.yale.edu /insights/is-germany-s-world-cup-triumph-triumph-of-management.

"Brazil v Germany (2014 FIFA World Cup)," *Wikipedia*, last modified June 23, 2017, https://en.wikipedia.org/wiki/Brazil_v_Germany_(2014_FIFA _World_Cup)#cite_note-TELEmatch-18.

Conner, Daryl, "The Real Story of the Burning Platform," *Conner Partners*, last modified August 15, 2012, http://www.connerpartners.com /frameworks-and-processes/the-real-story-of-the-burning-platform.

Forbringer, Louis R. "Overview of the Gallup Organization's Q-12 Survey" *O.E. Solutions*, Inc. (2002): 1–5. http://daveatwood.com/uploads/2/8 /4/4/2844368/overview_of_the_gallup_organization_s_q-12_survey.pdf.

"Gallup Q12 Employee Engagement Survey, The Right Questions," *Gallup*, last modified 2016, https://q12.gallup.com/public/en-us/Features.

"Germany national football team," *Wikipedia*, last modified February 14, 2017, https://en.wikipedia.org/wiki/Germany_national_football_team.

"GlaxoSmithKline CEO: Business Stabilising Despite China Slowdown," *The Guardian*, July 29, 2015, https://www.theguardian.com/business/2015 /jul/29/glaxosmithkline-ceo-business-stabilising-despite-china-slowdown

"GSK China Investigation Outcome," *GSK*, last modified September 19, 2014, http://www.gsk.com/en-gb/media/press-releases/gsk-china-investigation -outcome/.

Hampton, Karen, publisher, "Mulally Shares ONE Ford Plan, Encourages Focus and Teamwork," *FORD World*, January 21, 2008, p. 4-5.

Hoffman, Bryce G., *American Icon: Alan Mulally and the Fight to Save Ford Motor Company*. (New York: Crown Publishing Group, 2012). p. 57, 68, 94, 102, 107, 175.

"Nick Saban Coaching Record," *Sports Reference*, last modified September 14, 2016, https://www.sports-reference.com/cfb/coaches/nick-saban-1.html.

Saban, Nick with Brian Curtis, *"How Good Do You Want to Be?: A Champion's Tips on How to Lead and Succeed at Work and in Life,"* (New York: Ballantine Books, reprint edition 2007).

Stanford Graduate School of Business, "Alan Mulally of Ford: Leaders Must Serve, with Courage," YouTube video, 52:19. Posted February 7, 2011. https://www.youtube.com/watch?v=ZIwz1KlKXP4

ENDNOTES

1   "Pederson Pumps up Locker Room after Super Bowl Win, Minneapolis, Minnesota." Doug Pederson addresses his team and congratulates them on bringing the first Super Bowl title to Philadelphia. February 4, 2018, Super Bowl LII, ESPN Video http://www.espn.com/video/clip?id=22327039

2   "Leicester City Story Retold: An Ultimate Guide to a Premier League Season from Heaven," *Fox Sports*, last modified May 2016, https://www.foxsports .com.au/football/premier-league/leicester-city-story-retold-an-ultimate-guide -to-a-premier-league-season-from-heaven/news-story/e78c5808dc15109c3cb 3a4a71b5b24dc.

3   Oliver Yew, "Quotes of the Season," *Sky Sports*, last modified May 2016, http:// www.skysports.com/football/news/11661/10282956/quotes-of-the-season.

4   Geoff Colvin, "The World's 50 Greatest Leaders" *Fortune*, March 22, 2017. http://fortune.com/2017/03/23/worlds-50-greatest-leaders-intro/.

5   Brazil v Germany (2014 FIFA World Cup) http://fifaworld.wikia.com/wiki /Brazil_v_Germany_(2014_FIFA_World_Cup)#cite_note-BBCmatch-17

6   "Germany National Football Team," *Wikipedia*, last modified February 14, 2017, https://en.wikipedia.org/wiki/Germany_national_football_team.

7   "World Cup 2014: Germany's Purpose-built Training Camp Has Given Them Extra Edge," www.telegraph.co.uk/sport/football/teams/germany/10962216 /World-Cup-2014-Germanys-purpose-built-training-camp-has-given-them-extra -edge.html

8   David Bach, "Is Germany's World Cup Triumph a Triumph of Management?" *Yale Insights*, July 15, 2014.

9   Tony DeMeo, "How Good Do You Want To Be? By Nick Saban," Tony DeMeo, last modified February 17, 2011, http://tonydemeo.com/book-reviews/how -good-do-you-want-to-be-by-nick-saban/

10 "Nick Saban Coaching Record," *Sports Reference*, last modified September 14, 2016, www.sports-reference.com.

11 "Jeffrey Lurie: Trust and Hard Work Led to Super Bowl Title", February 4, 2018 after winning the Super Bowl, NFL video http://www.nfl.com/videos/nfl-super -bowl/0ap3000000914596/Jeffrey-Lurie-Trust-and-hard-work-led-to-Super-Bowl-title

12 Bryce G. Hoffman, *American Icon: Alan Mulally and the Fight to Save Ford Motor Company*. (New York: Crown Publishing Group, 2012), p. 57.

13 Ibid., p. 68.

14 Ibid., p. 94.

15 Ibid., p. 175.

16 Hoffman, *American Icon: Alan Mulally and the Fight to Save Ford Motor Company*, p. 102.

17 Ibid., p. 107.

18 "Alan Mulally of Ford: Leaders Must Serve, with Courage," YouTube video,

52:19. Posted by "Stanford Graduate School of Business," February 7, 2011. https://www.youtube.com/watch?v=ZIwz1KlKXP4.

19 Hoffman, *American Icon: Alan Mulally and the Fight to Save Ford Motor Company,* p. 380.

20 Ibid., p. 247.

21 "Mulally Shares ONE Ford Plan, Encourages Focus and Teamwork". FORD World, January 21, 2008.

22 Ibid.

23 Ibid.

24 Ibid.

25 Ibid.

26 Mary Connelley, "Where Jacques Nasser Went Wrong," Automotive News, last modified October 15, 2001, http://www.autonews.com/article/20011015/SEO/110150788/where-jacques-nasser-went-wrong

27 Daryl Conner, "The Real Story of the Burning Platform," Conner Partners, last modified August 15, 2012, http://www.connerpartners.com/frameworks-and-processes/the-real-story-of-the-burning-platform.

28 "Gallup Q12 Employee Engagement Survey, The Right Questions," *Gallup,* last modified 2016, https://q12.gallup.com/public/en-us/Features.

29 Louis R. Forbringer, "Overview of the Gallup Organization's Q-12 Survey" O.E. Solutions Inc., published 2002. http://daveatwood.com/uploads/2/8/4/4/2844368/overview_of_the_gallup_organization_s_q-12_survey.pdf .

30 "GSK Investigation Outcome," *GSK,* last modified September 19, 2014, http://daveatwood.com/uploads/2/8/4/4/2844368/overview_of_the_gallup_organization_s_q-12_survey.pdf .

31 "GlaxoSmithKline CEO: Business Stabilising Despite China Slowdown," *The Guardian,* July 29, 2015, https://www.theguardian.com/business/2015/jul/29/glaxosmithkline-ceo-business-stabilising-despite-china-slowdown

32 "Hospital Authority," last modified January 7, 2017, http://www.ha.org.hk/visitor/ha_visitor_index.asp?Content_ID=10009&Lang=ENG&Dimension=100&Parent_ID=10004.

33 "Hands on Hong Kong," last modified 2016, https://www.handsonhongkong.org/.

34 "Starbucks: Our Heritage," last modified 2017, https://www.starbucks.com/about-us/company-information.

35 "Virgin Atlantic: Our Mission Statement," last modified 2017, https://www.virginatlantic.com/gb/en/footer/our-story.html.

36 "Roche: Our Purpose," last modified 2017, http://www.roche.com/about/our_purpose.htm.

37 "BSD Code and Design Academy," last modified 2017, hk.bsdacademy.com.

38 "Melville: What Is Sustainability?" last modified 2015, http://melvillejewellery.com/.

39 Chris Geary, personal interview, May 2016.

40 Richard Preston, "Smiley Culture: Pret A Manger's Secret Ingredients," *The Telegraph,* last modified March 9, 2012, http://www.telegraph.co.uk/food anddrink/9129410/Smiley-culture-Pret-A-Mangers-secret-ingredients.html.

41 Ibid.

42 Dudley Slater, personal interview, August 2016.

43 IBID.

44 Harrison Assessments, "Harrison Assessments—Paradox Technology," last modified October 15, 2016, http://www.harrisonassessments.com/paradox -technology.html.

45 Mary Right, "Paradox Graph—Communication," June 8, 2005. http://www .trustedcoach.com/wp-content/uploads/2013/11/ParadoxReport.pdf.

46 Harrison Assessments' Team Paradox Graph: 'Communication.' http:// thethinkspot.com/communication-2011/chapters/11.

47 "Bayer: Science For a Better Life," last modified November 3, 2016, https:// www.bayer.com/en/bayer-mission-science-for-a-better-life.aspx.

48 "MTR: Our Business," last modified 2014, www.mtr.com.hk

49 "Radar Chart," *Wikipedia*, last modified November 28, 2016, https://en .wikipedia.org/wiki/Radar_chart.

50 Glenn Frommer, personal interview, August 2016.

51 Achal Agarwal, personal interview, August 2016.

52 Ibid.

53 "Yogi Berra," *Wikiquote*, last modified September 27, 2016, https://en .wikiquote.org/wiki/Yogi_Berra.

54 Penny Wan, personal interview, December 2016.

55 Abigail Brenner, "E~motions of Change = Energy in Motion," *Psychology Today*, last modified June 3, 2011, https://www.psychologytoday.com /blog/in-flux/201106/emotions-change-energy-in-motion.

56 Geoff Ziezulewicz, "Unique Camaraderie Forged by Troops Downrange Lasts Far Beyond Deployment," *Stars and Stripes*, last modified June 12, 2009, http://www.stripes.com/news/unique-camaraderie-forged-by -troops-downrange-lasts-far-beyond-deployment-1.92442.

57 "Harrison Assessments—Enjoyment performance Methodology," last modified February 8, 2017, http://www.harrisonassessments.com/enjoyment-performance .html.

58 Ibid.

59 "Global Sources: About Global Sources," last modified August 25, 2014, http://www.corporate.globalsources.com/PROFILE/BGROUND2.HTM?source =GSOLHP_Footer.

60 "Global Sources: Press Release," September 26, 2017. http://www.corporate .globalsources.com/INFO/INFO_IDX.HTM.

61 Merle Hinrich, personal interview, February 2016.

62 "Kohl's," *Wikipedia*, last modified February 10, 2017, https://en.wikipedia .org/wiki/Kohl%27s.

63 Dan Booher, personal interview, November 2014.

64 "Mission Control: The Unsung Heroes of Apollo. Official Trailer 1 (2017)— Documentary," Movieclips Film Festivals and Indie Films on YouTube video, 2:20. Posted March 2017, https://www.youtube.com /watch?v=GVDTSfyFTTY.

INDEX